RENNY DARLING'S

Cooking GREAT!

Looking GREAT!

Feeling GREAT!

———

The Moderation Diet

(The Only Sensible Way To Stay
SLIM & HEALTHY)

———

350 Deliciously LIGHT Recipes
Low-Calorie, Low-Cholesterol, Low-Fat,
Low-Sugar, Low-Sodium

Other Simply Delicious Cookbooks
by Renny Darling

The Joy of Eating
The Love of Eating
The Joy of Entertaining
The Joy of Eating French Food
Great Beginnings & Happy Endings
With Love from Darling's Kitchen
Easiest & Best Coffee Cakes & Quick Breads
Entertaining! Fast & Fancy

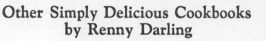

With sincere appreciation to the
Distinguished Paul J. Geller M.D.,
for his belief in and endorsement of "The Moderation Diet".

With thanks to Leonore Smith, gifted artist and friend

❤ ❤ ❤

IMPORTANT NOTE TO THE READER
The recipes in this cookbook were created to be low in calorie, fat, cholesterol, sugar and sodium content, which are within the guidelines of The Surgeon General's Report on Nutrition and Health. This cookbook is not intended, nor should it be considered, to be medical advice. Before starting any change in your eating habits, it is advised that you confer with your doctor for approval.

This cookbook is dedicated to your good health and long life...and
May your long life be longer.

First Edition

Published by Royal House Publishing Co., Inc.
P.O. Box 5027
Beverly Hills, CA 90210
Printed in the United States of America
Library of Congress Catalog Card Number: 90-60365
ISBN: 0-930440-30-7

The Foreword

Paul Geller, M.D.

When I first saw the manuscript of Renny Darling's new cookbook, "Cooking Great! Looking Great! Feeling Great! - The Moderation Diet", I was so excited that I wanted to write a few words to endorse the book from a medical point of view.

Finally a cookbook has been written with the basic premise of "moderation" and "common sense", which happens to be my personal philosophy concerning food and health. As a doctor, in practice for 25 years, I have always stressed, to my patients, moderation and common sense as the ultimate diet. I had hoped for a long time that someone would write a book such as this. This is a wonderful cookbook.

The relationship of diet and nutrition to good health is the subject of increasing interest and research. Americans are being reminded constantly of how food relates to their good health and well-being. But food is also a tremendous source of pleasure and enjoyment. In this cookbook, you will find the best of these two worlds:

1. Eating for health...and

2. Eating for pleasure.

Using Renny Darling's delicious recipes will not only be beneficial to your health but a source of pure pleasure and enjoyment, as well. She is showing us how we can enjoy mouth-watering dishes that will also help us stay slim and healthy. What a great combination.

To drastically reduce our food intake by low-calorie fasting-type diets, or to sacrifice texture and flavor with strange eating programs, can cause more harm than good. Diet food is often bland and boring and delivers very little enjoyment. Maybe that's why most diets fail.

Ms. Darling's approach to attain nutritional balance is to keep in mind that fats, cholesterol, sugar and salt should be limited, but not eliminated. Most foods can be enjoyed occasionally and in moderation (and that includes desserts).

Renny Darling shows us how we can eat a pleasurable and varied diet, how we can enjoy great tasting dishes...and still keep a low calorie, fat, cholesterol, sugar and salt content.

I would recommend that you browse through the contents, as I did, and note the variety and interest of the recipes. This is not a "diet", but good food, deliciously prepared, that is good for you, too.

Although much has yet to be scientifically proved about nutrition, the evidence today impels us to change our eating habits, if, indeed, we want to be healthy and live longer.

And yet, eating is one of civilization's greatest pleasures...and this creative cookbook allows us to partake of this pleasure, with the added bonus that this pleasure is healthy, too.

Paul J. Geller, M.D.
Beverly Hills, California

The Contents

FOREWORD PAUL GELLER, M.D. 3

INTRODUCTION 13

NOTES ON INGREDIENTS 15-22

SURGEON GENERAL'S REPORT 23-25

POSITIVE THINKING 26

SAMPLE MENUS 27-34

BASICS 35-42
   (*Numbers in parentheses indicate calorie value.*)
   Seasoned Flour for Chicken or Fish (25 per T), 36
   Sun-Dried Tomatoes (13), 36
   Basic Chicken Broth (4 per cup), 37
   Extra-Rich Chicken Broth (8 per cup), 37
   Low Calorie Cheese & Chives Spread (15 per T), 38
   Low-Calorie Mayonnaise-Like Spread (7 per T), 38
   Low-Calorie Sour Cream (9 per T), 38
   Low-Calorie Hollandaise Sauce (12 per T), 39
   Food Processor Method, 39
   Hollandaise with Chives (12 per T), 39
   Hollandaise with Dill (12 per T), 39
   Hollandaise with Basil (12 per T), 39
   Low Calorie Béarnaise Sauce (12 per T), 40
   Horseradish Sauce for Roast Beef (8 per T), 40
   Mayonnaise-Hollandaise & Chive Sauce (21 per T), 41
   Low-Calorie Sauce with Dill & Chives (13 per T), 41
   Light Mayonnaise (25 per T), 41
   Low-Cal Fresh Strawberry Jam (8 per T), 42
   Fresh Strawberry Sauce (9 per T), 42

BREADS & MUFFINS 43-56
   (*Numbers in parentheses indicate calorie value.*)
   Zucchini Oatmeal Muffins, (130), 44
   Oat Bran & Carrot Muffins (140), 44
   Butter-less, Egg-less Wheat Muffins with Walnuts (139), 45
   Bran & Oatmeal Date Nut Muffins (133), 46
   Spicy Orange Bran & Oatmeal Muffins (133), 46
   Cinnamon Cranberry & Orange Muffins (112), 47
   Buttermilk Oat Bran Muffins with Orange & Bananas (125), 47
   Buttermilk Orange Bran Muffins with Raisins (133), 48
   Apple & Orange Whole Wheat Muffins (139), 49
   Low-Cal Cinnamon Orange Bran Muffins (120), 49
   Spicy Apricot & Carrot Bread (72), 50
   Focaccio-Italian Flatbread with Red Peppers (97), 51

Greek Sesame Flatbread with Lemon, Onions & Cheese (96), 52
Italian Flatbread with Onions & Cheese (110), 53
Flatbread with Garlic & Rosemary (110), 53
Flatbread with Caraway Seeds (110), 53
Flatbread with Onions & Poppy Seeds (110), 53
Basic Non-Fat Whole Wheat Yeast Bread (63), 54
Basic Whole Wheat Quick Bread (78), 55
Oven-Baked French Toast (110), 55
Whole Wheat Buttermilk Biscuits (76), 56
Hardy Whole Wheat Biscuits with Chives (77), 56

CASSEROLES & SMALL ENTREES 57-72

(Numbers in parentheses indicate calorie value.)
Eggplant Lasagna with Tomatoes & Ricotta Cheese (145), 58
Chili Beef with Red Beans (254), 59
Pink Rice (138), 59
Royal Artichoke & Spinach Casserole (113), 60
Eggplant Frittata with Onions & Cheese (70), 60
Tomatoes Stuffed with Turkey in Light Tomato Sauce (223), 61
Crustless Tart with Tomatoes & Goat Cheese (103), 62
Frittata with Artichokes & Red Peppers (190), 62
The Big Chile Chicken Relleno (210), 63
Pink Chile Rice (139), 63
Old Fashioned Stuffed Peppers in Tomato Sauce (273), 64
Cabbage Rolls in Sweet Sour Tomato Sauce (200), 65
Spinach Frittata with Cheese & Onions (184), 66
Crustless Quiche with Eggplant, Onions & Cheese (108), 66
Paella Valencia with Shellfish (331), 67
Cauliflower with Tomatoes & Potatoes (100), 67
Jambalaya Creole with Shellfish (297), 68
Vegetable Paella with Artichokes & Yellow Rice (269), 69
Fresh Vegetable Pizza (183), 69
Eggplant Stuffed with Ricotta (209), 70
Greek Omelet with Tomatoes, Peppers & Feta (161), 71
Onion-Flavored Baked Baby Potatoes (115), 71
High Protein Cottage Cheese Pancakes (53), 71
Omelet with Spinach & Cheese (135), 72
Light Crepes for Cheese Blintzes (38), 72

PIZZAS & PASTAS 73-80

(Numbers in parentheses indicate calorie value.)
Lowest Calorie No-Oil Pizza Crust (77), 74
Basic Pizza Crust (93), 75
Mediterranean Pizza with Sun-Dried Tomatoes (189), 76
Pizza with Eggplant, Mushrooms, Leeks & Feta (134), 77
Pizza with Sun-Dried Tomatoes & Chevre (188), 78
Pasta with Artichoke, Red Pepper, Sun-Dried Tomatoes (200), 78
Pasta Primavera with Tomato Basil Sauce (207), 79
Pasta with Eggplant, Red Peppers & Sun-Dried Tomatoes (266), 80

SOUPS 81-92

(Numbers in parentheses indicate calorie value.)
Healthy & Homey Lentil Soup with Tomatoes, Carrots (99), 82
Cioppino - Italian Fisherman's Chowder (147), 83
Italian Croustades with Tomatoes, Chives & Cheese (90), 83
Best Country Cabbage & Tomato Soup (54), 84
Cucumber & Chive Soup with Lemon & Dill (50), 84
Easiest & Best Clam Chowder with Tomatoes (72), 85
Crispettes of Cheese (123), 85
The Best Old-Fashioned Chicken Soup/Stew (117/235), 86
Italian Vegetable & Bean Soup (94), 87
Leek & Tomato Soup with CiCi Peas (100), 88
Spinach Soup with Lemon & Vermicelli (97), 88
Thanksgiving Honey Apple Pumpkin Soup (89), 89
Carrot Soup with Apples & Cinnamon (61), 89
Mexican Chicken & Chili Bean Soup/Stew (148/296), 90
Leek & Potato Soup with Chives (59), 90
Low-Calorie Farmhouse Vegetable Soup (61), 91
Chicken CiCi Pea Stew (262), 91
Cold & Creamy Dilled Zucchini Soup (54), 92
Dilled Potato & Cucumber Soup (72), 92

SALADS 93-106

(Numbers in parentheses indicate calorie value.)
Cucumber Salad with Parsley & Chives (19), 94
Salad of Tomatoes, Onions & Feta Cheese (72), 94
Tomato, Mushroom & Mozzarella Salad (71), 94
Pasta Salad with Chicken & Cooked Vegetables (190), 95
Raw Vegetable Salad (61), 95
Artichoke, Red Pepper & Potato Salad (78), 96
Spinach, Mushroom & Red Onion Salad (74), 96
Chicken Salad with Cous Cous & Currants (169), 97
Carrot & Snow Pea Salad (43), 97
Confetti Cole Slaw in Horseradish Vinaigrette (44), 98
Eggplant Salad with Tomatoes & Cheese (69), 98
Marinated Red Pepper Salad (30), 99
Tomato & Onion Salad with Basil Vinaigrette (43), 99
Eggplant & Tomato Salad with Lemon & Dill (38), 100
Leeks & Tomatoes in Lemon Dressing (48), 100
Tomatoes with Garlic Croutons & Parmesan (38), 101
Low-Calorie Pineapple Cole Slaw (44), 101
Asparagus Vinaigrette with Cheese & Chives (21), 102
Shrimp in Honey Yogurt Lemon Dressing (75), 102
Middle Eastern Cracked Wheat Salad with Tomatoes (145), 103
White Bean Salad with Tomatoes & Scallions (74), 103
Basil Pimiento Dressing (3 per T), 104
Cucumber Sauce with Dill for Poached Salmon (5 per T), 104
Lemon-Dill Yogurt Sauce (6 per T), 104
Imperial Sauce Verte (7 per T), 105
Tomato & Chile Salsa for Dipping Fresh Vegetables (4 per T), 105

Basil Garlic Vinaigrette (27 per T), 106
French Mustard Vinaigrette (23 per T), 106
Yogurt Lemon Dressing (6 per T), 106

FISH & SHELLFISH 107-128
(Numbers in parentheses indicate calorie value.)
Costa del Sol Mediterranean Chowder (156), 108
Croustades of Olive Oil & Parmesan (130), 108
New Orleans Hot & Spicy Fish Stew (167), 109
Bouillabaisse (175), 110
Broiled Croustades with Cheese (42), 110
Fillets of Sole Stuffed with Spinach & Cheese (190), 111
Sole with Sun-Dried Tomato & Pepper Sauce (125), 112
Sole with Garlic, Lemon & Chive Sauce (128), 112
Fillets of Sole with Leeks & Tomato Sauce (152), 113
Mousse of Sole in Yogurt, Spinach & Chives (129), 113
Sole Italienne with Red Pepper Tomato Sauce (162), 114
Fillets of Sole in Artichoke & Tomato Sauce (163), 115
Sole Provencale with Tomatoes & Onions (151), 116
Brown Rice with Mushrooms, Onions & Carrots (147), 116
Tuna Steaks with Tomato Vinaigrette (277), 117
Fillets of Sole in Lemon Dill Cream Sauce (140), 117
Sea Bass in Salsa Español (143), 118
Sea Bass with Tomato, Currants & Pine Nuts (177), 119
Bass with Mushrooms, Tomatoes & Leeks (161), 119
Sea Bass Persillade with Yogurt & Tomatoes (159), 120
Sea Bass with Low Calorie Basil Sauce (191), 120
Chinese Whole Fish Steamed in Oven (160), 121
Red Snapper Teriyaki with Ginger & Scallions (121), 121
Red Snapper Sesame with Ginger & Scallions (132), 122
Fillets of Red Snapper with Crumb Topping (156), 122
Cajun Shrimp in Red Hot Garlic Clam Sauce (148), 123
Red Hot Baby Shrimp Creole (166), 124
Shrimp in Honey Barbecue Sauce (128), 124
Shrimp Greco with Lemon & Feta (214), 125
Lobster with Chile Tomato Salsa & Garlic Cheese (146), 125
Best Herbed Scampi with Leeks, Shallots (128), 126
Scallops in Wine Sauce (125), 127
Scallops & Mushrooms in Herb & Wine Sauce (168), 127
Mexican Tomato Salsa for Fish & Shellfish (6 per T), 128
Honey Mustard Dill Sauce for Fish & Shellfish (13 per T), 128
Tartar Sauce for Fish & Shellfish (8 per T), 128

POULTRY 129-160
(Numbers in parentheses indicate calorie value.)
Plum-Glazed Teriyaki Chicken (241), 130
Chicken in Honey Lemon Yogurt Sauce (258), 130
Chicken Parmesan in Light Tomato Sauce (254), 131
Chicken in Dill & Wine Sauce (217), 132
Chicken Paella with Tomatoes & Chiles (305), 133
Chicken with Red Cabbage, Apples & Cranberries (255), 134

Potato & Onion Cake (96), 134
Caribbean Chicken with Apricots (269), 135
Brown Rice with Onions & Cinnamon (106), 135
Kung Pao Chicken with Peanuts (262), 136
Moroccan Chicken with Raisins (263), 137
Cous Cous with Chick Peas (118), 137
Country Chicken with Potatoes & Carrots (215), 138
Old-Fashioned Chicken Stew (216), 138
Chicken Italienne in Red Pepper Tomato Sauce (279), 139
Angel Hair Pasta (110), 139
Chicken & Mixed Vegetable Stir-Fry (198), 140
Chicken with Tomatoes, Cabbage & Onions (287), 141
Enchiladas with Chicken, Chiles & Cheese (325), 142
Hot & Spicy Cajun Chicken Wings (265), 143
Dirty Rice (118), 143
Chicken Breasts Stuffed with Spinach & Cheese (249), 144
Chicken Breasts with Mushrooms, Red Peppers (247), 145
Chicken Indienne with Yogurt & Lemon (244), 146
Chicken Stuffed with Mushrooms
   in a Delicate Champagne Sauce (234), 147
To Make Low-Calorie Creme Fraiche (20 per T), 147
Chicken Breasts with Herbed Stuffing (241), 148
Dilled Mushroom Cream Sauce (34 per 2 T), 148
Chicken in Tomato Vinaigrette Sauce (230), 149
Chicken with Honey Mustard Dill Sauce (252), 149
Baked Chicken Breasts in Tomato Artichoke Sauce (230), 150
Chicken Romano with Red Pepper & Garlic (230), 151
Chicken Dijonnaise with Mushroom, Pepper, Tomato (238), 151
Chicken with Yogurt, Lemon & Garlic (246), 152
Chicken New Orleans with Apricots & Pecans (290), 153
Chicken with Carrots, Apples & Prunes (293), 153
Chicken in Mushroom Wine Sauce (270), 154
Mexican Chicken with Tomatoes & Chiles (219), 155
Chicken Smothered in Honey Onions (259), 155
Rock Cornish Hens with Mushrooms, Carrots (417), 156
Chicken with Apples & Honey Ginger Sauce (241), 157
Normandy Chicken with Apples & Wine (282), 157
Chicken Creole in Hot Pepper Tomato Sauce (239), 158
Chicken with Mushrooms & Onions in Burgundy Wine (274), 159
Chicken Baroness with Artichokes & Mushrooms (275), 160
Rich Basting Mixture for Chicken or Turkey (Negligible), 160

MEATS 161-174
   (Numbers in parentheses indicate calorie value.)
Sweet & Sour Boiled Beef & Cabbage (212), 162
Oven-Baked Stew with Carrots & Potatoes (302), 162
Paupiettes de Boeuf in Mushroom Wine Sauce (232), 163
German-Style Sweet & Sour Potted Beef (215), 164
Old-Fashioned Hungarian Goulash (202), 164
Beef with Peppers & Onions (206), 165
Irish Beef Stew with Mashed Potatoes (218), 165

Beef & Red Peppers Romano with Cheese (254), 166
Moroccan Lamb Dumplings in Apple, Raisin, Vegetable (231), 167
Cous Cous (104), 167
Leg of Lamb with Lemon, Garlic & Rosemary (270), 168
Lamb Indienne with Garlic & Yogurt (257), 168
Honey Glazed Pork Roast with Baked Apples (295), 169
Pork with Red Cabbage & Apples (290), 169
Veal Shanks in Tomato Wine Sauce (302), 170
Veal with Roasted Leeks & Carrots (299), 170
Veal Dumplings in Light Tomato Sauce (197), 171
Veal Italienne with Onions, Carrots, Tomatoes (249), 171
Veal & Vegetable Pate with Spinach & Tomato Sauce (184), 172
Veal Roast Persillade with Garlic, Tomato & Wine (292), 173
Paupiettes of Veal Filled with Apple Stuffing (218), 174

NOODLES & RICE 175-186
    (*Numbers in parentheses indicate calorie value.*)
Brown Rice with Pimiento & Parsley (129), 176
Brown Rice & Lentils with Onions (122), 176
Confetti Brown Rice with Scallions & Peppers (144), 176
Cracked Wheat with Mushrooms & Onions (134), 177
Brown Rice with Leeks & Onions (Stove-Top Method) (136), 178
Brown Rice with Leeks & Onions (Oven Method) (139), 178
Toasted Egg Barley with Onion & Mushrooms (120), 179
Lentils with Tomatoes, Carrots & Onions (159), 179
Toasted Fideos (157), 180
Bulgur with Lemon, Currants & Pine Nuts (156), 180
Confetti Rice with Onions, Peppers & Peas (131), 181
Lemon Rice with Onions & Pine Nuts (148, 181
Pink Rice with Chives & Parsley (138), 182
Rice with Lemon & Chives (129), 182
Pink Rice & Mushrooms (135), 182
Fried Rice with Green Onions (128), 183
Herbed Rice (117), 183
Lemon Rice with Leeks & Herbs (143), 183
Rice with Cheese & Chives (110), 184
Emerald Rice with Parsley & Chives (129), 184
Rice with Mushrooms (144), 184
Pastina with Fresh Tomato & Basil Sauce (126), 185
Toasted Orzo with Mushrooms & Onions (157), 185
Pink Orzo with Tomatoes & Onions (159), 186

VEGETABLES 187-208
    (*Numbers in parentheses indicate calorie value.*)
Artichokes & Mushrooms with Cheese (48), 188
Artichokes & Potatoes with Green Onions (68), 188
Asparagus in Lemon Chive Sauce (41), 189
Asparagus with Lemon, Garlic & Cheese (43), 189
Green Beans with Tomatoes & Onions (46), 190
Green Beans with Parsley Sauce (35), 190
Lima Beans with Onions & Tomatoes (79), 190

Broth-Fried Broccoli with Ginger (35), 191
Broccoli with Garlic & Shallot Cream Sauce (39), 191
Frittata of Broccoli, Mushrooms & Tomatoes (49), 192
Brussel Sprouts with Lemon Chive Sauce (60), 192
Brussel Sprouts with Mushrooms & Shallots (59), 193
Pureed Carrots with Cinnamon (79), 193
Carrot & Potato Cake (74), 194
Honey & Butter Glazed Carrots with Parsley (41), 194
Celery in Lemon Dill Sauce (20), 195
Cucumbers with Lemon, Parsley & Chives (20), 195
Sweet & Sour Red Cabbage with Apples & Currants (49), 196
Cauliflower with Tomatoes & Onions (55), 196
Baked Eggplant with Tomatoes & Ricotta (145), 197
Mushrooms & Tomatoes in Wine (41), 198
Mushrooms with Dill & Yogurt Stuffing (43), 198
Honey & Brandy Glazed Carrots (54), 199
Onions with Raisins (51), 199
Onion & Mushrooms Saute (44), 199
Potatoes Roasted with Garlic (104), 200
Country Baked Potatoes (104), 200
Sweet Potatoes Baked with Sugar & Spice (112), 200
Roasted Red Pepper, Potato & Onion Cake (84), 201
Potato & Onion Cake (79), 201
Garlic Potatoes with Onions & Rosemary (109), 202
Steamed Baby Potatoes with Parsley & Dill (104), 202
Spinach Pate with Onions, Peppers, Carrots (97), 203
Broiled Tomatoes with Garlic Cheese Crumbs (46), 204
Baked Zucchini in Lemon Tomato Sauce (53), 204
Zucchini Frittata with Tomatoes Vinaigrette (93), 205
Ramekins of Zucchini, Onions & Cheese (55), 206
Baked Zucchini with Tomatoes & Cheese (49), 206
Zucchini with Tomatoes & Onions (48), 207
Baked Zucchini Crisps (50), 207
Broiled Mixed Vegetable Platter (53), 208
Stir-Fried Mixed Vegetable Platter (62), 208

DESSERTS 209-244
(Numbers in parentheses indicate calorie value.)
Walnut Cake with Raspberry & Lemon Glaze (163), 210
Orange & Walnut Torte with Orange Glaze (150), 211
Angel Cake with Fresh Strawberry Sauce (92), 212
Skinny Chocolate Torte ala Sacher (156), 213
Chocolate Sponge for Jelly Rolls (113), 214
Cinnamon-Marbled Orange Walnut Cake (166), 215
Apple Cinnamon Coffee Cake (149), 215
Orange & Apple Oatmeal Cake (95), 216
Spicy Applesauce Cake (161), 217
Lady Finger Spongecake Base (40), 217
Basic Orange & Lemon Sponge Cake (98), 218
Old-Fashioned Raisin Ginger Cake (143), 219
Cranberry, Orange & Walnut Cake (150), 219

Peach & Macaroon Crumb Cobbler (102), 220
Spicy Peach Cobbler with Oat Topping (160), 221
Vanilla Cream Sauce (7 per T), 221
Blueberry & Lemon Cobbler (129), 221
Chocolate Cheesecake with Creme Vanilla (150), 222
Creme Vanilla (15 per 2 t), 222
Lemon Cheesecake with Strawberry Sauce (145), 223
Chocolate Marbled Cheesecake (136), 224
Basic Brownies (72), 225
Oatmeal & Raisin Bar Cookies (35), 226
Oat Bran & Apricot Cookies (37), 226
Ginger-Spice Apple Cookies (56), 227
Spiced Compote of Dried & Winter Fruit (98), 228
Spiced Peaches with Cinnamon & Cloves (57), 228
Baked Apples with Orange, Macaroon, Walnut (120), 229
Baked Bananas with Orange & Walnuts (126), 229
Apples Baked in Orange Juice (82), 230
Mocha Parfaits with Kahlua (77), 230
Iced Vanilla Glace (40), 231
Basic Berry Granité (60), 232
Basic Fruit Juice Ices (42), 232
Espresso Granité with Kahlua (64), 232
Banana Iced Cream (58), 233
Frozen Yogurt in Meringue Shells (150), 233
Basic Lemon Ice (68), 234
Pineapple Sherbet (58), 234
Basic Tea Sherbet (24), 235
Low-Calorie Pumpkin Orange Mousse (71), 236
Oatmeal & Raisin Cookie (58), 236
Peach & Strawberry Vanilla Rum Mousse (101), 237
Low-Calorie Vanilla Creme Fraiche (22 per T), 237
Crisp Cookie Crust for Fruit Tarts (92), 238
Flaky Crust (90), 238
Strawberry Tart on Cookie Crust (120), 239
Apple Tart on Cookie Crust (126), 239
Basic Fruit Souffle (39), 240
Low-Calorie Whipped Cream (2 per T), 241
No Sugar Hot Chocolate Fruit Sauce (14 per t), 241
Low-Calorie Devonshire Cream (21 per T), 242
Fresh Apple & Cinnamon Sauce (10 per T), 242
Chocolate Sauce (12 per T), 243
Meringue Shells (50), 243
Meringue Kisses (12), 243
Hot Spiced Apple Cider with Orange & Lemon (50), 244
Cappuccino (35), 244
Café Kahlua (25), 244

CALORIE CHART 245-248

INDEX 249

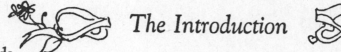

The Introduction

Dear Friends,

Welcome! to "Cooking Great! Looking Great! Feeling Great! - The Moderation Diet" It has been a labor of love, researching this project for the past years. Recently, "The Surgeon General's Report on Nutrition and Health" has affirmed some of the basic principles of nutrition that have been evolving during the past years. The recommendations made in The Surgeon General's Report are not revolutionary, but a summary of principles that have been developing during the past 15 years.

The latest findings in the Surgeon General's Report on Nutrition and Health find a compelling relationship between good food and good health. And there is some excellent "good news" in this connection.

The first is that making changes in the diet can produce "substantial gains in good health" and second is that reducing bad eating habits can reverse or lessen disease that is already present.

The best "good news" of all is that Americans are becoming more and more aware of the role of nutrition and exercise in good health. And while in the past, the siren call was just to be thin (and at any expense to our health), the emphasis now is a siren call to be healthy and fit. Slimness **is** achieved as a benefit and result of the healthier lifestyle. Americans are eating lighter and healthier foods, exercising regularly and enjoying the benefits of increased energy and vitality.

The basic features advised by the Surgeon General and the accepted health standards today are:

1. Moderation, no excess or imbalanced use of any food group
2. Variety, to assure balance, interest and excitement to meals
3. Very low fat, saturated fat and cholesterol to lessen the
        risk of chronic disease and to reduce the risk of obesity
4. Increased use of complex carbohydrates, grains and fibers
5. Vastly reduced amounts of sugars
6. No added sodium

The accent is...
Keep it Light...Keep it Varied...Keep it Delicious and Satisfying.

The key is...
Moderation and Common Sense.

These are the guidelines used throughout "Cooking Great", to maintain desired weight, good health and lessen the risk of chronic disease. Moderation and common sense are at the heart of this cookbook. Most of us (not all) would hardly be satisfied with an apple for dessert for the rest of our lives. Or for a celery stick as an hors d'oeuvre. Or celebrate a special date with club soda and a twist of lemon. Common sense dictates that pleasurable eating should be part of our lifestyle, but with moderation and good sense.

This is not a diet book in the ordinary sense, but a creative and inventive way to cook and serve, with unique recipes that are low in calories, fat, cholesterol, salt and sugar. These are recipes that promise pleasure and excitement and promise to be light, also.

These are recipes that are "normal and natural" and, while low in calories, are still delicious and satisfying. They are good for reducing weight or maintaining weight...for it is the **quantity** that we eat that makes the difference.

As noted in the Surgeon General's Report, "Food sustains us, it can be a source of considerable pleasure, . . . it adds valued dimensions to our lives." In short, food is a source of sustenance and considerable pleasure. But so often, it has been loaded with guilt. The recipes in this cookbook are **delicious, easy to prepare** and **guilt-free. This cookbook is dedicated to those...**

1. Who find pleasure and satisfaction from food.
2. Who choose to cook creatively for health and pleasure.
3. Who choose to change their eating behavior and attitude toward food.
4. Who choose to eat moderately for slimness and health, not by going "on a diet" (which infers you will soon be going "off a diet") or by eliminating a food group, but by changing their eating habits, in light of present accepted nutritional standards.

Unless you have a particular health problem, you can eat practically any food, provided you eat it in moderation and with a little common sense. Good quality ingredients, combined in an exciting and original manner, sparkled with herbs and spices can produce a low-calorie feast at anytime. The great pleasures of the table can be prepared with vegetables, mustards, lemon, vinaigrettes...very delicious and satisfying. The fact that they happen to be low in calories has nothing to do with it. Good taste is good taste...period!

Good taste produces satisfaction, and satisfaction is your closest ally when trying to lose weight or keep it off. Satisfaction allows you to consume smaller portions resulting in fewer calories. Delicious food satisfies cravings.

We must think sensibly about priorities. Few can disagree that good health and long life ranks first. And it must surely follow that with good health as a goal, slimness will surely follow. The emphasis should be on eating good food that is good for you, too...in moderation, because we love to be healthy and slim.

We aren't exercising because we want to be slim. We are exercising because it is beneficial to our circulation, metabolism, cardiovascular fitness and to our general feeling of well-being. We invest this time in ourselves because we're worth it. Slimness is a healthy fringe benefit of healthy eating and exercise. (Exercise is recommended in The Surgeon General's Report, but the kind of exercise best suited to your health, should be taken up with your doctor or an expert in the field.)

I hope this cookbook helps you in the quest for good health and slimness. I hope it will be a friend that will serve you well. I hope it will make your life healthier and more delicious. I hope it will help you take charge and control of your eating habits because you value your good health. And when you take charge and control, you will feel strong and confident...and when you feel strong and confident, it radiates... In other words, you will feel happy inside and out.

As always, enjoy with love,

Renny Darling

Ingredients

From my notebook:

Alcohol

In the few instances where wine or liquor is used for flavoring, the alcohol content is cooked off, leaving only the flavor. The flavor of wine does not improve with cooking, so, as a rule, don't use any wine for cooking that you would find unacceptable to drink.

Chicken & Chicken Products

Chicken

All recipes were tested with lean fryer chickens, about 2 1/2 pounds with all separable fat removed. Skin was removed before cooking, where indicated. If not indicated, chicken was baked with skin. If you do bake the chicken with the skin (to prevent its drying out), be certain to remove the skin before serving. I like to prebake chicken before putting it into a sauce. Baking chicken before it is put into a sauce, serves to defat it, as all the fat is left in the pan.

Chicken Broth

There are many benefits to making your own chicken broth. Besides being richer, more flavorful and less caloric, you can control the amount of sodium. If you must severely restrict your intake of sodium, be certain to either prepare your own broths, or purchase those that are salt-free.

The calories are markedly lower in homemade chicken broth, at 4 calories per cup, as compared to 6 to 8 calories per cup for broth made with seasoned stock base and 30 calories per cup for the canned.

Recipes in this book were calculated and tested with canned broths at 30 calories per cup, just in case you use the higher-caloried canned broths. In the event that you do prepare and use homemade broths (see Index), (preparing them is not as time-consuming as one would think), reduce 26 calories for each cup of broth used, divide it by the number served, and subtract this number from the total calories per serving.

Homemade broths freeze beautifully. Premeasure in 1/2 cup quantities and freeze for later use.

Dairy Products

Low-Fat Sour Cream
This is a real bounty at 20 calories per tablespoon. It tastes quite rich and flavorful, adds a good deal of flavor with markedly less fat, and was the sour cream I used. With low-fat cream cheese it produced a marvelous cheesecake, velvety smooth, extremely delicious and very satisfying.

Low-Fat Cream Cheese
Also known as Neufchatel cheese, this lower-calorie, lower-fat version of cream cheese is a fairly decent substitute. But it is still caloric, so use it sparingly. It produced a lovely cheesecake, that was every bit as satisfying as the original.

Non-Fat Yogurt
Non-fat yogurt is very available nowadays. There was a time when it could only be found in health food stores. Unless otherwise stated, non-fat yogurt was used throughout this book. At 110 calories per cup it is a caloric bargain.

Non-Fat Cottage Cheese
Non-fat cottage cheese is also very available nowadays. It used to be hard to find, but is now sold in most markets. It is truly good tasting and recommended, at only 70 calories per 1/2 cup. Non-fat cottage cheese was used throughout this book.

Eggs

Eggs
The number of eggs recommended for weekly consumption has been increased from 3 to 4. However, if you must severely restrict your intake of cholesterol, then, substitute 2 egg whites for 1 whole egg. There will be some difference in the finished product, so you might have to experiment a little with this substitution.

Fats, Oils & Cholesterol

The Surgeon General's Report recommends reduced consumption of fat (especially saturated fat) and cholesterol. But "reduced consumption" does not mean "no fat". A certain amount of fat is needed in the diet to perform necessary body functions. A diet too low in fat can be dangerous.

Most of the recipes in this book are made with fish, chicken, lean meats, vegetables, fruits and whole grains. A teaspoon or 2 of oil was added to most dishes, to be certain that you do not go overboard in avoiding fats. All the recipes were tested with olive oil, canola oil (Puritan) or safflower oil. If olive oil is not stated, then canola or safflower oil was used.

The American Heart Association and the American Cancer Society recommends that the daily intake of fat should be 30% of the total calories. In other words, if you are on 1500 calories a day, your intake of fat calories should be around 450. Use as a guideline that 1 tablespoon of oil is about 124 calories.

Fats used in baking make everything more tender (including people) and they have been reduced markedly in the breads and desserts included here. Butter has been used, for flavor, in several recipes, but in minute quantities. Good oils to choose from: Olive, canola (with the lowest amount of saturated fat), safflower, sunflower, soybean, or corn. Avoid coconut oil, palm oil, and hydrogenated vegetable oils.

There is also some evidence that olive oil, the best source of monounsaturated fat, can help raise the "good cholesterol". But remember, it is still high in calories and should be kept within the recommended daily allowance.

Low-Fat Mayonnaise
There are many brands of low-fat mayonnaise on the market today. Also, many companies are featuring no-cholesterol mayonnaise. Mayonnaise that was both low-fat and low-cholesterol was used throughout the testing.

Cholesterol
The Surgeon General's Report states, "Dietary cholesterol is found only in foods of animal origin, such as eggs, meat, poultry, fish and dairy products. To help reduce consumption of total fat, especially saturated fat and cholesterol, food choices should emphasize intake of fruits, vegetables and whole grain products and cereals. They should also emphasize consumption of fish, poultry prepared without skin, lean meats and low-fat dairy products. Among vegetable fats, those that are more unsaturated are better choices."

Fish & Shellfish

Fish and Shellfish
The results of recent studies seem to indicate that the Omega-3 fatty acids found in fish and shellfish may help to reduce blood cholesterol levels. Findings are not yet conclusive, so moderation is still the best policy.

Shellfish...shrimps, scallops, lobster should be used in moderation because of their content of cholesterol. For comparison, 1 large egg yolk has 272 milligrams of cholesterol and a 4-ounce serving of shrimp has 171 milligrams of cholesterol. If you must severely restrict your intake of cholesterol, use only lean fish.

Fish have varying amounts of fat, as indicated by their calorie count. The following will serve as a guide.

Lean Fish	Sole
	Flounder
	Halibut
	Pollack
	Cod
	Haddock
	Red Snapper
	Sea Bass
Moderately Fat Fish	
	Swordfish
	Tuna
	Shark
	Whiting
Fat Fish	Mackerel
	Salmon

Fruits & Peels

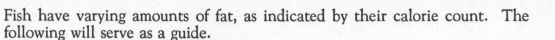

Orange Zest

In many recipes you will find the ingredient "orange zest". The "zest" is the outer peel of the orange and has the essence of the orange flavor. It is best removed by grating. (It can be peeled off and ground in a food processor, but it is hard to get it as fine as grating.) It does not include the "pith" which is the white part.

Very often you will need the ingredient "grated orange". This means that you will grate the whole orange and use the juice, fruit and peel. Of course, you will remove any large pieces of membrane. When using fruit, juice and peel, try not to use a very thick-skinned orange, or you will have too much of the white part, which can be bitter. I use the whole fruit, because in certain breads and cakes you want the "accent" of the peel.

Canned Fruit & Frozen Fruit

Both can be purchased unsweetened. Do not use fruit packed in syrup.

Grains & Complex Carbohydrates

Complex carbohydrates come in many forms of pastas and grains. In this cookbook, you will find a great variety...bulgur, cous cous, pastina, rice, orzo, barley. Each are a delight with different sauces and accompaniments. Use them often. Breads are made with wheat bran, oat bran, wheat germ, and whole wheat flours.

Oat Bran

A recent study indicated that oat bran could lower blood cholesterol levels. However, results are not conclusive.

Breads

Many low-calorie breads are included in this cookbook. Remember, you can substitute whole wheat pastry flour for the all-purpose unbleached flour. Also, the amounts of oil have been reduced to a minimum and sugar is reduced markedly.

Cracker & Cracker Crumbs

Many crackers contain coconut oil, palm oil, hydrogenated animal fats, lard which are all high in saturated fats. Be certain to look at the label and if these ingredients are present, avoid the product. Bread crumbs can be substituted for cracker crumbs. To make bread crumbs, toast bread in a 350-degree oven until crisp, and then make into crumbs in a food processor. Melba toast does not contain hydrogenated fats and can be used to make crumbs.

Flours

Whole wheat pastry flour can be substituted for all-purpose flour with good results. Whole wheat flour that is stone-ground or mill-ground can be substituted for part of the flour in certain bread recipes, but the amount of flour should be reduced by about 1 tablespoon per cup. Using the coarser flour in cakes will require some experimentation as a denser cake will be produced.

To measure flour, spoon it loosely into a cup and do not pack it. I like to store whole wheat flours in the refrigerator or freezer, as this prolongs their shelf life.

Pastas

The darlings of complex carbohydrates, and loved by almost everyone, are the many pastas available today. Fresh, frozen or dried, in every shape imaginable, they can be made with an infinite number of vegetables and flours. Spinach pasta, beet pasta, yes, even chocolate pasta. Whole wheat pasta is available in almost every supermarket.

Serve it hot, serve it cold, serve it at room temperature. It can be delicious in any manner...prepared with sauce, in salads, in soups. Pasta shops are springing up everywhere, featuring fresh pastas, which is the most tender and succulent. With pastas, fresh is better than fresh frozen and fresh frozen is better than dried. Cook pasta al dente, tender but firm. Fresh pasta cooks in minutes. Dried pasta, much longer.

Rice
Long grain white and brown rice were used throughout.

Meat & Meat Products

Meat
Trim every trace of separable fat. Meat prepared in stews or in sauces should be chilled and then every bit of congealed fat should be removed.

Beef Broth
Making homemade beef broth is more time-consuming than chicken broth. There are a few very fine prepared broths you could use. These contain about 16 calories per cup and are quite flavorful. They are used sparingly throughout this book. Use only salt-free broths if you must severely restrict your intake of sodium.

Nuts & Seeds

Walnuts
Walnuts are high in polyunsaturated fats, and it is believed they lower the "bad" blood cholesterol. However, they do contain a small amount of saturated fat.

Seasonings

Salt
No added salt was used in preparing these recipes. Herbs and spices, seasonings and broths, fruits and vegetables, shallots and garlic, were used in abundant quantities, imparting good solid flavor with no added salt. Canned broths, however, do contain salt, so if you must restrict your intake of salt, prepare homemade broth. Salt has not been added to cake or bread recipes. However, self-rising flour does contain salt as do some margarines.

Herbs
Fresh herbs are better than dried...and dried are better than none at all. So few of us can afford the luxury of a garden with fresh herbs. Window boxes or indoor planters are a close second, and are recommended.

Some of the fresh herbs found in plastic bags in the markets are wilted and unsatisfactory. If you can find healthy, fresh herbs, of course, buy them. And if you cannot, know that dried herbs are available at any time. Please know, that the shelf life of dried herbs is not as long as one would guess. In 3 to 6 months they lose their potency and should be replaced. Use 3 times the amount of fresh herbs when converting from dry herbs.

Vinegars

Herb or garlic scented vinegars add depth to salads, and they are easy to make at home. Use 1 quart cider or white vinegar or any unflavored vinegar and add a small bouquet of fresh herbs. Tarragon, dill, thyme or basil are all good. To make garlic vinegar, add 6 large cloves garlic, thinly sliced. Allow to stand for about 1 week before using.

Sugars & Sweets

Sugars

In most dessert and muffin recipes, the amount of sugar can be reduced without noticeably affecting the characteristics of the finished product. In the recipes included here, sugar has been reduced significantly and spices have been added in abundance for flavor.

Honey

While honey is a natural product, it is very high in calories and without significant nutrients. Substituting it for sugar is a personal decision, but, then, the liquid in a recipe will have to be adjusted.

Vegetables

Vegetables, basically low in calories and high in fiber and nutrients, should take a prominent place in one's diet. In the recipes included in this book, I have tried to add numerous vegetables to meat, chicken, pasta, soups, casseroles, for their nourishment and fiber and low-calorie content. In this manner, animal protein can be lessened (not omitted). Pasta dishes benefit from vegetable additions in flavor and bulk as do casseroles and soups.

Vegetables prepared in small amounts of broth have a rich and satisfying flavor. A sprinkling of shallots or chives, a squeeze of lemon, a dash of herbs will transform a vegetable dish to delicious heights.

As a general rule, fresh vegetables are superior to frozen vegetables and frozen vegetables are superior to canned. Frozen vegetables are good, if you do not have the time to shop and prepare fresh ones. In certain cases where you simply want the florets of a vegetable or a combination of mixed vegetables, using the frozen vegetables is certainly recommended. Cook vegetables until firm, but tender.

Artichoke Hearts
In several recipes, I call for a 6-ounce jar of marinated artichoke hearts. While in most cases they are drained, the artichoke still maintains a very agreeable flavor and it adds a terrific taste to the dish. The calories were calculated at 175 which is on the high (but safe) side.

Dried Beans and Peas
It is indicated in several reports that the soluble fiber in peas, beans and legumes will help to lower cholesterol, and these are used extensively throughout.

Onions and Shallots
Yellow onions, green onions and shallots are used often for flavor. However, and I am strict about this, green onions do not substitute for shallots. Shallots have a perfume and flavor of their very own, and they will enrich a dish with marvellous depth.

Tomatoes and Tomato Products
Tomatoes and tomato products are used in abundance. If you must restrict your intake of salt, use fresh tomatoes where canned tomatoes are called for. You can substitute 1 pound of fresh tomatoes for a 1-pound can of stewed tomatoes. Slice them and cook them in their own juice for 5 minutes, and then use as directed.

Tomato paste (which is basically salt-free) is a good substitute for tomato puree or tomato sauce. Dilute 1 can (6 ounces) tomato paste with 3/4 cup water to make tomato puree or with 1 1/4 cups water to produce tomato sauce. For extra flavor, dilute with chicken or beef broth, using the appropriate broth to blend with the dish.

Summarized from:

SURGEON GENERAL'S
REPORT ON NUTRITION AND HEALTH

1. Diseases such as coronary heart disease, stroke, cancer, and diabetes remain leading causes of death and disability in the United States.

2. **Substantial scientific research over the past few decades indicates that diet can play an important role in prevention of such conditions.**

3. The Public Health Service has now reviewed this research and has produced a comprehensive analysis of the relationship between dietary factors and chronic disease risk.

4. This *Surgeon General's Report on Nutrition and Health* summarizes research on the role of diet in health promotion and disease prevention. Its findings indicate **the great importance of diet to health.**

5. They demonstrate that **changes in present dietary practices of Americans could produce substantial gains in the health** of the population.

...Food sustains us, it can be a source of considerable pleasure, it is a reflection of our rich social fabric and cultural heritage, it adds valued dimensions to our lives.

...Undernutrition remains a problem in several parts of the world, as well as for certain Americans. But for most of us the more likely problem has become one of overeating--too many calories for our activity levels and an imbalance in the nutrients consumed along with them.

...As the diseases of nutritional deficiency have diminished, they have been replaced by diseases of **dietary excess and imbalance.**

...The Report's main conclusion is that overconsumption of certain dietary components is now a major concern for Americans. While many food factors are involved, chief among them is the disproportionate consumption of foods high in fats, often at the expense of foods high in complex carbohydrates and fiber that may be more conducive to health.

Recommendations for Most People

❦*Fats and cholesterol:* **Reduce consumption of fat (especially saturated fat)** and cholesterol. Choose foods relatively low in these substances, such as vegetables, fruits, whole grain foods, fish, poultry, lean meats and low-fat dairy products. Use food preparation methods that add little or no fat.

❦*Energy and weight control:* **Achieve and maintain a desirable body weight.** To do so, choose a dietary pattern in which energy (caloric) intake is consistent with energy expenditure. To reduce energy intake, limit consumption of foods relatively high in calories, fats, and sugars, and minimize alcohol consumption. Increase energy expenditure through regular and sustained physical activity.

❦*Complex carbohydrates and fiber:* **Increase consumption of whole grain foods and cereal products, vegetables (including dried beans and peas) and fruits.**

❦*Sodium:* **Reduce intake of sodium** by choosing foods relatively low in sodium and limiting the amount of salt added in food preparation and at the table.

❦*Alcohol:* **To reduce the risk for chronic disease, take alcohol only in moderation (no more than two drinks a day), if at all.** Avoid drinking any alcohol before or while driving, operating machinery, taking medications, or engaging in any other activity requiring judgment. Avoid drinking alcohol while pregnant.

Key Findings and Summary of Recommendations

1. Even though the results of various individual studies may be inconclusive, the preponderance of the evidence presented in the Report's comprehensive scientific review, substantiates an association between dietary factors and rates of chronic diseases.

2. In particular, the evidence suggests strongly that a dietary pattern that contains excessive intake of foods high in calories, fat (especially saturated fat), cholesterol, and sodium, but that is low in complex carbohydrates and fiber, is one that contributes significantly to the high rates of major chronic diseases among Americans.

3. It also suggests that reversing such dietary patterns should lead to a reduced incidence of these chronic diseases.

This *Surgeon General's Report on Nutrition and Health* provides a comprehensive review of the most important scientific evidence in support of current Federal nutrition policy as stated in the *Dietary Guidelines for Americans*. These *Guidelines*, issued jointly by the Department of Agriculture and the Department of Health and Human Services recommend:

- ❦ Eat a variety of foods.

- ❦ Maintain desirable weight.

- ❦ Avoid too much fat, saturated fat, and cholesterol.

- ❦ Eat foods with adequate starch and fiber.

- ❦ Avoid too much sugar.

- ❦ Avoid too much sodium.

- ❦ If you drink alcoholic beverages, do so in moderation.

The Surgeon General's Report on Nutrition and Health, 017-001-11465-1, can be purchased for $22.00. The Summary and Recommendations of the Surgeon General's Report 017-001-00466-9 can be purchased for $2.75. Send order to

Superintendent of Documents
Government Printing Office
Washington, D.C. 20402-9325

Call Order and Information Desk at 202-783-3238 for more information.

Positive Thinking

The relationship between positive attitude and good health is the subject of considerable research today. One study out of Stanford University Medical Center notes that good humor, positive attitude, laughter and pleasure can contribute to good health by strengthening the immune system and warding off disease. Laughter can strengthen the immune system with the beneficial effect of fighting disease.

The idea of mind-made immunity is the exciting new theory of Mood Medicine or Mood Therapy. The theory of the power of positive thinking and positive attitude is not new, but it is fast growing into a discipline. That healthy pleasures triggers the pharmacy of the brain, to release brain chemicals, that reduce the compounds that suppress the immune system, and as a result of this suppression, strengthen the immune system, is fascinating.

Health optimism can be a predictor of future health and longevity. There is a physiology of optimism and hope. People with a confident, positive outlook may have stronger immune functions and may ward off disease better. But how can you have a positive and confident attitude about the events in your life, if you do not have a positive and confident attitude about yourself. So, the better you feel about yourself, the better you feel, the healthier you are, the better you feel about yourself....a wonderful chain reaction of optimism and hope.

The following resolutions might be helpful, if you repeat them, to yourself or aloud, and often. Little by little, they offer more positive attitudes and some inner strength. I don't want to dwell on it, because it is not the scope of this book, but of my next work. Read this through once and if it has no impact on you, turn the page.

A Dozen Resolutions

1. I am the only one who chooses the food I eat.
2. I am in control.
3. I am excited by my new power.
4. I am in charge.
5. I love myself and who I am.
6. I honor myself and appreciate who I am.
7. I cherish who I am, and I will take the best care of my body.
8. I value who I am, for I am good.
9. Everyday, I will give myself a kiss...for I deserve it.
10. I am always free to choose and I am choosing to be healthy and slim.
11. I will do it!
12. I will do it NOW!

A few more words before you begin:

Most people go "on diets" which implies it is something they will eventually go "off". This cookbook is dedicated to "normal" "happy" eating that you will never need to go "on" or "off" because the recipes incorporate all the food groups, are designed to be low in fats, cholesterol, sodium AND CALORIES and can serve you well for as long as they give you pleasure.

This book is for those who are basically healthy and want to stay that way. If you have a particular dietary problem, of course, follow the guidelines of your doctor.

"Cooking Great!" stresses MODERATION which is also known as "COMMON SENSE". With moderation you can eat well, with an infinite variety of light foods, light desserts, an occasional glass of wine...all leading to pleasure and satisfaction.

Healthy Eating is Here to Stay
Eating foods that are low-calorie, low-fat, low-cholesterol, low-sodium are not to be considered a fad or passing fancy. From all indications it would appear that healthful eating, feeling fit, looking slim, vital, and energetic is now firmly rooted in the conscience of more and more Americans. More than ever before, Americans are more concerned and more aware about health and its relationship to food.

There has been compelling and increasing evidence over the past few decades, that healthy eating and exercising regularly plays an important role in maintaining good health. And now the Surgeon General's Report has found that while results of certain studies may be inconclusive, there is a preponderance of evidence suggesting a close association between diet and health.

Findings Still Inconclusive
However, reading all the reports on nutrition and fitness, can make your head whirl. The results of many studies create a lot of confusion. We are bombarded with findings. Oat bran can lower cholesterol but perhaps not necessarily more than any complex carbohydrate. Caffeine will give you the jitters but decaffeinated coffee can raise cholesterol. Eggs are high in cholesterol, well maybe not as high we think. Eat more fruits and vegetables but fruits and vegetables sprayed with pesticides can increase the risk of cancer. Fish is a good low-fat protein but fish may have a high content of mercury. Beef has too much saturated fat...but some of it may be good saturated fat.

Much of what is believed today is incomplete and still to be researched. The jury is still out on many studies and theories. Before you go overboard on oat bran or fish or on calcium supplements or any ingredient or group of ingredients, more evidence needs to be furnished. Therefore, moderation in diet and exercise is the only sensible way to approach the broad spectrum of good health. Think in terms of moderation and balance. Overeating and undereating can lead to health problems and both are to be avoided.

The 5 Basic Food Groups

1. Breads

This is the carbohydrate group, high in dietary fiber and includes breads, cereals, rice, grains, pastas. Supplies the body with energy. Should be eaten in generous quantities.

2. Fruits and Vegetables

Raw fruits and vegetables are complex carbohydrates, also high in dietary fiber. Supplies the body with vitamins and minerals. Should be eaten in generous quantities.

3. Lean Meats, Fish & Poultry

These are high-protein foods that supply the body with proteins that help build bones, muscles, nails and hair. Should be eaten in moderate quantities.

Included in this protein group are legumes, (such as dried beans, peas, soybeans, lentils), and tofu. Legumes are also complex carbohydrates and good sources of fiber. Should be eaten in generous quantities.

4. Milk & Dairy Products

These are protein foods, rich in calcium, minerals and fortified with vitamins. The low-fat and non-fat dairy products should be used, for they provide the same nourishment as whole-milk products but without the fat. Use in moderate quantities.

5. Sugars, Alcohol and Fats

This is the group that must be used with care. Sugar and alcohol offer little or no nutrition for their calories, so it is advised they be used sparingly.

How Much Food Do I Need?

Good question. At best, this is only a general guide as individual needs will vary from person to person. Age, body type, amount of daily activity, metabolism all contribute to your daily needs.

For a general idea of how much food you need, multiply your present weight by 15. This will give you a rough idea of how many calories you need to maintain your present weight. For example, if you weigh 150 pounds, to maintain that weight, you will have to consume about (150x15) or 2250 calories a day. Reducing (or increasing) that amount, by 500 calories a day, will result in a 1 pound weight loss (or gain) per week. It is recommended that you do not go under 1200 calories per day without being under the care of a physician.

You will have to ask your doctor to recommend the number of calories to get you started. If you have been on very low calorie, fasting-type diets, your metabolism might be affected. Let's use a daily intake of 1500 calories as an example.

1500 Calorie Sample Menus

On the following 1500 Calorie Sample Menus, you will note many options and a few "musts". The options were chosen with a range of calorie values (some considerably higher than others), to illustrate how you can choose a higher-caloried dish and balance it with a lower-caloried accompaniment and still keep a low total for the meal.

The 1500 Calorie Sample Menus are roughly guided by the following outline with approximately 1300 to 1350 calories. The extra 150 to 200 calories can be chosen from any food group except fats or oils. It can include an occasional wine, a little dessert, an extra salad, some whole-grain bread. Keep track of the calories.

Breakfast - 200 calories
Mid-Morning Snack - 110 calories
Lunch - 250 to 300 calories
Mid-Afternoon Snack - 110 calories
Dinner - 500 calories
Night Snack - 130 calories

Consider the daily total calorie intake.
If you choose a dish for lunch or dinner that is higher in calories, then choose a low-calorie salad or soup as an accompaniment. Or go lighter on another meal. You can choose from a vast number of options, just keep the total calories in mind.

Keep it Varied and Interesting
Considering the number of options, please eat as varied and interesting diet as possible. Be happy and excited about food. It is one of the pleasures of life and, heavens knows, who is so abundant in pleasure and can afford to give up a single one. Besides chicken and fish, which are now the most popular, choose meat, legumes, an occasional vegetarian dinner like Vegetable Paella or Chile & Rice.

Plan Your Meals and Write it Down
Don't trust this to memory. On a piece of paper, plan your meals, for 1 day, 2 days, or whatever. Figure the calories and then follow your plan.

Sample Menus
1500 calorie

	Total	Daily Totals
Breakfast		
Breakfast Fruit (Choose 1)		
1/2 papaya (8 ounces)	60	
1 cup strawberries	53	✓
1 peach-4 ounces	38	

Breakfast (Choose 1)

2 Cottage Cheese Pancakes with	106	
2 tablespoons Fresh Strawberry Sauce	18	124
Cinnamon Cranberry & Orange Muffin		112
Buttermilk Oat Bran Muffins with Orange & Banana		125 ✓
Oat Bran Cereal made with 1/3 cup oat bran		100

Total Breakfast	**178**

Mid-Morning Snack (See "Daily Musts")

1/3 cup non-fat cottage cheese	47	✓
1 small orange	60	✓
Total Mid-Morning Snack		**107**

Lunch

Lunch (Must)

Large Raw Vegetable Salad with Dressing	62	✓

Lunch (Choose 1)

Eggplant Lasagna	145	✓
Royal Artichoke & Spinach Casserole	113	
Eggplant Frittata with Onions & Cheese	88	

Lunch Dessert (Choose 1)

4 ounces non-fat frozen yogurt	56	✓
Oatmeal & Raisin Bar Cookie	35	
Total Lunch		**263**

Mid-Afternoon Snack (See "Daily Musts")

1 apple	60	✓
1/2 cup non-fat yogurt	55	✓
Total Mid-Afternoon Snack		**115**

Dinner

Dinner-Soup or Salad (Choose 1)

Best Country Cabbage & Tomato Soup	54
Easiest & Best Clam Chowder	72
Leek & Potato Soup with Chives	59
Carrot Soup with Apples	61
Low-Calorie Farmhouse Vegetable Soup	61 ✓
Leeks & Tomatoes in Lemon Dressing	48
Eggplant & Tomato Salad	38
Asparagus Vinaigrette	32
Cucumber Salad with Parsley & Chives	19
Tomatoes with Garlic Croutons	38
Marinated Red Pepper Salad	30
Raw Vegetable Salad	62

———————

Dinner-Main Course & Carbohydrate (Choose 1 Pair)

Costa del Sol Mediterranean Chowder	156
2 slices Croustades of Olive Oil & Parmesan	130
Sea Bass with Tomato, Currants & Pine Nuts	177
Pink Rice with Chives & Parsley	138
Fillets of Sole with Leeks & Tomato Sauce	152 ✓
Pastina with Fresh Tomato & Basil Sauce	126 ✓
Sole with Sun-Dried Tomato & Pepper Sauce	125
Herbed Orzo with Tomatoes & Onions	159
Fillets of Sole in Artichoke & Tomato Sauce	122
Garlic Potatoes with Onions & Rosemary	109
Old Fashioned Hungarian Goulash	202
Cracked Wheat with Mushroom & Onions	134
Moroccan Lamb Dumplings with	231
Vegetable Cous Cous	104

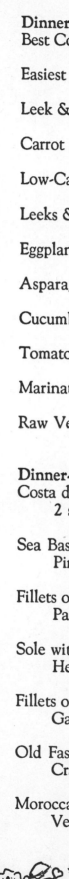

Tomatoes Stuffed with Turkey in Light Tomato Sauce	223
Brown Rice with Leeks & Onions	139
Kung Pao Chicken with Peanuts	262
Steamed Rice	110
Chicken in Dill & Wine Sauce	209
Rice with Lemon & Chives	129
Plum-Glazed Teriyaki Chicken	241
Fried Rice	128
Chicken with Red Cabbage, Apples & Cranberries	255
Potato & Onion Cake	96
Vegetable Paella	269
Jambalaya Creole	297

_____

Desserts (Choose 1)

Orange Apple and Oatmeal Cake	95	
Walnut Cake with Raspberry & Lemon Glaze	163	✔
Orange & Walnut Torte with Orange Glaze	150	
Skinny Chocolate Torte ala Sacher	156	
Angel Cake with Strawberry Sauce	92	
Peach & Macaroon Crumb Cobbler	102	
Lemon Cheesecake with Strawberry Sauce	145	
Banana Iced Cream	58	
Iced Vanilla Glace with Strawberries Grand Marnier	40	
Basic Fruit Souffle	39	
Apple Tart	126	
Total for Dinner	**502**	

Evening Snack (See "Daily Musts")

1 small banana	81	✓
2/3 cup non-fat milk	53	✓
Total Evening Snack	**134**	

YOU WILL NOTICE THAT THE ITEMS CHECKED OFF ON THE MENU TOTAL APPROXIMATELY 1300 CALORIES. THIS ALLOWS YOU AN EXTRA 200 CALORIES, THAT CAN BE CHOSEN FROM ANY OF THE FOOD GROUPS, EXCEPT OILS OR FATS. IT CAN INCLUDE SOME WHOLE GRAIN BREAD, A GLASS OF WINE (OCCASIONALLY), ADD A SALAD AT DINNER, OR AN EXTRA FRUIT. JUST KEEP TRACK OF THE CALORIES.

"Daily Musts"

(Each of the following must be eaten every day, whenever desired, but preferably as mid-morning, afternoon or evening snacks.)

2 cups non-fat milk (160) or 1 1/2 cups non-fat yogurt (165) or 1 cup non-fat cottage cheese (140) - (average)	160
1 small orange (4 ounces)	64
1 small banana (6 ounces)	81
1 small apple (4 ounces)	60
	365

Important - Please note that mid-morning, mid-afternoon and evening snacks are a must. Also, note, these are a combination of a protein and a complex carbohydrate. Snacks were chosen, with the idea in mind, that you would be at work during the day, and these are easy to take to work. Also, mid-meal snacks help to keep the blood sugar and energy levels more constant.

How to Use the "Table of Contents" to Plan Menus

To help you plan your menus in the most convenient way, each recipe is listed in the Table of Contents with its calorie value. When you plan your meals, for the day or week, run through the contents of each chapter, pick the dishes that appeal to you, write them down, and note their calorie value. Be sure to pick from each food group as described earlier. If you choose a higher calorie main course, choose a salad or soup with a lower calorie value. You will have to experiment on the totals for the day. Start with 1500 and adjust from there. Be certain to include foods from each food group. The "Sample Menus" will be a guide.

A Few Last Words - To make changes in life-style and eating habits is never easy. But the following may help to make the shift more successful.

1. Do not skip meals or snacks. It is important to keep blood sugar levels constant. Avoid becoming ravenously hungry.

2. Authorities recommend drinking 6 to 8 glasses of water per day. About tea or coffee, caffeine or decaffeinated, keep it moderate (2 cups a day) until more is known.

3. If there are times when you feel exceptionally hungry, there are many healthy choices you can make. A raw vegetable salad, with low-calorie dressing, can be very filling, and will give your jaws a good work-out, too. Any of the low-calorie soups are very nourishing and satisfying. A cup of hot tea with a low-calorie muffin is good. A baked apple, or 1/2 cup of non-fat frozen yogurt or light ice milk is a terrific snack.

4. Do not eat anything that isn't enjoyable for you. Don't waste your calories on foods that do not satisfy you.

5. When dining out, remember to order food seasoned with lemon, mustard, vegetables or fruit. Dishes named "Provencal" are relatively safe as they are laden with vegetables. Restaurants, today, are very aware of the trend toward healthier food, and it is very acceptable and common to order dishes "prepared without oil." To be especially safe, ask the waiter to bring the salad dressings, sauces or gravies on the side and use them with moderation. Dipping the tip of your fork into the dressing and then into the salad, is a common way of managing salad dressings and is very economical calorically.

Dessert can be difficult. If you can't stop with a reasonable taste, share it with a friend (or two). You will be amazed how a small taste can satisfy. It would be unreasonable to believe that fresh fruit will be your only dessert for the rest of your life.

6. Chicken (without the skin) and fish are lower in calories than beef, pork or lamb.

7. After a while you will know what 4 ounces of chicken looks like, but until you do, it is a good idea to weigh your food.

8. At dinner parties or cocktail parties, vegetable platters are often included. But common sense dictates that you cannot be expected to only eat vegetables, or drink club soda with a dash of lemon at every party. Plan to eat lighter (don't skip a meal) the day of the party and save a few calories for a glass of wine or a special hors d'oeuvre. Remember, you can satisfy your taste buds, but with moderation.

9. Stock your freezer with pre-measured portions of breads, muffins, frittatas, lasagna, soups, main courses and desserts for meals or snacks. Mark the calories on each portion. A snack of Spinach Frittata or Eggplant Frittata is truly satisfying. It heats in minutes in a toaster oven, and Voila!... a low-calorie and delicious snack.

10. Confer with your doctor and start an appropriate exercise program today.

Basics

From my notebook:

In this chapter you will find many basic sauces that will sparkle a bland vegetable and give zest to certain dishes. The Seasoned Flour for Chicken or Fish is strongly flavored with garlic and paprika. A little goes a long way. The Sun-Dried Tomatoes is one of the most delicious accompaniments to salads, pastas, pizza, and sauces and I recommend you keep it handy in the refrigerator. As mentioned earlier, using homemade chicken broth is strongly recommended because of its flavor and richness and low calorie content. Also, the amount of sodium can be controlled.

Spreads, (Low-Calorie Cheese and Chives or Mayonnaise-Like) are good to use on toast, baked potatoes or in tuna. Using whipped non-fat cottage cheese for sour cream (Low-Calorie Sour Cream) is much more delicious than it sounds and it is pure and wholesome.

Low-Calorie Hollandaise and Béarnaise Sauce are beautiful to serve on vegetables. They can be prepared without the little amount of butter, but that is a personal preference. Also included are variations which will add excitement and variety to meals. The Horseradish Sauce for Roast Beef will also add a marvelous touch to the roast and is exceedingly low in calories. A few more sauces round out the chapter.

Low-Calorie Strawberry Jam is a little gem that I keep available at all times. It is truly benign and very satisfying. It is good to serve on toast, sponge cakes, even frozen yogurt or ice milk. Fresh Strawberry Sauce can be used in the same manner and is, also, low in calories and very tasty.

Seasoned Flour for Chicken or Fish

1/2	cup flour
1/2	teaspoon garlic powder
1/2	teaspoon onion powder
1	teaspoon paprika
1/8	teaspoon cayenne pepper
1/8	teaspoon white pepper

In a plastic bag, shake together all the ingredients until blended. This is an excellent coating for fish or chicken. Stored in the freezer, it will keep for months.

(About 25 calories per tablespoon)

Sun-Dried Tomatoes

Sun-dried tomatoes add an intense flavor to casseroles and pastas. Sometimes they are packed in a salty solution and sometimes in oil. Never buy the salty ones, for their flavor is less than satisfactory. Those packed in oil are more acceptable, but their is still a wide variation between the different companies. This is a pure and wholesome recipe that you can make, without adding salt or preservatives. While these are stored in a little olive oil, they can be drained before using. Use them in pastas, casseroles, rice, salads, sauces. The added flavor is well worth their few calories. This recipe is from my "Entertaining Fast & Fancy".

2	pounds Italian plum tomatoes (about 8 to the pound)
2	cloves garlic, minced
4	tablespoons champagne vinegar
1	teaspoon sweet basil flakes
4	tablespoons olive oil

Cut tomatoes in half, lengthwise, and remove stem and seeds. Place tomatoes, cut side up, on a non-stick shallow baker and place in a very low oven at 140-degrees, until tomatoes are shriveled and dehydrated, but not completely dried to a crisp, about 6 to 8 hours, depending on the size of the tomato. Tomatoes should retain just a little moisture.

Place tomatoes in a glass jar, with a tight-fitting lid, and add the remaining ingredients. Seal jar and shake contents so that tomatoes are fully coated with oil/vinegar mixture. Refrigerate until ready to use. Can be stored in the refrigerator for several weeks, shaking contents from time to time. Use in pastas, sauce, salads, casseroles for an intense tomato flavor.

(About 25 calories per 2 tomatoes-drained)

Basic Chicken Broth

Homemade chicken broth has markedly fewer calories than the broth from cans. It, also, has far less salt. But making broth can be time-consuming, and somehow, time is becoming more and more of a problem. However, if you are inclined to make broth, the following is a simple recipe. Broth can be frozen in 1/2 cup containers and is used in numerous recipes throughout this book to enhance the flavor of vegetables, casseroles, rice and the like. It is not necessary to peel the vegetables. Water should be cold and heated slowly. The stock should not boil, but simmer. Pot should be uncovered or with cover ajar, or stock will become bitter.

1   fryer chicken (about 3 pounds) cut into serving pieces
2   pounds chicken back bones
3   quarts cold water

2   large onions, cut into slices
4   carrots, sliced
2   stalks celery, without leaves, sliced
2   leeks, split and washed to remove sand
4   cloves garlic, peeled and cut in half
1/2   teaspoon thyme flakes

In a stockpot, place chicken, bones and water and bring to a slow boil. Skim away any scum that has formed. Add the remaining ingredients and simmer soup for 2 hours, uncovered. Allow to cool enough to handle. Remove chicken, skin it and bone it. It has lost a lot of flavor by now, so shredding it and using it in a soup or salad is all you could do with it.

Place double thicknesses of cheesecloth in a strainer and strain soup. Discard vegetables and refrigerate broth. When cold, remove every trace of fat that has congealed on top. Store in 1/2 cup containers and freeze. Yields about 8 cups.

(About 3 or 4 calories per cup)

To make Extra-Rich Chicken Broth:
In the above recipe use 3 quarts of chicken broth instead of water. This will make the broth exceedingly rich and flavorful. Store as above.

(About 8 calories per cup)

Low-Calorie Cheese & Chives Spread

    8   ounces low-fat or skimmed-milk ricotta cheese
    1/3   cup non-fat unflavored yogurt
    1   teaspoon lemon juice (or a little more to taste)
    4   tablespoons chopped chives

In a food processor, blend all the ingredients for 10 seconds, or until chives are pureed. Spread on toast or baked potatoes. Yields 1 1/2 cups.
(About 15 calories per tablespoon)

Low-Calorie Mayonnaise-Like Spread

    3/4   cup unflavored low-fat yogurt
    2   tablespoons lemon juice (or more to taste)
    3   tablespoons chopped chives

In a food processor, blend all the ingredients for 10 seconds, or until chives are pureed. Use on salads or mix with tuna. Yields about 1 cup.
(About 7 calories per tablespoon)

Low-Calorie Sour Cream

While this is not as rich as its high-calorie cousin, it tastes really delicious and pure. In some parts of the country, you can purchase prepared whipped cottage cheese. It is getting more and more difficult to find in Southern California. And I cannot imagine why, as it is an excellent alternative to sour cream.

    1   cup non-fat cottage cheese
    2   tablespoons lemon juice

Beat cottage cheese and lemon juice in the container of a food processor and blend until mixture is very smooth and creamy. Use as you would sour cream, over potatoes, or in dips and salad dressings. Yields about 1 cup.
(About 9 calories per tablespoon)

Low-Calorie Hollandaise Sauce

This is an excellent sauce to serve over fish, chicken or vegetables...and it will save you a thousand calories. It is simple to prepare, but care should be taken to avoid curdling the sauce. Follow the instructions exactly and you will savor the lowest-calorie Hollandaise in history. To further reduce calories, this sauce can be prepared without the butter, in which case, it would resemble the Greek Lemon and Egg Sauce. This sauce will sparkle the blandest dish. Also note, that by using the whole egg, instead of the traditional egg yolks, the amount of cholesterol drops markedly.

2	tablespoons lemon juice
6	tablespoons chicken broth
1	egg
1 1/2	teaspoons butter, melted (optional)

In a saucepan, heat together lemon juice and chicken broth to boiling point. In another saucepan, beat egg with a whisk or a fork, until thoroughly blended. Drizzle hot broth mixture into egg, whisking constantly, until blended. Place pan over low heat and cook, stirring constantly, until sauce thickens slightly, about 2 to 3 minutes. (This is not a thick sauce.) Stir in the melted butter and serve warm. Sauce can be refrigerated and heated before serving. Heat just until warm and do not overheat. Yields 3/4 cup sauce.

Food Processor Method:
This can be prepared in a food processor. Beat the egg until foamy. Bring lemon juice and broth to a boil, and drizzle it in slowly, with the motor running, until it is incorporated. Transfer mixture to a saucepan, and over low heat, stirring constantly, cook sauce for 2 to 3 minutes or until it thickens slightly. Stir in the melted butter (optional).

Hollandaise with Chives:
Add 2 tablespoons minced chives to the finished sauce.

Hollandaise with Dill:
Add 1/2 teaspoon dried dill weed (or 2 teaspoons fresh dill weed) to the finished sauce and serve with fish or vegetables.

Hollandaise with Basil:
Add 1/2 teaspoon dried sweet basil flakes (or 2 teaspoons chopped fresh basil) to the finished sauce and serve with fish or vegetables.

(About 12 calories per tablespoon-using butter)
(About 8 calories per tablespoon-without butter)

Low-Calorie Béarnaise Sauce

You will never feel deprived when you lavish this sauce on a tender, medium-rare tenderloin. It will also sparkle broiled fish and chicken. As with the Hollandaise, to avoid curdling, use low heat and stir constantly.

2 eggs

2 tablespoons tarragon vinegar
3/4 cup chicken broth
1 shallot, minced (about 1 tablespoon)
1/4 teaspoon dried tarragon (or 3/4 teaspoon fresh)
     pinch of white pepper

1 tablespoon butter, melted

In a food processor, beat eggs until foamy. In a saucepan, cook together next 5 ingredients until shallots are softened. Slowly, drizzle broth mixture into the eggs, with the machine running constantly, until it is incorporated. Transfer sauce to a saucepan, and over low heat, stirring constantly, cook sauce for 2 to 3 minutes, or until it has thickened slightly. Beat in the melted butter. Yields about 1 1/2 cups sauce.

(About 12 calories per tablespoon)

Variations (Insignificant increase in calories):
1. Add 1 teaspoon of prepared horseradish to the finished sauce and serve cold with roast beef.

2. Add 2 teaspoons of ketchup and 1 tablespoon chopped chives to the finished sauce and serve with roast chicken or meats.

Horseradish Sauce for Roast Beef

1 cup non-fat unflavored yogurt
2 tablespoons half and half cream
1 tablespoon chopped chives
1 tablespoon finely chopped parsley (no stems)
2 tablespoons prepared horseradish sauce
   white pepper to taste

Stir together all the ingredients until blended. Refrigerate sauce for several hours before serving. Yields 1 1/3 cups sauce.
(About 8 calories per tablespoon)

Mayonnaise-Hollandaise & Chive Sauce

This is not a real low-calorie sauce, but a small amount will sparkle a bland vegetable. Actually, 1 tablespoon will go a long way to flavor 1 portion of vegetables.

- 1/2 cup low-calorie mayonnaise
- 3 tablespoons lemon juice or a little more to taste
- 2 tablespoons unflavored non-fat yogurt

- 3 tablespoons chopped chives

Just before serving, in a saucepan, over low heat, stir together first 3 ingredients and heat, stirring, just until sauce is warm. Do not allow to boil. Stir in the chives. Serve over asparagus or broccoli. Yields 1 cup sauce.

(About 21 calories per tablespoon)

Low-Calorie Sauce with Dills & Chives

This is a sour-cream-type sauce that is nice to serve over fish, baked potatoes, or asparagus.

- 1 cup non-fat cottage cheese
- 1/4 cup unflavored non-fat yogurt
- 2 tablespoons low-fat milk

- 3 tablespoons chopped chives
- 1 tablespoon lemon juice
- 1/2 teaspoon dried dill weed

In a food processor, place first 3 ingredients and blend until cottage cheese is pureed. Blend in chives, lemon juice and dill. Yields 1 1/2 cups sauce.

(About 13 calories per tablespoon)

Light Mayonnaise

- 1 egg
- 3 tablespoons lemon juice
- 1/4 cup chopped chives

- 1/4 cup oil
- 1 cup unflavored non-fat yogurt

In a blender, beat together first 3 ingredients until blended. Drizzle in the oil, a few drops at a time, until completely incorporated. Beat in the yogurt, in 4 batches, until blended. Yields 1 3/4 cups sauce.

(About 25 calories per tablespoon)

Low-Cal Fresh Strawberry Jam

This little gem is very much like the expensive fruit spreads that are cropping up all over. Be certain that the strawberries are thoroughly cooked, or the jam will not last more than 2 days.

1	envelope unflavored gelatin
1/4	cup water
1/4	cup orange juice

2	tablespoons sugar or honey
2	tablespoons lemon juice
1	very thin slice lemon (about 1/8-inch)
2	cups (1 pint) strawberries, sliced

In a 1-cup metal measuring cup, soften gelatin in water and orange juice. Place cup in a larger pan with simmering water and stir until gelatin is dissolved.

Meanwhile, in a saucepan, place the remaining ingredients and simmer mixture, stirring now and again, for about 20 minutes, or until strawberries are cooked through. Discard lemon slice. Stir in gelatin mixture until thoroughly blended and simmer for 1 minute, stirring. Place jam in a jar with a tight-fitting lid and store in the refrigerator. Serve with toast, over crepes or on sponge cake. Yields about 2 cups.

(About 8 calories per tablespoon)

Fresh Strawberry Sauce

This sauce is tart and fruity and very good on pancakes or French toast.

1/2	cup orange juice
1/4	cup lemon juice
2	tablespoons sugar or honey
1	tablespoon cornstarch

1	pint strawberries, hulled and sliced

In a saucepan, stir together first 4 ingredients until blended. Simmer mixture, stirring, for about 5 minutes, or until slightly thickened. Stir in strawberries and simmer for an additional 10 minutes, stirring now and again, until syrup is clear. Refrigerate until ready to use. Serve over ice milk, pancakes or sponge cake. Yields about 2 cups sauce.

(About 9 calories per tablespoon)

Breads & Muffins

From my notebook:

Here you will find lots of muffins, sweet and savory breads, French toast made in the oven, plus a few biscuits to accompany meals. The muffins are all delicious and range in calories from real low at 112 to a moderate 140. These are good choices for breakfast or snacks as they are filled with bran, oat bran, rolled oats, bran flakes, wheat germ or whole wheat flour. These are generous in size and not like little thimbles which will leave you wanting more. Muffins are flavored with many fresh fruits, orange, cranberries, bananas. Dried fruits, like apricots, dates, raisins, currants can also be found. Fresh vegetables include carrots and zucchini.

Butter-less, Egg-less Whole Wheat Muffins are really delicious and accented with walnuts and raisins. The Spicy Apricot Bread is a real caloric bargain, for a 1-inch slice is only 72 calories. Spread with a little Devonshire Cream, will still keep the calories low. There is an important little note on the bottom of the recipe that I do not want you to miss. Any of the muffins, or breads can be sliced very thin, and toasted in the oven. This will give you small amounts to munch on and the crunch will make your jaws happy, too.

The flatbreads are wonderful and I promise they will add a good deal of excitement and pleasure to your meals. The three I included use 3 basic principles. They use yeast, baking powder or self-rising flour (which has the baking powder already included.) These can be varied with different herbs or spices, onions or garlic, lemon or cheese, to match you meal. Whole wheat pastry flour works exceedingly well in these recipes.

The two basic whole wheat breads are just fabulous. They are good for slicing or toasting into melbas or crackers. They also are fine and pure to use as crumbs. Basic Whole Wheat Bread was designed as a dinner bread and Basic Whole Wheat Bread with the honey and orange flavor is great for breakfast. They freeze beautifully.

I will tell you, right at the start, that the Oven-Baked French Toast is not as good as making it on a griddle. If you have a non-stick griddle, I prefer the texture. Making it in the oven is a bit tricky, for if you overbake it, it becomes rubbery. So keep this little tip in mind.

And the two biscuit recipes are also basic and can be made with various additions...onion, garlic, sesame seeds, a little cheese. All these breads and muffins will add interest and pleasure to your meals.

Zucchini Oatmeal Muffins

Zucchini adds moistness, but no taste to these muffins. To make these into Chocolate Zucchini Muffins, substitute 2 tablespoons cocoa for 2 tablespoons of the flour. This will produce a moist chocolate muffin with no evidence of the zucchini.

1	cup buttermilk
1/2	cup sugar
2	tablespoons oil
1	egg
2	tablespoons grated orange peel
1	teaspoon vanilla
1	cup peeled and grated zucchini
1	cup flour
1	cup oats
1	tablespoon baking powder
2	teaspoons cinnamon

Beat together first 6 ingredients until blended. Stir in zucchini. Beat in the remaining ingredients until blended. Do not overbeat. Divide batter between 12 paper-lined muffin cups and bake at 400-degrees for 20 minutes. Yields 12 muffins.

(About 130 calories per muffin)

Oat Bran & Carrot Muffins

These are moist and tasty muffins and are a good choice for breakfast or afternoon snack. If you like to make these spicy, add 2 teaspoons of pumpkin pie spice to the batter. To make these into Apple Muffins, substitute 1 cup grated apple for 1 cup grated carrots.

1	egg
2	tablespoons oil
3/4	cup buttermilk
1/2	cup sugar
1	cup grated carrots
1	teaspoon vanilla
3/4	cup oat bran
1	cup whole wheat flour
2	teaspoons baking powder
1	teaspoon baking soda
1/4	cup dried currants

Beat together first 6 ingredients until blended. Beat in the remaining ingredients until blended. Divide batter between 12 paper-lined muffin cups and bake at 400 degrees for 20 minutes, or until a cake tester, inserted in center comes out clean. Yields 12 muffins.

(About 140 calories per muffin)

Butter-less, Egg-less Whole Wheat Muffins
with Walnuts & Raisins

This is an interesting and unusual muffin as it does not contain any butter or eggs. It contains the simplest of cupboard ingredients and yet produces a dark, chewy, fine-tasting muffin with an unusual character.

3/4   cup hot tap water
1/2   cup molasses
1 1/4   cups buttermilk (or sour milk)
3/4   cup brown sugar
1   teaspoon vanilla

2   cups whole wheat flour
1   cup flour
3   teaspoons baking powder
1   teaspoon baking soda
1/4   teaspoon salt (optional)
1/4   cup chopped walnuts
1/4   cup yellow raisins

In the large bowl of an electric mixer, beat together water and molasses until blended. Beat in milk, sugar and vanilla. Beat in remaining ingredients until blended. Do not overbeat.

Divide batter between 18 paper-lined muffin cups and bake in a 325-degree oven for about 35 minutes, or until a cake tester, inserted in center comes out clean. Allow to cool in pan for 10 minutes, and then remove from pan and continue cooling on a rack. Yields 18 muffins.

(About 139 calories per muffin)

To Make Sour Milk: Stir together 1 1/4 cups lo-fat milk and 1 teaspoon lemon juice.

Bran & Oatmeal Date Nut Muffins

These muffins are filled with bran and oats and an excellent source of fiber. They are exceedingly tasty and good for breakfast or snacking.

1 1/2	cups 100% Bran Cereal
1	cup quick-cooking oats
1 1/2	cups orange juice
1	egg
1/4	cup oil
1/3	cup sugar
1	cup flour
1	tablespoon baking powder
2	teaspoons cinnamon
1/2	cup chopped pitted dates
1/4	cup coarsely chopped walnuts

Beat together first 6 ingredients until blended. Stir together and add the remaining ingredients until blended. Do not overmix. Divide batter between 18 paper-lined muffin cups and bake at 400-degrees for about 25 minutes, or until tops are browned. Allow to cool in pan for 10 minutes, and then remove from pan and continue cooling on a rack. Yields 18 muffins.

(Each muffin approximately 133 calories)

Spicy Orange Bran & Oatmeal Muffins

Another delicious, healthy, fiber-filled muffin that is a treat for breakfast.

1 1/2	cups unprocessed bran flakes
1	cup oats
1 1/2	cups non-fat milk
1	egg
1/3	cup sugar
1/4	cup oil
1	medium orange, grated
1 1/4	cups flour
1	tablespoon baking powder
1/4	cup coarsely chopped walnuts
2	teaspoons cinnamon
1/4	teaspoon ground nutmeg
1/4	teaspoon ground cloves

Beat together first group of ingredients until blended. Stir together and add the remaining ingredients until blended. Do not overmix. Divide batter between 18 paper-lined muffin cups and bake at 400-degrees for 25 minutes, or until tops are browned. Allow to cool in pan for 10 minutes, and then remove from pan and continue cooling on a rack. Yields 18 muffins.

(About 133 calories per muffin)

Cinnamon Cranberry & Orange Muffins

This muffin has a really low number of calories and one would never guess it. It is delicious and healthy, too, with whole wheat, bran, fruit and buttermilk.

2	tablespoons oil
3/4	cup buttermilk
1/2	cup sugar
1	egg
2	tablespoons grated orange peel

3/4	cup all-bran cereal
1	cup whole wheat flour
1	teaspoon cinnamon
2	teaspoons baking powder
1	teaspoon baking soda

1	cup fresh or frozen cranberries, sliced in half

In the large bowl of an electric mixer, beat together first group of ingredients until mixture is blended. Stir together next 5 ingredients and add, all at once, beating just until blended. Stir in the cranberries. Divide batter between 12 paper-lined muffin cups. Bake at 400-degrees for 20 minutes or until a cake tester, inserted in center, comes out clean. Yields 12 muffins.

(About 112 calories per muffin)

To make into Peach or Apricot Muffins:
Substitute 1 cup chopped peaches or apricots for the cranberries.

Buttermilk Oat Bran Muffins with Orange & Bananas

These flavorful muffins are made with oat bran and whole wheat flour, sparkled with orange, banana and cinnamon and crunchy with raisins and nuts. They are really good...and good for you, too.

2	cups oat bran
1/2	cup water
1	cup buttermilk
4	tablespoons oil
1/4	cup honey
2	eggs

3	tablespoons grated orange (fruit, juice and peel)
1/4	cup yellow raisins

More →

Buttermilk Oat Bran Muffins (Continued)

1 1/2	cups whole wheat flour
1 1/2	teaspoons cinnamon
1	teaspoon baking soda
1/2	teaspoon baking powder
1	medium banana, coarsely mashed

In a large bowl, beat together first 6 ingredients until blended. Stir in orange and raisins. Stir together next 4 ingredients, add to bran mixture and beat just until blended. Do not overmix. Stir in banana. Divide batter between 18 paper-lined muffin cups and bake at 350-degrees for 25 minutes. Yields 18 muffins.

(About 125 calories per muffin)

Buttermilk Orange Bran Muffins with Raisins & Walnuts

A lovely breakfast muffin, sparkling with the flavor of orange and spices. And good for you, too, with lots of fiber.

1	egg
1	cup buttermilk
1	tablespoon oil
4	tablespoons grated orange. (Use fruit, juice and peel.)
1/4	cup dark molasses
3	tablespoons sugar

1 1/2	cups whole wheat flour
1/3	cup Miller's Unprocessed Bran Flakes
1	teaspoon baking powder
1	teaspoon baking soda
1	teaspoon cinnamon
1	teaspoon ground nutmeg
1/4	cup chopped raisins
1/4	cup chopped walnuts

In the large bowl of an electric mixer, beat together first 6 ingredients until blended. Stir together the remaining ingredients and add, all at once. beating until blended. Do not overmix.

Divide batter between 12 paper-lined muffin cups and bake at 350-degrees for 25 to 30 minutes, or until a cake tester, inserted in center, comes out clean. Allow to cool for 10 minutes and then remove from pan and continue cooling on a rack. Yields 12 muffins.

(About 133 calories per muffin)

Note: -Buttermilk can be substituted with 1 cup low-fat milk stirred with 1 teaspoon lemon juice.

Apple & Orange Whole Wheat Muffins

These heavenly muffins are fragrant with cinnamon and orange and richly flavored with apples, currants and walnuts. They freeze beautifully and are nice to have on hand.

1   egg
1   cup buttermilk
1/4   cup honey
1   tablespoon oil

1/2   medium orange, grated
1   small apple, peeled, cored and grated
1/4   cup currants
1/4   cup chopped walnuts

1 1/2 cups whole wheat flour
1/2   cup Miller's bran flakes
2   teaspoons baking powder
1   teaspoon cinnamon
      pinch of ground nutmeg and ground cloves

Beat together first 4 ingredients until blended. Stir in the next 4 ingredients until blended. Stir together remaining ingredients and add, all at once, stirring just until blended. Do not overmix. Divide batter between 12 paper-lined muffin cups and bake at 350-degrees for 25 minutes, or until tops are browned. Yields 12 muffins.

(About 139 calories per muffin)

Low-Cal Cinnamon Orange Bran Muffins

When you taste these marvelous muffins, you will hardly believe that they are roughly 120 calories each. You won't feel deprived or left wanting. And, they are chock-full of fiber and fruit.

1 1/2 cups all-bran cereal
1   cup skimmed milk
2   tablespoons oil
2   tablespoons sugar
1   egg
1   medium orange, grated. (Use fruit, juice and peel.)

1 1/3 cups flour
3   teaspoons baking powder
1   teaspoon cinnamon
2   teaspoons cinnamon sugar

Beat together first 6 ingredients until blended. Beat in next 3 ingredients until blended. Do not overbeat. Divide batter between 12 paper-lined muffin cups and sprinkle tops with a little cinnamon sugar. Bake in a 400-degree oven for 20 minutes, or until a cake tester, inserted in center, comes out clean. Allow to cool in pan for 10 minutes, and then remove from pan and continue cooling on a rack. Yields 12 muffins.

(About 120 calories per muffin)

Spicy Apricot & Carrot Bread

In many cases, 2 egg whites can be substituted for 1 whole egg. It does change the character and color of the loaf a bit. But if cholesterol is a problem, then the substitution will not let you feel deprived. You can still enjoy many breads and cakes using only egg whites. In this recipe, which is basic, carrots can be substituted with zucchini or apples. The apricots can be substituted with raisins or currants.

4	egg whites
1/4	cup oil
1	cup unflavored non-fat yogurt
1/4	cup orange juice
3/4	cup sugar
2	teaspoons vanilla
1	cup grated carrots
1 1/2	cups all-purpose flour
1 1/2	cups whole wheat flour
1	tablespoon baking powder
3	teaspoons pumpkin pie spice
1/2	cup chopped apricots (2 ounces)

Beat together first group of ingredients until blended. Beat in the carrots. Beat in the remaining ingredients until blended. Do not overbeat. Divide batter between 5 mini-loaf pans (6x3-inches) and bake at 350-degrees for 40 minutes, or until a cake tester, inserted in center, comes out clean. Allow to cool in pan for 5 minutes, and then remove from pans and continue cooling on a rack. Yields 5 mini-loaves and about 30 1-inch slices.

(About 72 calories per 1-inch slice)

To make into Mandelbread:
This bread is delicious, sliced very thin and toasted until crisp. Slice bread into 1/2-inch slices and place on a cookie sheet. Toast in a 350-degree oven until lightly browned. Turn and brown other side. (Yields 144 slices and about 36 calories per slice.)

Focaccio-Italian Flatbread
with Red Peppers, Garlic & Cheese

An excellent accompaniment to dinner in an Italian mood. This bread, studded with red peppers and green onions and flavored with garlic and rosemary, will appeal to all your senses. It is assembled in minutes and produces a truly delicious bread. It can be prepared earlier in the day or 1 day earlier, securely wrapped in foil and stored in the refrigerator. Heat bread in a 350-degree oven for 10 minutes before serving.

1/3	cup chopped green onions
2	cloves garlic, minced
2	eggs
1	cup buttermilk
2	teaspoons sugar
2	cups flour
3 1/2	teaspoons baking powder
1	teaspoon Italian herb seasoning
1	jar (2 ounces) sliced pimientos (slivered sweet red pepper)
2	tablespoons grated Parmesan cheese
1	teaspoon rosemary

Beat together first group of ingredients until blended. Add the next 4 ingredients and beat until nicely blended, about 30 seconds. Do not overbeat.

Spread batter into a lightly oiled 12-inch round baking pan and brush top with a little oil. Sprinkle top with grated Parmesan and rosemary and gently press topping into the batter. Bake at 350-degrees for about 40 minutes, or until top is browned. Serve warm, or at room temperature. Cut into wedges to serve. Serves 12.

(About 97 calories per serving)

Greek Sesame Flatbread with
Lemon, Green Onions & Parmesan Cheese

Using whole wheat flour produces a denser, heartier bread. White flour or a combination of both can be substituted. If you are using only white flour, increase the quantity by 1/4 cup. The flavor of onions and cheese are balanced with the lemon. This delicious bread has very little oil and therefore, must be eaten in a day or two after baking. Store in double plastic bags to help keep it moist.

1	package dry yeast
1 1/4	cups warm water (105-degrees)
1	teaspoon sugar
1	tablespoon olive oil
2 1/2	cups whole wheat flour
2	tablespoons grated lemon
1/2	cup chopped green onions
2	tablespoons grated Parmesan cheese
1	tablespoon sesame seeds

In the large bowl of an electric mixer, stir together first 3 ingredients and allow to stand for 10 minutes, or until yeast starts to bubble. If yeast does not bubble, it is inactive and should be discarded.

Beat in oil and flour, and beat for 5 minutes. (This will take the place of kneading.) Beat in lemon and onions. Spread batter evenly in a lightly oiled 12-inch round baking pan, cover loosely with a towel and allow to rise in a warm place for 1 hour. Sprinkle top with Parmesan and sesame seeds and bake at 350-degrees for about 35 minutes, or until top is nicely browned. Cut into wedges to serve. Yields 12 servings.

(About 96 calories per serving)

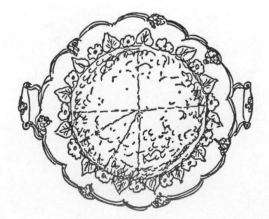

Italian Flatbread with Onions & Cheese

This is a variation of the classic Beer Bread, made a lot more delicious and exciting. It is is very simple to prepare and the possible variations are endless. Using different seasonings and flavors, it can be transformed to fit into any dinner you are serving. Use caraway seeds and it is a delicious rye bread. Onions and poppy seeds, garlic and rosemary, different herbs and spices, all change the character of the bread. Traditionally it is made into a loaf, but, I find preparing it as a flatbread is far more interesting. Also, it is traditionally made with 1/4 cup butter and I have changed this to 2 tablespoons oil, reducing the fat and cholesterol. Now that I think of it, there is very little left of the original recipe, but I thought you would like to know its origin.

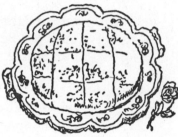

3	cups self-rising flour
2	tablespoons sugar
1	bottle (12 ounces) beer
1/2	cup chopped green onions
2	tablespoons oil
2	tablespoons grated Parmesan cheese

In the large bowl of an electric mixer, beat together first 3 ingredients until mixture is blended. Do not overbeat. Beat in the green onions. Spread a little oil on the bottom of a 12-inch round baking pan and spread batter evenly in pan. Drizzle remaining oil on top of the batter and sprinkle with grated cheese. Bake at 350-degrees for 40 to 45 minutes, or until top is golden brown. Allow to cool in pan. Serve warm or at room temperature. Cut into wedges or squares. Serves 16.

(About 110 calories per serving)

To make Flatbread with Garlic & Rosemary:
Prepare the bread as above but add a sprinkle of garlic powder and rosemary on the top before baking. Do this in addition to the cheese. Bake for the same amount of time.

To make Flatbread with Caraway Seeds:
Prepare the bread as above, substituting 2 tablespoons of caraway seeds for the green onions.

To make Flatbread with Onions & Poppy Seeds:
Prepare the bread as above, adding 2 tablespoons of poppy seeds to the batter. Everything else remains the same.

Basic Non-Fat Whole Wheat Yeast Bread

A delicious sturdy bread that does not have to be kneaded and is easy to prepare. It is dense and needs some rising time. The best way I have found to allow dough to rise is to heat the oven to 140-degrees, turn it off, wait 5 minutes and then put the pans in. Rising takes half the time this way. Be certain oven is not too hot or yeast will not rise. Loaves can also be placed in refrigerator and will slowly rise overnight. Bake in the morning as described. As this is like a batter bread, it does not peak, but is level, and good for sandwiches.

1/2	cup warm water (105-degrees)
1	teaspoon sugar
1	envelope dry yeast
2	cups water
4	cups whole wheat flour
1	cup whole wheat flour

Optional:

1. 2 tablespoons sesame seeds or poppy seeds or onion flakes
2. 1/4 cup chopped chives or green onions
3. 1 tablespoon sweet basil flakes, thyme flakes or rosemary

In a large bowl of an electric mixer, stir together first 3 ingredients. Allow to stand for 10 minutes to soften yeast. Beat in 4 cups of whole wheat flour and beat for 3 minutes. Beat in remaining flour until blended. (Dough will be stiff, but a little sticky.) Beat in seeds, herbs or onions (optional).

Divide dough between 2 lightly oiled 8x4-inch loaf pans and drizzle a drop or 2 of oil on top. Cover with plastic wrap and put in a warm place to rise. When doubled in bulk, (dough will almost reach top of the pan), bake at 350-degrees for 35 minutes or or until top is golden brown. Allow to cool in pan for 15 minutes, and then remove from pan and continue cooling on a rack. Cut into 1/2-inch slices. Yields 32 slices.

(About 63 calories per slice)

Basic Whole Wheat Quick Bread

This is nice fragrant, low-calorie breakfast bread that prepares in minutes. You can add cinnamon or a few nuts to the batter. Serve it warm with a little Devonshire Cream and sliced strawberries.

    2   eggs
    1   tablespoon oil
    1/4   cup honey
    1/2   grated orange, about 3 tablespoons (use fruit juice and peel)
    1/2   cup water

    1 3/4   cups whole wheat flour
    1   tablespoon baking powder

Beat together first 5 ingredients until blended. Beat in the remaining ingredients until blended. Place batter into a lightly oiled 8x4-inch loaf pan and bake at 350-degrees for about 35 minutes or until top is golden brown. Allow to cool in pan for 15 minutes, and then remove from pan and continue cooling on a rack. To serve, cut into 1/2-inch slices. Yields 16 slices.

(About 78 calories per slice)

Oven-Baked French Toast

Baking the French toast in the oven eliminates the use of any fat or oil. However, these can be prepared in a skillet, with just a wiping of oil and the toast will be a little more tender. Cook until browned on both sides.

    1   egg
    1/2   cup non-fat milk

    4   slices whole wheat bread, cut in half

Beat together egg and milk until blended. Place bread in a 7x11-inch non-stick shallow pan and pour egg mixture over all. Allow to stand for about 5 minutes, or until egg is absorbed, turning once. Place pan in a 350-degree oven and bake for 10 minutes, turn and bake for another 3 or 4 minutes, or until puffed and golden. Serve each slice with 1 tablespoon Fresh Apple & Cinnamon Sauce or a sprinkle of cinnamon sugar. Serves 4.

(About 110 calories per slice French Toast)
(About 10 calories per tablespoon sauce)

Whole Wheat Buttermilk Biscuits with Poppy Seeds & Onions

1 1/2	cups whole wheat pastry flour
1/2	cup unsweetened wheat germ
1	tablespoon baking powder
6	tablespoons cold margarine, cut into 6 pieces
1	cup buttermilk
1	tablespoon dried onion flakes
1	teaspoon poppy seeds

In the bowl of a food processor, mix first 3 ingredients. Add margarine, and blend, with quick on/off pulses, until margarine is the size of small peas. Add the buttermilk, and pulse again, until mixture is blended. Pulse in the onion and poppy seeds. Do not overmix.

Drop biscuits by rounded tablespoonful on a lightly greased cookie sheet and bake at 450-degrees for 15 minutes, or until tops are flecked with brown. Yields 20 biscuits.

(About 76 calories per biscuit)

Note: As these are made with whole wheat flour and wheat germ, the biscuits are dark and appear browned. Bake for the full amount of time.

Hardy Whole Wheat Biscuits with Chives

These are like small whole wheat rolls. While they are not heavy, they do have a good deal of character and are hardy and satisfying.

2	cups whole wheat pastry flour
1/4	cup wheat germ
1	tablespoon baking powder
6	tablespoons cold margarine, cut into 6 pieces
1 1/3	cups buttermilk
3	tablespoons chopped chives

In a food processor, place first 3 ingredients and pulse once or twice until mixed. Add the margarine and pulse until margarine is the size of small peas. Add the milk and chives and pulse only until mixture is blended. Do not overprocess or biscuits will toughen up.

Drop batter by rounded tablespoon onto a lightly greased 10x15-inch baking pan and bake at 450-degrees for 15 minutes, or until biscuits are flecked with brown. Yields about 22 biscuits.

(About 77 calories per biscuit)

Casseroles & Small Entrees

From my notebook:

Casseroles are one of the true joys of the culinary experience. They are homey, casual, informal, great for buffets and can be varied with, different vegetables, or with chicken for beef or fish for shellfish. There are some very special ones in this chapter and I want to point them out to you.

Eggplant Lasagna is a fine vegetarian choice for lunch or dinner. The Pink Orzo with Basil & Chives is a delicious accompaniment. Who doesn't love Chili? Chili with Red Beans & Pink Rice is one of the best. And if beef is not your choice, it is equally good with chunks of chicken.

Lots of vegetable frittatas and crustless quiches...Royal Artichoke & Spinach, Eggplant Frittata, Crustless Tart with Tomatoes & Goat Cheese, Frittata with Artichokes & Red Peppers, Spinach Frittata and many more, are all excellent for lunch or dinner.

Lots of Stuffed Vegetables...The Big Chile Relleno with Salsa and Pink Rice is a taste treat and very easy to prepare. Tomatoes stuffed with Turkey is an excellent light meal and serving it with sauteed mushrooms and a generous portion of another vegetable will still keep the calories low. Old-Fashioned Stuffed Peppers, Cabbage Rolls, Eggplant Stuffed with Ricotta are all exciting and delicious and excellent family meals.

And several casseroles that serve as complete meals and are truly enjoyable. Paella Valencia, made without the usual sausage or ham is lovely with seafood. It is equally good with chunks of a firm-fleshed fish. Hot and spicy Jambalaya Creole with Shellfish can also be made with fish. Vegetable Paella is a very light and very satisfying casserole. It has all the flavor of Paella without meat or fish.

A couple of interesting omelets, Cottage Cheese Pancakes, and a wonderful Cheese Blintze recipe will help make breakfast, brunch or lunch a happier time. The crepes are light and thin and can be filled with any number of fillings from savory to sweet. Example: Slices of any of the frittatas can be wrapped with crepes for a different presentation. They can be filled with iced milk and topped with a little sauce for dessert.

Eggplant Lasagna with
Tomatoes, Onions & Ricotta Cheese

This casserole yields 6 very generous servings, is low in calories and very high in nourishment. Serve with Pink Orzo with Basil and Chives for a truly satisfying and pleasurable accompaniment.

1	medium eggplant, cut into quarters and thinly sliced. Do not peel.
1	can (1 pound) stewed tomatoes, chopped. Do not drain.
1	can (8 ounces) tomato sauce
1	onion, chopped
3	cloves garlic, minced
1/2	teaspoon, each, sweet basil flakes and Italian Herb Seasoning
1	teaspoon sugar
	pepper to taste

1	pint low-fat Ricotta cheese
1	egg
1/3	cup grated Parmesan cheese
1	teaspoon sweet basil flakes

In a Dutch oven casserole, simmer together first 9 ingredients for 30 minutes, or until eggplant is soft. Meanwhile, beat together the Ricotta, egg, Parmesan and sweet basil until blended.

In a 9x13-inch baking pan, spread 1/2 the eggplant mixture. Top with Ricotta cheese mixture and then, remaining eggplant mixture. Sprinkle top with 1 tablespoon grated Parmesan (optional, but nice). Bake in a 350-degree oven for about 20 minutes, or until casserole is set and top is browned. Cut into squares to serve. Serves 8 as a small entree or 6 for dinner.

(About 145 calories per serving-serving 8)
(About 193 calories per serving-serving 6)

Note: -Casserole can be baked earlier in the day and heated at serving time.

Chili Beef with Red Beans & Pink Rice

Here's a nice healthy chili to satisfy your cravings for a strong taste. Although it contains no oil and very little fat, it is immensely delicious. The amounts of chili powder and cumin are average, and a lot more can be added for fiery palates. Cubes of chicken or turkey can be substituted for the chuck, but these must be added at the last 5 or 10 minutes of cooking time.

2	large onions, chopped (1/2 pound)
1/2	cup chopped green onions
2	tomatoes, chopped (fresh or canned)
1	can (7 ounces) diced green chiles
3	cloves garlic, minced
2	tablespoons chopped parsley
1 1/4	cups beef broth
1/2	teaspoon dried oregano flakes
1 1/2	tablespoons chili powder (or more to taste)
3/4	teaspoon ground cumin (or more to taste)
1/4	teaspoon black pepper
3	shakes cayenne pepper
2	cans (15 ounces, each) red kidney beans, thoroughly rinsed and drained
1	pound boned, lean chuck steak cut into 1/2-inch cubes

In a Dutch oven casserole, place all the ingredients, cover pan and simmer mixture for about 1 hour, or until onions are very soft and meat is tender. Serve on a bed of Pink Rice. Serves 8.

(About 254 calories per serving)

Pink Rice:

1 1/2	cups rice
3	cups chicken broth
2	tablespoons tomato sauce
1	tablespoon chopped parsley

In a saucepan, stir together all the ingredients, cover pan and simmer rice for 30 minutes, or until rice is tender and liquid is absorbed. Generously serves 8.

(About 138 calories per serving)

Royal Artichoke & Spinach Casserole

This serves well on a buffet, for brunch or lunch. It is a tempting combination of vegetables, cheese, eggs, yogurt, bread and a little oil...a little from each food group.

   1   cup part-skimmed Ricotta cheese
  1/4 cup unflavored non-fat yogurt
   1   egg
   1   slice bread, (1 ounce) made into crumbs
  1/3 cup grated Parmesan cheese
  1/4 cup chopped chives

   1   package (10 ounces) frozen spinach, defrosted and drained
   1   jar (6 ounces) marinated artichoke hearts, drained, rinsed
           and cut into fourths
        pepper to taste
   1   teaspoon oil

Stir together first 6 ingredients until blended. Stir in spinach, artichokes and pepper. Spread mixture into an oiled 10-inch deep-dish pie plate and bake in a 350-degree oven for about 40 to 45 minutes or until top is golden brown. Cut into wedges to serve. Serves 8.

(About 113 calories per serving)

Eggplant Frittata with Onions & Cheese

This is truly delicious, healthy and soul-satisfying. Excellent for lunch. Serve warm.

   1   medium eggplant (about 1 pound), peeled and thinly sliced
  1/2 cup chicken broth

   2   cups non-fat cottage cheese
  1/3 cup grated Parmesan cheese
   1   egg, beaten
  1/3 cup soda cracker crumbs
        pepper to taste

   2   tablespoons grated Parmesan cheese

In a 9x13-inch baking pan, place eggplant and drizzle with broth. Cover pan tightly with foil and bake in a 350-degree oven for about 30 minutes, or until eggplant is soft.

In a large bowl, place the eggplant and the next 5 ingredients and stir until blended. Spread mixture evenly in an oiled 9x13-inch pan and sprinkle top with grated cheese. Bake at 350-degrees for about 50 minutes to 1 hour or until top is golden brown. Cut into squares to serve. Excellent as an accompaniment to roast chicken. Serves 8 to 10.

(About 70 calories per serving-serving 10)
(About 88 calories per serving-serving 8)

Tomatoes Stuffed with Turkey in Light Tomato Sauce

Using the ground turkey meat instead of beef reduces the number of calories and cholesterol. But the taste is divine. This is a good dish to consider serving as a main course with rice or as an accompaniment to dinner.

8   medium-sized firm tomatoes, 1 1/2 pounds

1/2 pound ground turkey, white meat
1   slice bread (1 ounce) made into crumbs
1   small onion, grated
1   egg, beaten
1   tablespoon chopped parsley
     pepper to taste

Cut 1/4-inch off the tops of the tomatoes and scoop out pulp. Chop tomato pulp coarsely and set it aside for the sauce. Combine the remaining ingredients until blended and stuff tomatoes loosely with turkey mixture.

In an 10-inch round oven-proof casserole, place the tomatoes in one layer. Spoon Light Tomato Sauce over the top and bake in a 350-degree oven for about 30 minutes, or until meat is cooked through. Serves 4.

Light Tomato Sauce:
1   teaspoon oil
     reserved chopped tomato pulp
1   can (1 pound) stewed tomatoes, chopped and drained. Reserve
      juice for another use.
1/4 teaspoon, each Italian Herb Seasoning and sweet basil flakes
1/8 teaspoon, each, garlic powder and onion powder
     pinch of cayenne pepper
     freshly ground black pepper to taste

Stir together all the ingredients until blended

(About 223 calories per serving)

Crustless Tart with Tomatoes & Goat Cheese

Goat cheese (Chevre) is somewhat like Feta cheese (made from sheep's milk). It is intensely flavorful and very popular. Here it is paired with tomatoes, onions and herbs for a delicious tart that serves well for lunch or brunch.

1	can (1 pound) stewed tomatoes, chopped. Do not drain.
1	onion, minced
2	shallots, minced
1	clove garlic, minced
1	tablespoon lemon juice
1	tablespoon chopped parsley leaves
1/2	teaspoon sweet basil flakes
	pepper to taste
4	eggs, beaten
1/4	cup crumbled goat cheese (2 ounces)

In an uncovered saucepan, simmer together first group of ingredients for 20 minutes, or until onion is soft. If most of the juice has not evaporated, cook over high heat until very little liquid remains. Of course, watch carefully not to scorch. Allow to cool for about 5 minutes.

Stir in the beaten eggs and place mixture into a lightly oiled 9-inch quiche pan. Sprinkle top with cheese. Bake at 350-degrees for about 30 minutes, or until eggs are set. Serve with a vegetable salad. Serves 6.

(About 103 calories per serving)

Frittata with Artichokes and Red Peppers

4	eggs
1	cup low-fat milk
1/2	teaspoon oregano flakes
	white pepper to taste
1	jar (6 ounces) marinated artichoke hearts, rinsed, drained and cut into fourths
4	marinated red peppers, drained and cut into strips
1/2	cup chopped green onions
1	clove garlic, minced
2	tablespoons grated Parmesan cheese

Beat together first group of ingredients in a large bowl. Stir in next 4 ingredients until blended. Pour mixture evenly into a lightly greased 10-inch quiche baker or 9x9-inch baking pan and sprinkle top with grated cheese. Bake at 350-degrees for 20 to 25 minutes or until eggs are set and top is browned. Serves 4 for lunch.

(About 190 calories per serving)

The Big Chile Chicken Relleno with Tomato & Chile Salsa & Pink Rice

There is no way you would judge this delicious Mexican dish as a diet casserole, but at approximately 350 calories, including the rice, it most assuredly is. This will appeal to those with a keen and spicy palate. You may add an extra dash or two of Tabasco Sauce to the salsa, if you like it very hot.

> 4 ounces low-fat Mozzarella cheese, grated
> 6 ounces cooked chicken, coarsely chopped (white meat only)
> 2 tablespoons grated Parmesan cheese
> 2 tablespoons chopped green onions
> 2 tablespoons chopped cilantro
>
> 1 can (7 ounces) whole green chiles. Carefully remove seeds.
> 4 teaspoons low-fat sour cream

In a bowl, stir together first 5 ingredients until nicely mixed. Divide mixture and stuff the chiles. Place chiles in one layer in an 8x12-inch baking pan and spread Tomato & Chile Salsa over the top.

Bake in a 350-degree oven for about 15 minutes, or until cheese is melted. Serve with a teaspoon of sour cream on top. Pink Chile Rice is an excellent accompaniment. Serves 4.

Tomato & Chile Salsa:
> 1/2 cup canned chopped stewed tomatoes
> 1 can (4 ounces) diced green chiles
> 4 tablespoons finely chopped green onions
> 4 tablespoons finely chopped cilantro
> 2 tablespoons vinegar
> 1/8 teaspoon garlic powder
> dash of Tabasco Sauce

Stir together all the ingredients until blended.

Pink Chile Rice: In a saucepan, stir together 3/4 cup rice, 1 1/2 cups chicken broth, 1/4 cup chopped stewed tomatoes, 1/2 teaspoon chili powder, 1/2 teaspoon ground cumin. Cover pan and simmer mixture for 30 minutes, or until rice is tender and liquid is absorbed. Serves 4.

(Chile Rellenos - About 210 calories per serving)
(Pink Chile Rice - About 139 calories per serving)

Note: -*If the whole chiles are small, then sprinkle any left-over stuffing over the tops of the chiles in the pan.*
-*1 can (1 pound) stewed tomatoes, drained and chopped will be sufficient for the rice and salsa. Use juice for another use.*
-*Entire dish can be assembled earlier in the day and heated before serving.*

Old-Fashioned Stuffed Peppers in Tomato Sauce

6 medium green bell peppers, cut in half lengthwise (top to bottom).
Remove seeds and membranes. You will have 12 halves.

1 pound ground turkey
1 tomato, peeled, seeded and chopped (fresh or canned)
3/4 cup rice (par-boiled in 3 cups water for 15 minutes), drained
1 tablespoon minced parsley leaves
1/2 teaspoon sweet basil flakes
pepper to taste

Place peppers in a 9x13-inch pan. Combine the remaining ingredients and divide stuffing between the peppers, smoothing the tops. Pour Quick Tomato Sauce over the tops, cover pan with foil, and bake at 350-degrees for 40 minutes. Uncover pan and continue baking for 20 minutes, basting now and again. Serves 6 as a main course or 12 as a side dish.

Quick Tomato Sauce:
1 can (1 pound) stewed tomatoes, chopped. Do not drain.
3 tablespoons tomato paste
1 small onion, grated
1 teaspoon sugar
1 clove garlic, minced
1 tablespoon minced parsley leaves
1/2 teaspoon sweet basil flakes
1/2 teaspoon Italian Herb Seasoning flakes
pinch of cayenne pepper

In an uncovered saucepan, simmer together all the ingredients for 10 minutes.

(About 273 calories per serving-serving 6)
(About 137 calories per serving-serving 12)

Cabbage Rolls in Sweet & Sour Tomato Sauce

1   large head cabbage (about 1 pound), rinse and remove the core
1   pound ground turkey
1/2 cup raw rice, partially boiled*
1/2 small onion, grated, about 3 tablespoons
1   egg
1/8 teaspoon garlic powder
    black pepper to taste

Stand cabbage up on core end and cook it in 2-inches of boiling water for 10 to 12 minutes or until softened. Remove from pan and refresh under cold water. Carefully remove the outer leaves. When the leaves are too small to roll, chop them finely and place them in a Dutch oven casserole.

Mix together the remaining ingredients until nicely blended. Place about 2 tablespoons meat mixture on the bottom of the cabbage leaf. Tuck in the sides and roll it. Place rolls on top of minced cabbage in Dutch oven and pour Sweet & Sour Tomato Sauce over all. Cover pan and simmer for 1 hour. Serve with Pink Rice with Chives. Yields about 12 to 16 cabbage rolls and generously serves 6 to 8.

Sweet & Sour Tomato Sauce:
1   can (1 pound) stewed tomatoes, chopped. Do not drain.
1   can (8 ounces) tomato sauce
3/4 cup chicken broth
3   tablespoons lemon juice
1   teaspoon sugar
    black pepper to taste

Stir together all the ingredients until blended.
            (About 200 calories per serving-serving 8)
            (About 265 calories per serving-serving 6)

*To partially boil rice:
Stir 1/2 cup rice in 1-quart rapidly boiling water, lower heat to medium, simmer for 5 minutes and drain.

Note: Any leftover meat filling can be shaped into balls and cooked with the rolls.

Spinach Frittata with Cheese & Onions

This simple little casserole will furnish you with a fine vegetable accompaniment to dinner. It is also a very satisfying snack, and you will feel virtuous nibbling on this marvelous combination of vegetables, cheese, egg, and whole wheat bread.

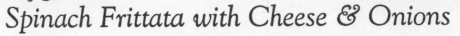

2 packages (10 ounces, each) frozen chopped spinach, drained
1 pint low-fat Ricotta cheese
3 tablespoons grated Parmesan cheese
1 egg, beaten
2 slices fresh whole wheat bread, crumbed (1 cup crumbs)
1/3 cup chopped green onions
1/2 teaspoon each, sweet basil flakes and oregano flakes
    pepper to taste
1 teaspoon oil

In a large bowl, stir together all the ingredients (except the oil) until mixture is nicely blended. Spread oil on the bottom of a 9x13-inch baking pan and spread spinach mixture evenly in pan. Bake at 350-degrees for about 50 to 55 minutes, or until top is browned and casserole is set. If not serving at this time, allow to cool in pan. When cool, cut into squares. This is nice served warm. Will serve 6 for lunch or 12 as an accompaniment to dinner.

(About 184 calories per serving-serving 6)
(About 92 calories per serving-serving 12)

Crustless Quiche with Eggplant, Onions & Cheese

This is a gutsy quiche, with good solid character. It yields a very generous serving and is excellent for lunch or an afternoon snack.

1 medium eggplant (about 1 pound), peeled and sliced
1/2 cup chicken broth

2 cups non-fat cottage cheese
2 ounces crumbled feta cheese
2 eggs, beaten
1/3 cup cracker crumbs
    pepper to taste

2 tablespoons grated Parmesan cheese

In a 9x13-inch baking pan, place eggplant and drizzle with broth. Cover pan tightly with foil and bake in a 350-degree oven for about 30 minutes, or until eggplant is soft.

In a large bowl, place the eggplant and the next 5 ingredients and stir until blended. Spread mixture evenly in a 10-inch quiche pan and sprinkle top with grated cheese. Bake at 350-degrees for about 50 minutes to 1 hour or until top is golden brown. Cut into wedges to serve. Serves 8 to 10.

(About 108 calories per serving-serving 8)
(About 87 calories per serving-serving 10)

Paella Valencia with Shellfish

This colorful, intensely delicious paella, made with very little oil and no sausage, ham or pork is just as delicious as the original. The yield is also generous and satisfying.

2 onions, chopped
3 cloves garlic, minced
1 teaspoon oil
1 can (4 ounces) diced green chiles
2 medium tomatoes, peeled, seeded and chopped

1 1/2 cups rice
2 cups chicken broth
1/4 teaspoon black pepper
1 teaspoon ground turmeric
1/4 teaspoon ground cumin

1 1/2 pounds cooked shellfish (shrimp, lobster, etc.)
1 package (10 ounces) baby peas, defrosted

In a Dutch oven casserole, saute onions and garlic in oil until onions are soft. Stir in chiles and tomatoes and heat through. Stir in the next 5 ingredients, cover pan and simmer mixture for about 30 minutes, or until rice is tender and liquid is absorbed. Fluff rice with a fork, stir in shrimp and peas and heat through. Serves 6.

(About 331 calories per serving)

Cauliflower with Tomatoes & Potatoes

This delicious and homey casserole serves well on a buffet for a very informal dinner. Serve it with roast chicken or veal. Dieters will love its blend of flavors.

1 can (1 pound) stewed tomatoes, chopped. Do not drain.
1 teaspoon chicken-seasoned stock base
4 medium potatoes, peeled and cut into 1/2-inch slices
1 large onion, chopped
4 tablespoons lemon juice
1 teaspoon sugar
4 tablespoons chopped parsley
1/2 teaspoon dried dill weed
freshly ground pepper to taste

2 packages (10 ounces, each) frozen cauliflower florets, defrosted

2 tablespoons dry bread crumbs mixed with
2 tablespoons grated Parmesan cheese

More →

Cauliflower with Tomatoes & Potatoes (Continued)

In a Dutch oven casserole, place first 9 ingredients, and simmer mixture for 30 minutes, or until potatoes are almost tender. Stir in the cauliflower and simmer for an additional 5 minutes.

In a 12-inch oval porcelain baker, or 9x13-inch baking pan, lay cauliflower mixture in a shallow layer and sprinkle top with bread crumbs and grated cheese. Heat in a 350-degree oven until heated through. Serves 8.

(About 100 calories per serving)

Note: -This can be prepared earlier in the day, and stored in the refrigerator (except for the sprinkling of the bread crumbs and cheese, which should be done just before reheating).

Jambalaya Creole with Shellfish

This tasty casserole eliminates sausage, pork and ham from the traditional Jambalaya. The amount of oil is insignificant. Add a little hot pepper for more bite.

2	onions, chopped
1	medium sweet red bell pepper, chopped
1/3	cup chopped green onions
3	large cloves garlic, minced
2	tablespoons chopped parsley
1	teaspoon vegetable oil

1 1/2	cups rice
2 1/4	cups water
3/4	cup clam broth
1	teaspoon chili powder (or more to taste)
1/2	teaspoon dried thyme flakes
1/4	teaspoon, each, black pepper and ground cumin
2	shakes, each, cayenne and ground cloves

1 1/2	pounds cooked shellfish (shrimp, lobster, etc.)

In a covered Dutch oven casserole, cook together first 6 ingredients, until onions are soft, about 20 minutes. Stir in the next group of ingredients, cover pan, and simmer mixture for 30 minutes, or until rice is tender and liquid is absorbed. Fluff rice with a fork, stir in the cooked shellfish and heat through. Serves 6.

(About 297 calories per serving)

Vegetable Paella with Artichokes & Yellow Rice

Artichokes, tomatoes and rice sparkled with lemon and cheese give this vegetable casserole the feeling of a complete meal...which it could well be. Leftover diced cooked chicken, beef or fish can be stirred in after cooking, but the fullness of the flavor stands alone quite well. It is a lovely dish to serve on a buffet, with its myriad of colors and textures.

1	package (10 ounces) frozen artichoke hearts, cooked tender in 2 cups water and 2 tablespoons lemon juice, drained and quartered.
1	cup rice
2	cups chicken broth
2	medium tomatoes, peeled, seeded and chopped
2	large marinated red peppers, cut into strips
1/3	cup chopped green onions
1	clove garlic, minced
2	teaspoons oil
2	tablespoons lemon juice
1	teaspoon turmeric, or a little more to taste
1/4	teaspoon ground cumin
	black pepper to taste
4	teaspoons grated Parmesan cheese
2	tablespoons minced parsley

In a Dutch oven casserole, stir together first group of ingredients, cover pan and simmer mixture for 30 minutes, or until rice is tender and liquid is absorbed. Fluff rice with a fork and serve, sprinkled with grated cheese and parsley. Serves 4.

(About 269 calories per serving)

Fresh Vegetable Pizza

If you are craving a special taste, this is nice dish to consider. Don't think for one moment that this is anything but a delicious and healthy lunch.

6	flour tortillas, (6-inch rounds)
1/2	pound mushrooms, cleaned and sliced
2	medium tomatoes, cut into thin slices
4	tablespoons sliced black olives (1/4 cup)
6	ounces lo-fat Mozzarella cheese, grated
1	teaspoon oregano flakes
	cayenne pepper to taste
	freshly ground black pepper to taste
6	teaspoons grated Parmesan cheese

More →

Fresh Vegetable Pizza (Continued)

Place tortillas on a 12x16-inch cookie sheet and toast in a 350-degree oven for about 4 minutes, or until lightly crisped. Now, divide the remaining ingredients, in order listed, equally over the tortillas and bake in a 350-degree oven for 5 minutes or until cheese is bubbly. Serve at once. Serves 6.

(About 183 calories per serving)

Note: -This is also delicious with broccoli, cauliflower, carrots, etc. but vegetables must first be blanched by placing in boiling water for 3 to 4 minutes or until firm tender.

Eggplant Stuffed with Ricotta

This delicious dish is a fine entree for vegetarian lunch or light supper. It is exceedingly low in calories when you consider the huge portion. It is rather a complete food, too, as it contains vegetables, eggs, cheese and bread. If serving for dinner, pasta is a nice accompaniment.

3 medium eggplants, (about 3/4 pound, each), cut in half lengthwise. Scoop out the vegetable, leaving a 1/3-inch thick shell. Finely chop the scooped out eggplant.

1 teaspoon, each, oil and water

1 pound low-fat Ricotta cheese (also called "part-skimmed")
1/4 cup grated Parmesan cheese
2 eggs, beaten
1/2 cup fresh bread crumbs (1 slice)
1/2 teaspoon Italian Herb Seasoning
1 tablespoon minced parsley leaves
white pepper to taste

2 tablespoons grated Parmesan cheese

In a 9x13-inch baking pan, place chopped eggplant. Drizzle with 1 teaspoon of oil and 1 teaspoon of water, cover pan tightly with foil and bake in a 400-degree oven for about 25 minutes or until eggplant is very soft.

In a large bowl, mix together cooked eggplant and next 7 ingredients until blended and divide mixture between the 6 eggplant shells. Sprinkle tops with grated cheese. Place in a baking pan and bake, uncovered, for 45 minutes, or until shells are softened and top is browned. Serves 6.

(About 209 calories per serving)

Greek Omelet
with Tomatoes, Peppers & Feta Cheese

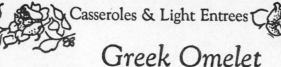

1/4 cup chopped red bell peppers
1/4 cup chopped green bell peppers
1/4 cup finely minced onions
1 tomato, peeled, seeded and chopped
    freshly ground black pepper to taste
1 teaspoon olive oil

4 eggs, beaten
3 ounces feta cheese, crumbled
1/4 teaspoon dried dill weed

In a covered saucepan, cook together first 6 ingredients until vegetables are soft. Spread mixture evenly in 9x2-inch round baking pan or deep-dish pie plate. Stir together the remaining ingredients, and pour evenly over the vegetables. Bake in a 350-degree oven for about 20 minutes or until eggs are set. Serve with Onion-Flavored Baby Baked Potatoes. Serves 4.
(About 161 calories per serving)

Onion-Flavored Baked Baby Potatoes:
8 baby potatoes (about 1 pound), scrubbed. Peel off 1-inch of skin
    from around the center.
1 tablespoon melted butter
1/4 teaspoon onion powder, or to taste

In an 8-inch round baking dish, toss together all the ingredients. Bake in a 350-degree oven for about 40 minutes, or until potatoes are tender and the peeled band is golden brown. Serves 4.
(About 115 calories per serving)

High Protein Cottage Cheese Pancakes

1 cup non-fat cottage cheese
2 eggs
2 egg whites
1/3 cup whole wheat pastry flour
1 tablespoon sugar
1 tablespoon melted margarine
1 teaspoon baking powder
1/4 teaspoon vanilla

In a mixing bowl, mix all the ingredients with a fork until combined. Do not overmix. Spoon about 1/8 cup batter on a preheated non-stick griddle pan. When the bottom of the pancake is golden brown and top is bubbly, turn and brown other side. Serve with with Low-Calorie Sour Cream and Fresh Strawberry Sauce. Yields 12 pancakes.
(About 53 calories per pancake)

Omelet with Spinach & Cheese

More than an omelet, this is much like the Italian Frittata, filled, as it is, with vegetables and cheese. High in protein and very low in fats, this is a good dish to consider for lunch or brunch.

6	eggs,
1	package (10 ounces) frozen chopped spinach, defrosted and drained
3/4	cup non-fat cottage cheese
1/4	cup grated Parmesan cheese
1/4	cup chopped green onions
	pepper to taste
2	teaspoons margarine
2	teaspoons grated Parmesan cheese

Beat eggs until nicely blended. Stir in the next 5 ingredients until blended. In a 10-inch round baking pan, melt margarine until sizzling hot. Pour in egg mixture and spread evenly. Sprinkle top with 2 teaspoons grated cheese. Bake in a 350-degree oven for about 20 to 25 minutes, or until eggs are set. Serves 6 for breakfast or lunch.

(About 135 calories per serving)

Light Crepes for Cheese Blintzes

2	eggs
1 1/4	cups water
1	cup all-purpose unbleached flour
2	teaspoons sugar
1/4	teaspoon vanilla

In a bowl, place all the ingredients and beat until blended. Refrigerate batter for 1 hour. Remove from the refrigerator and stir. Lightly butter a 6-inch omelet pan with a napkin or paper towel. Pan should be very hot but not smoking. Pour 1/8 cup batter into the pan and quickly tilt and turn the pan so that the bottom is completely covered. Cook crepe for about 45 seconds or until top is dry. Turn and cook other side for 15 seconds. Remove crepe onto a platter. Repeat with remaining batter. Yields 24 crepes.

(About 25 calories per crepe without filling)

To make Cheese Blintzes:

1 1/2	cups non-fat cottage cheese
2	tablespoons sugar
2	tablespoons lemon juice

Stir together all the ingredients until blended. Place 1 tablespoon filling on each crepe and roll up. In a non-stick pan, heat blintzes until browned on both sides.

(About 13 calories per tablespoon filling)
(About 38 calories per blintze with filling)

Pasta & Pizza

From my notebook:

I bet you thought you couldn't have any pasta or pizza on a healthy diet. Well, you most certainly can. While you will have to watch the calories, pasta or pizza is basically a complex carbohydrate with a "little" sauce or topping. Unfortunately, the accent is on the word "little."

The pizza crusts are basic and one slice of pizza is like a slice of bread. The dough can be used to make flatbreads. These can be soft and chewy or brittle and crisp, depending on the amount of baking time. Flatbreads can be made with any number of flavors, onion, garlic, cheese, hot pepper, etc. It is important to note that pizza crusts can be prepared with whole wheat pastry flour and are very good, indeed.

If you use fillings with lots of vegetables and strong flavored accents, a little goes a long way. Sun-dried tomatoes is one of the best for flavor. The pizzas in this chapter are basically filled with eggplant, leeks, mushrooms and sparkled with a little Mozzarella or Feta cheese. Lots of flavor, but not low in calories, so use with moderation.

Now, the pastas also fit into this category. One way of handling pastas to control calories is to fill it up with vegetables or vegetable sauces. A little pasta with a variety of vegetables in a light sauce can still deliver a lot of pleasure and in this manner, a little pasta goes a long way. Besides, it is only the sauce that delivers the taste. Pasta does not stand alone. So, you will find some interesting sauces in this chapter. Artichokes, Red Pepper and Sun-Dried Tomatoes are just delicious together. Carrots, broccoli and cauliflower with Tomato Basil Sauce make a lovely Primavera. Eggplant with Red Peppers and Sun-Dried Tomatoes is another interesting sauce.

At this time, I did not include a recipe for making your own pasta. There are so many pasta shops, featuring freshly made pasta, at very reasonable prices, that I felt, let it go for now. As a general rule, fresh pasta is better than fresh-frozen, and fresh-frozen is better than dried. Cooking times will vary with each style. Do not overcook pasta, but then again, don't undercook it either. It should be firm to the bite, but cooked through.

Lowest Calorie No-Oil Pizza Crust
(Made in a Mixer)

If you're the type that can be intimidated by kneading, my way of beating the dough in the mixer will dispel all fears. If you own a heavy-duty mixer with a paddle, this crust can be prepared without a dough hook. Kneading will be taking place during the first beating period when the dough is still in a soft stage. Adding the remaining flour is then easily achieved. This crust does not contain any oil and is on the crisp side.

1	package dry yeast
1	teaspoon sugar
1/4	cup warm water (105-degrees)
3/4	cup warm water (105-degrees)
	pinch of salt
2 1/2	cups flour
1/2	cup flour, a little more or less

In a bowl, proof yeast in sugar and water for 10 minutes, or until mixture starts to bubble. (If yeast does not bubble, it is inactive and should be discarded.) In the large bowl of an electric mixer, beat together yeast mixture and next 3 ingredients for 3 minutes. Continue beating (with a dough hook, if necessary), adding the remaining flour, until the dough is smooth and elastic.

Place dough in a lightly oiled bowl, and turn to coat all sides. Cover with plastic wrap and let rise in a warm place until doubled in bulk, about 1 hour. (Or dough can be held in the refrigerator overnight at this point.)

Punch dough down and divide in half. On a lightly floured surface roll each half into a 12-inch circle, with the edges thicker than the center. Place dough in a very lightly floured 12-inch pizza pan, build up the edges a little and let dough rest for 20 minutes. Now, proceed to fill with your favorite ingredients. Bake at 450-degrees for about 20 minutes or until edges are crisp and browned. Makes 2 large 12-inch pizzas or 4 smaller 8-inch pizzas and will yield 16 generous slices.

(About 77 calories per slice)

To make flatbreads:
This dough can be used to make flat breads of many styles. In this case, follow directions above. After placing dough into a 12-inch pan, brush it with a little oil, sprinkle and lightly press into the dough, either garlic powder, Parmesan cheese, poppy seeds, onion flakes, hot pepper, Cajun seasoning, sesame seeds, chives, green onions, herbs, or any combination that will harmonize with your meal. Bake for 15 minutes for a chewy bread or 20 minutes for a very crisp one.

Note: Whole wheat flour can be substituted for the all-purpose flour.

Basic Pizza Crust
(Made in a Processor)

1   package dry yeast
1   teaspoon sugar
1/4   cup warm water (105-degrees)

2 1/2   cups flour
3/4   cup warm water (105-degrees)
2   tablespoons oil
    pinch of salt

1/2   cup flour

In a bowl, proof yeast in sugar and water for 10 minutes, or until yeast starts to bubble. (If yeast does not bubble, it is inactive and should be discarded.) In a food processor bowl, place the flour. With the motor running, slowly pour in yeast mixture and next 3 ingredients and process for 1 minute. Now add the remaining flour and process until dough forms a ball around the blade. Add a little more flour if dough appears sticky.

Place dough in a lightly oiled bowl and turn to coat all sides. Cover bowl with plastic wrap and let rise in a warm place for 1 hour or until doubled in bulk. (It can be refrigerated overnight at this point, and it will rise slowly in the refrigerator.) Punch dough down and divide in half.

On a lightly floured surface, roll dough out to a 12-inch circle, with the edges slightly thicker than the center. Place dough in a very lightly floured 12-inch pizza pan, build up the edges a little and let dough rest for 20 minutes. Now proceed to fill with your choice of ingredients. Bake at 450-degrees for about 20 minutes or until edges are crisped and browned. Makes 2 large 12-inch pizzas or 4 smaller 8-inch pizzas and yields 16 generous slices.

(About 93 calories per serving)

To make flatbreads:
Follow instructions in preceding recipe to convert this dough into flatbreads.

Important Note:
Whole wheat flour can be substituted for the all-purpose flour.

Mediterranean Pizza with Sun-Dried Tomatoes, Pine Nuts & Mozzarella

The sun-dried tomatoes add an intense flavor and color to this fresh and delicious-tasting pizza. The flavor is so rich and satisfying, that a small amount delivers a lot of pleasure. Mozzarella cheese can be sprinkled on top before baking, but it develops a crust, which is not satisfactory for my taste. I like the cheese melted and bubbling and not crusty brown.

1	12-inch pizza crust (Basic or No-Oil)
2	teaspoons olive oil
1/2	teaspoon red pepper flakes (or to taste)
1/2	cup sun-dried tomatoes, cut into strips
1	clove garlic, peeled
3	tablespoons pine nuts, (about 1 ounce)
2	tablespoons grated Parmesan cheese
6	ounces Mozzarella cheese, grated
12	fresh basil leaves

Preheat oven to 450-degrees. Brush crust with oil and sprinkle with red pepper. In a food processor, blend together next 4 ingredients until blended and spread over prepared crust. Bake for 10 minutes. Sprinkle top with Mozzarella cheese and basil leaves and continue to bake for 10 minutes longer, or until edges are browned and cheese is bubbling. Yields 8 slices.

(About 189 calories per slice-using No-Oil Crust)
(About 205 calories per slice-using Basic Crust)

Pizza with Eggplant, Mushrooms, Leeks & Feta Cheese

Very Greek in feeling with the flavors of eggplant, leeks and feta cheese. Feta is a low-calorie cheese, at only 76 calories per ounce. If you are only serving 4, freeze the second pizza in double thicknesses of plastic wrap and foil.

2	12-inch pizza crusts (Basic or No-Oil)
4	small Japanese eggplants, unpeeled, cut into 1/4-inch slices, or 1 pound eggplant, cut in half and into 1/4-inch slices
1/2	pound mushrooms, sliced
2	leeks, white parts and 1-inch of tender green parts, thoroughly washed and thinly sliced
2	cloves garlic, minced
1	tablespoon olive oil
2	tablespoons lemon juice
2	tomatoes, thinly sliced
8	ounces feta cheese, crumbled (2 cups)
2	teaspoons sweet basil flakes (or 2 tablespoons fresh basil)

Prepare pizza crusts as directed and have them ready in their prepared pans. Place next 4 ingredients in a 9x13-inch pan and toss with oil and lemon juice. Broil for 8 to 10 minutes, turning once, until eggplant is softened and tops are beginning to brown. Preheat oven to 450-degrees. Divide vegetables between the pizza crusts. Top each with sliced tomatoes, feta cheese and sweet basil and bake for about 20 minutes, or until edges are browned. Truly delicious. Yields 16 slices.

(About 134 calories per slice-using No-Oil Crust)
(About 150 calories per slice-using Basic Crust)

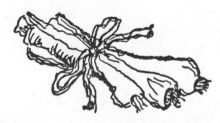

Pizza with Sun-Dried Tomatoes & Chevre

A marvellous combination of flavors and colors, this is one of my family's favorites. If you are only serving 4, freeze the second pizza in double thicknesses of plastic wrap and foil.

2	12-inch pizza crusts (Basic or No-Oil)
2	teaspoons olive oil
1	teaspoon red pepper flakes (or to taste)
1/2	cup sun-dried tomatoes (packed in oil) drained and chopped
8	ounces crumbled chevre cheese
1/4	cup minced chives
2	teaspoons sweet basil flakes (or 2 tablespoons fresh basil)
8	ounces grated part-skim Mozzarella cheese (2 cups)

Preheat oven to 450-degrees. Brush crusts with oil, sprinkle with red pepper, tomatoes, chevre, chives and basil and bake for 10 minutes. Sprinkle top with Mozzarella and continue to bake for 10 minutes longer, or until edges are browned and cheese is bubbling. Yields 16 slices.

(About 188 calories per slice-using Basic Crust)

(About 172 calories per slice-using No-Oil Crust)

Pasta with Artichoke, Red Pepper & Sun-Dried Tomato Sauce

This is a great sauce to serve over pasta. Mostacciola, a medium tube pasta, is a good choice, although any shape will do. Sauce can be prepared earlier in the day, or 1 day earlier and stored in the refrigerator. Cook the pasta and heat the sauce just before serving.

1	jar (6 ounces) marinated artichoke hearts, chopped. Do not drain.
1	jar (8 ounces) roasted red peppers, drained and cut into strips
2	tablespoons chopped sun-dried tomatoes
2	shallots, minced
2	cloves garlic, minced
1/4	teaspoon, each, Italian Herb Seasoning and sweet basil flakes black pepper to taste
8	ounces pasta, cooked al dente
4	teaspoons grated Parmesan cheese (optional)

In a saucepan, heat together first group of ingredients and simmer for 10 minutes or until shallots are soft. Serve hot over pasta and sprinkle with optional cheese. Serves 6

(About 200 calories per serving)

Pasta Primavera with Tomato Basil Sauce

One of the tricks in lowering calories is to take a marvelous pasta dish and build it up with a gorgeous array of vegetables. In this Primavera, the pasta is halved and the vegetables are tripled. The sauce is light and fresh and delicious. Using fresh vegetables is, of course, preferred. But the Del Sol mixture of vegetables makes this dish simple to prepare and economical, too. The carrots are pre-cut into perfect strips and only the florets of the cauliflower and broccoli are included.

1   pound bag frozen Del Sol vegetables (carrot strips, cauliflower and broccoli florets). Cook vegetables in boiling water for 5 minutes and drain.

1/4   pound whole wheat pasta (fresh or fresh-frozen is best). Cook in boiling water until firm but tender. Drain.

Tomato Basil Sauce:

6   shallots, minced

6   cloves garlic, minced (or more to taste)

1   teaspoon olive oil

4   medium tomatoes, peeled, seeded and diced

1   tablespoon tomato paste

1/4   cup minced fresh basil (or 2 teaspoons dried basil leaves) pinch of cayenne pepper

4   teaspoons grated Parmesan cheese

In a Dutch oven casserole, saute shallots and garlic in olive oil until shallots are transparent. Add the tomatoes, tomato paste, basil and pepper and simmer sauce for 10 minutes. Add the prepared vegetables and pasta to the sauce, toss to blend and heat through. Serve with a spoonful of cheese on top. Serves 4.

(About 207 calories per serving)

Pasta with Eggplant, Red Pepper & Sun-Dried Tomato Sauce

1   medium eggplant (a little under 1 pound), peeled and chopped
2   red bell peppers, cut into strips
1   can (1 pound) stewed tomatoes, chopped. Do not drain.
3   sun-dried tomatoes cut into strips
1   small onion, minced
2   cloves garlic, minced
1   tablespoon vinegar
1   teaspoon sugar
1   teaspoon oil
1/2   teaspoon sweet basil flakes
1/2   teaspoon oregano flakes
     freshly ground black pepper
     pinch of cayenne pepper

1/4   cup sliced black olives (optional)
2   tablespoons capers, thoroughly rinsed (optional)

1   pound linguini, cooked al dente
6   teaspoons grated Parmesan cheese

In a Dutch oven casserole, place first group of ingredients, cover pan and simmer mixture for about 40 to 50 minutes, or until eggplant is tender. Add the olives and capers (optional). Serve over a bed of linguini and spoon a little cheese on top. Yields 8 generous portions.

(About 266 calories per serving)

Soups

From my notebook:

The soups included here are wonderful allies in a healthy regimen. Soup is very filling, very satisfying, very healthy and low in calories. With 50 or 60 calories a serving, soup can be enjoyed at each meal. It is also a good snack.

This chapter features soups and a few stews. The soups are varied and range from around 50 to 100 calories. They are all pure and wholesome. If you choose a soup from the higher range, then choose a salad from the lower range. You are choosing the foods that are most appealing to you at that time so just watch the totals.

Low-Calorie Farmhouse Vegetable Soup is one that I make often. It is a very generous portion and filled with delicious vegetables. Best Country Cabbage & Tomato Soup is a true bargain at 54 calories. Clam Chowder with Tomatoes is another delicious soup in the mid-range at 72 calories. Carrots Soup with Apples is a little gem that I hope you enjoy. It is low in calories, at only 61.

Some substantial soups include Italian Vegetable & Bean Soup very filling and satisfying. Lentil Soup, filled with vegetables seasoned with turmeric and cumin is interesting and different. If those spices do not appeal to you, omit them. I know the basic soup will. It is homey and delicious. The Leek & Tomato Soup is filled with CiCi Peas, which is getting good press, lately. Spinach Soup with Vermicelli is another soup that is paired with a complex carbohydrate.

Thanksgiving Honey Apple Pumpkin Soup is pure pleasure, and while it does contain a little honey and cream, it is a minute quantity.

The stews are actually complete meals. Cioppino, the Italian Fisherman's Chowder is a low-calorie complete meal. If you want to omit the bread, you can add a small potato (4 ounces), sliced, for each serving, and the total main course will still be under 300 calories. The Best Old-Fashioned Chicken Soup (235 calories) is a complete meal as it includes chicken, vegetables and potatoes. It is so low in calories that you can enjoy a salad, some whole grain bread, and dessert and still keep dinner values under 500.

Mexican Chicken & Chili Bean Soup is a hefty stew filled with chicken, chiles, beans, and orzo. It is a taste sensation and the whole course is still under 300 calories. Chicken CiCi Pea Stew is another complete meal and only with 262 calories.

Healthy & Homey Lentil Soup with Tomatoes, Carrots & Onions

This hearty, zesty soup was one of our favorites when we were growing up and it is still one of my favorites. It is even delicious on the second day. Take care in reheating, stirring frequently, so that it doesn't scorch. This produces a bounteous amount of soup, about 12 cups, and yields a generous serving.

- 2 medium onions, finely chopped
- 3 large carrots, grated
- 1 stalk celery, finely chopped
- 6 cloves garlic, minced
- 1/2 pound brown lentils, washed and picked over for any foreign particles
- 1 can (1 pound) stewed tomatoes, chopped. Do not drain.
- 2 cups tomato juice
- 3 cups beef broth
- 2 cups chicken broth
- 2 tablespoons chopped parsley
- 1 teaspoon ground cumin
- 1 teaspoon ground turmeric
- 1 tablespoon vinegar
- pepper to taste

In a large, covered soup pot, cook together all the ingredients for about 1 hour or until the lentils are tender, stirring now and again. Serve with an assertive, crusty pumpernickel bread with raisins. Serves 12.

(About 99 calories per serving)

Cioppino - Italian Fisherman's Chowder

This is a keen and spicy soup, rich and flavorful. It is the essence of simplicity to prepare. While low in calories, it is high in nourishment. The Italian Croustades with Tomatoes, Chives & Cheese are a lovely accompaniment.

Soup Base:
- 2 onions, chopped
- 6 cloves garlic, minced
- 2 cups clam broth
- 2 cups tomato juice
- 1 can (8 ounces) tomato sauce
- 1 can (7 ounces) chopped clams. Do not drain.
- 1 teaspoon, each, sugar, oil, dried basil, Italian Herbs, turmeric, and parsley
- 1/8 teaspoon cayenne pepper
- pepper to taste

- 2 pounds fillets of sole, cut into 1 1/2-inch chunks

In a Dutch oven casserole, simmer together all the ingredients (except the fish) for 20 minutes. Bring to a rolling boil, add the fish, lower the heat, and simmer fish for about 4 to 5 minutes, or until fish becomes opaque. Do not over cook. Serve in deep bowls with a slice or two of Italian Croustades with Tomatoes, Chives & Cheese. Serves 6 to 8.

(About 147 calories per serving-serving 8)
(About 190 calories per serving-serving 6)

Note: -Soup base can be prepared earlier in the day and stored in the refrigerator. However, do not cook fish until a few minutes before serving.

Italian Croustades with Tomatoes, Chives & Cheese:
- 12 thin slices Italian bread, (1/2-ounce, each)
- 4 teaspoons olive oil
- 1 small tomato, finely chopped
- 6 teaspoons grated Parmesan cheese
- 6 tablespoons chopped chives

Spread each slice of bread with a thin coating of olive oil and place on baking sheet. Divide remaining ingredients over the tops of each slice of bread. Cover pan with foil and heat at 350-degrees for 10 minutes. Remove foil and broil for a few seconds to brown tops. Yields 6 to 8 servings.

(About 90 calories per 1 1/2 slice serving-serving 8)
(About 120 calories per 2 slice serving-serving 6)

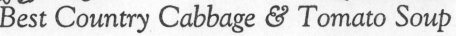

Best Country Cabbage & Tomato Soup

This is another sweet-and-sour-styled soup that is brimming with flavor and goodness. It is low in calories but very hearty and satisfying. It is a benign snack.

1	small cabbage (about 1 pound) coarsely chopped
1	can (1 pound) stewed tomatoes, chopped. Do not drain.
2	onions, chopped
6	shallots, minced
6	cloves garlic, minced
2	cups chicken broth
3	cups beef broth
2	tablespoons lemon juice
1	teaspoon sugar
1	teaspoon sweet basil flakes
1/2	teaspoon oregano flakes
	pepper to taste
2	sprinkles cayenne pepper

In a Dutch oven casserole, with the cover slightly ajar, simmer together all the ingredients, for about 1 hour, or until cabbage is soft. Serve in deep bowls with 1 teaspoon grated Parmesan on top (add 7 calories) (optional). Serves 8.
(About 54 calories per serving)

Cucumber & Chive Soup with Lemon & Dill

3	medium cucumbers, (about 1 pound), peeled and cut in half lengthwise. With a spoon, scrape out the seeds. Cut cucumbers into 1-inch chunks.
1/3	cup chopped chives
1	cup unflavored non-fat yogurt
1	cup buttermilk
3	tablespoons lemon juice
1	teaspoon dried dill weed
	pinch of salt
1	tablespoon, each chopped chives and minced parsley for garnish

Finely chop cucumbers in food processor. In a large bowl, stir together cucumbers with the next 6 ingredients until blended. Refrigerate until serving time. Serve in glass bowls with a dollup of yogurt and a sprinkle of chopped chives and parsley. Serves 4 to 6.
(About 50 calories per serving-serving 6)
(About 76 calories per serving-serving 4)

Easiest & Best Clam Chowder with Tomatoes

        1   onion, finely chopped
        2   medium carrots, grated
        4   shallots, minced
        3   cloves garlic, minced
        1   can (1 pound) stewed tomatoes, chopped. Do not drain.
        1   can (8 ounces) tomato sauce
        1   cup tomato juice
        1   cup bottled clam broth
      1/2   teaspoon sugar
        1   teaspoon ground turmeric
      1/2   teaspoon thyme flakes
      1/2   teaspoon sweet basil flakes

        1   can (7 ounces) chopped clams. Reserve broth.

In a Dutch oven casserole, with the cover slightly ajar, simmer together first group of ingredients, for 30 minutes, or until vegetables are tender. Add the clams and broth and heat through.   Serve with a sprinkling of grated Parmesan. Crispettes of Cheese are an excellent accompaniment. Serves 6.

(About 72 calories per serving)

Crispettes of Cheese:
     12   slices French bread (1/2 ounce each)
      6   teaspoons margarine
      9   teaspoons grated Parmesan cheese

Place bread in one layer in a 10x15-inch baking pan. Spread each slice with a thin layer of margarine (1/2 teaspoon) and a sprinkling of grated Parmesan cheese (3/4 teaspoon). Broil bread for about a minute or until lightly browned. Serves 6.

(About 123 calories per 2-slice serving)

The Best Old-Fashioned Chicken Soup

This grand soup is rich with the flavors of garlic, leeks, onions and tomatoes and is made substantial with the addition of potatoes. It can be prepared earlier in the day or 1 day earlier and stored in the refrigerator. Baking the chicken for 40 minutes to brown it and seal in the juices, is a technique I initiated years and years ago. It takes the place of browning the chicken in oil, reducing markedly the amount of oil needed. It also will defat the chicken. Notice also that the potatoes are cooked separately. This will eliminate the potato starch in the soup.

1   fryer chicken (about 2 1/2 pounds) cut into serving pieces, sprinkled with pepper, paprika, garlic and onion powders

1   leek, white and 1 1/2-inches of tender green part, thoroughly washed and thinly sliced
1   large onion, chopped
4   cloves garlic, minced
1   can (1 pound) stewed tomatoes, chopped. Do not drain.
6   carrots, peeled and thinly sliced
1   stalk celery, thinly sliced
6   cups chicken broth
    white pepper to taste

1/2   pound potatoes (2 medium), peeled, cubed and cooked in boiling water until tender
2   tablespoons chopped parsley or chives (optional)

In a 9x13-inch baking pan, bake chicken at 350-degrees for 40 minutes. Meanwhile, in a Dutch oven casserole, cook together the next 8 ingredients for 40 minutes. Add the chicken to the casserole, discarding the skin, bones and fat in the pan. Continue cooking for 15 minutes, or until chicken is tender. Add the potatoes and heat through. Sprinkle with parsley or chives, if desired. Serves 6 as dinner and 12 as an accompaniment to dinner.

(About 235 calories per serving-serving 6)
(About 117 calories per serving-serving 12)

Italian Vegetable & Bean Soup

This soup may appear to be a lot of work. In a way it is hefty with ingredients, but the result is so fantastic that it is well worth the extra effort of slicing the vegetables. It keeps for several days and somehow, the taste always improves. Cooking the vegetables in the broth eliminates sauteing them in oil and reduces markedly the fat (and calories).

2   onions, chopped
6   shallots, chopped
6   cloves garlic, sliced
2   leeks, white and tender green parts, thoroughly washed and sliced
2   carrots, sliced
1   stalk celery, sliced
2   cups shredded cabbage
1   can (1 pound) stewed tomatoes, chopped. Do not drain
2   cups chicken broth
3   cups beef broth
1   teaspoon dried basil flakes
1   teaspoon dried oregano flakes
3   tablespoons minced parsley
    pepper to taste
3   sprinkles cayenne pepper

1   can (1 pound) Northern white beans, rinsed and drained
1   package (10 ounces) frozen peas
2   zucchini, unpeeled and sliced, (1/2 pound)

In a covered Dutch oven casserole, simmer together first group of ingredients for 45 minutes or until vegetables are tender. Add the last 3 ingredients and continue simmering for 15 minutes. (This soup is very thick, and some chicken broth can be added to taste.) Serve with 1 teaspoon of grated Parmesan cheese (add 7 calories) (optional). Serves 10.
(About 94 calories per serving)

Note: Spinach adds a delicious dimension, and very few calories to this soup. Just before serving, add 1 cup coarsely chopped spinach to the soup and allow it to simmer for 5 minutes.

Leek & Tomato Soup with CiCi Peas

This is a complex soup, rich with the flavors of leeks, garlic, shallots and tomatoes. Using the canned cici peas (garbanzos) saves hours of preparation and loses nothing in the translation. Soup can be prepared earlier in the day or 1 day earlier and stored in the refrigerator.

2   leeks, (use the white and tender green parts) chopped
2   medium onions, finely chopped
4   shallots, minced
3   carrots, finely chopped
6   cloves garlic, minced
1   can (1 pound) stewed tomatoes, chopped. Do not drain.
4   cups chicken broth
1   teaspoon ground turmeric or more to taste
1/2 teaspoon ground cumin
    black pepper to taste
2   sprinkles cayenne pepper

1   can (1 pound) cici peas (garbanzos), drained

In a Dutch oven covered casserole, simmer together first group of ingredients until vegetables are softened, about 20 minutes. Add the cici peas and simmer mixture, with the cover slightly ajar, for another 10 minutes. Taste and adjust seasonings. This should have a little bite from the pepper, but should not be too overpowering. Serves 8.

(About 100 calories per serving)

Spinach Soup with Lemon & Vermicelli

1   onion, finely chopped
6   cloves garlic, minced
4   shallots, minced
1   teaspoon olive oil

4   cups chicken broth
2   packages (10 ounces, each) frozen chopped spinach
1/4 cup lemon juice
1   cup cooked vermicelli (or other fine noodle) (2 ounces dry)
    white pepper to taste

In a covered Dutch oven casserole, over low heat, cook together first 4 ingredients until onion is soft. (This is called "sweating" the vegetables.) Stir in the remaining ingredients and simmer mixture for 15 minutes. Serve with a spoonful of unflavored yogurt and a generous sprinkling of chives. Serves 6.

(About 97 calories per serving)

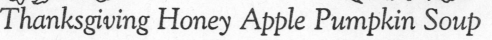

Thanksgiving Honey Apple Pumpkin Soup

This is one of the quickest and easiest soups to prepare, which is especially appreciated (considering the time crunch) around the holidays. Serve it with a fruity muffin or quick bread.

    3   cups chicken broth
    1   small onion, minced
    2   medium apples, peeled, cored and grated

    2   tablespoons honey
    2   cups canned pumpkin puree
    1   cup apple juice
   1/3   teaspoon pumpkin pie seasoning
   1/4   cup half and half cream

In a Dutch oven casserole, simmer together first 3 ingredients until onion and apple are soft. (This can be pureed in a food processor at this point, but it is not essential.) Stir in the remaining ingredients and heat through. Serve with a teaspoon of half and half sour cream on top (7 calories) and a sprinkling of cinnamon. Serves 8.

(About 89 calories per serving)

Carrot Soup with Apples & Cinnamon

This delicious soup, served hot, is a great choice for a Thanksgiving dinner. It is just as delicious served cold, as a lovely first course to a summer dinner on the patio.

    1   package (1 pound) carrots peeled and sliced
    1   large onion, chopped
    2   shallots, chopped
    3   cloves garlic, sliced
    1   small apple, peeled, cored and sliced
    4   cups chicken broth

   1/4   cup half and half cream
    6   teaspoons unflavored low-fat yogurt
         sprinkling of cinnamon for garnish

In a Dutch oven casserole, with cover slightly ajar, simmer together first 6 ingredients, until vegetables are very soft, about 30 minutes. Puree the soup, in batches, in a food processor. Stir in the cream. Serve, hot or cold, with a spoonful of yogurt and a sprinkling of cinnamon on top. Serves 8.

(About 61 calories per serving)

Mexican Chicken & Chili Bean Soup

1 fryer chicken (about 2 1/2 pounds) cut into serving pieces and
   sprinkled with garlic powder, pepper and paprika

2 onions, chopped
1 can (1 pound) stewed tomatoes, chopped. Do not drain.
6 cloves garlic, minced
1 can (8 ounces) tomato sauce
4 cups chicken broth
1 can (7 ounces) diced green chiles
1 can (1 pound) red kidney beans, rinsed and drained
1/4 cup raw rice or orzo
1 tablespoon chili powder (or more to taste)
1 teaspoon ground turmeric
1/2 teaspoon ground cumin
   black pepper to taste
3 sprinkles cayenne pepper

In a 9x13-inch baking pan, roast chicken in a 350-degree oven for 45 minutes
or until practically tender. Meanwhile, in a Dutch oven casserole with the
cover slightly ajar, simmer together the remaining ingredients for 30
minutes. Add the chicken, cut into bite-size pieces, discarding skin, bones
and fat in pan. Continue to simmer for 15 minutes, or until chicken is very
tender. Serve with 1 teaspoon of grated Parmesan cheese (add 7 calories)
(optional) on top. Serves 6 as dinner or 12 as a first-course.

(About 296 calories per serving-serving 6)
(About 148 calories per serving-serving 12)

Leek & Potato Soup with Chives

2 leeks, white and tender green parts only, rinsed and chopped
1 onion, chopped
1/2 cup chicken broth

1 medium potato, peeled and sliced
4 cups chicken broth
   white pepper to taste

4 tablespoons unflavored yogurt
4 tablespoons chopped chives

In a covered saucepan, over low heat, cook together first 3 ingredients for 10
minutes, or until vegetables are softened. Add the next 3 ingredients and
simmer mixture for about 30 minutes, or until vegetables are very soft.
Allow to cool to lukewarm and then puree mixture in a food processor.
Refrigerate until serving time. Serve with a dollup of yogurt, generously
sprinkled with chives. Serves 6.

(About 59 calories per serving)

Low-Calorie Farmhouse Vegetable Soup

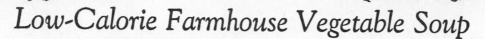

This is a soup I make often. It is a fine accompaniment to dinner and a great low-calorie snack, as well (1/2 cup 30 calories). Make it in large batches, for it freezes well. This yields over 10 cups of soup at about 60 calories per cup

> 6   cups chicken broth
> 2   medium onions, minced
> 6   cloves garlic, minced
> 2   stalks celery, thinly sliced
> 1   can (1 pound) stewed tomatoes, chopped. Do not drain.
> 2   tablespoons tomato paste
> 1   teaspoon sugar
> 1   teaspoon oregano flakes
> 1   teaspoon Italian Seasoning flakes
>   pinch of cayenne pepper
>
> 2   bags, (1 pound, each), frozen Del Sol vegetables (broccoli and cauliflower florets and carrot sticks). These can be found in the frozen food section of your market. Fresh is not better in this instance, as these are perfectly trimmed and do not contain any of the twiggy parts of the vegetables.

In a large covered soup pot, place first 10 ingredients, and bring soup to a simmer. Add the vegetables, and simmer soup, with the cover slightly ajar, for about 40 minutes, or until vegetables are tender. Serve with 1 teaspoon of grated Parmesan cheese (add 7 calories) (optional). Serves 10.

(About 61 calories per serving)

Chicken Ci Ci Pea Stew

Also known as "garbanzos" or "chick peas", ci ci peas are lovely in rice, excellent in salads and in this recipe they produce a grand soup that will satisfy and nurture. Using broth, instead of water, in the soup, enriches the flavor markedly.

> 1   can (1 pound) ci ci peas, rinsed and drained
> 3   onions, minced
> 6   carrots, peeled and sliced
> 3   cloves garlic, minced
> 1   can (1 pound) stewed tomatoes, chopped. Do not drain.
> 6   cups chicken broth
> 1   fryer chicken (about 2 1/2 pounds) cut into serving pieces

In a covered Dutch oven casserole, place all the ingredients and bring mixture to a rapid boil. Lower heat and simmer mixture for about 45 minutes to 1 hour or until chicken is tender. Remove chicken from stew and discard the skin and bones. Return boned chicken pieces to stew. Serves 6.

(About 262 calories per serving)

Cold & Creamy Dilled Zucchini Soup

Delicious served cold or hot. If serving hot, do not allow to boil after adding the buttermilk.

- 6   Italian zucchini, stemmed and partially peeled. (This means that you will leave a few strips of green for color.)
- 2   onions, chopped
- 4   shallots, chopped
- 6   cloves garlic, sliced
- 4   cups chicken broth
- 1/2   teaspoon dried dill weed or 1 tablespoon fresh dill weed

- 1   **cup buttermilk**

In a Dutch oven casserole, simmer together first 6 ingredients until vegetables are soft, about 30 minutes. Puree mixture in batches in a food processor. Return soup to pan, add the buttermilk and heat through. Do not boil after adding the buttermilk. Add a little dill to taste. Refrigerate soup until serving time. Serve with a dollup of yogurt and float a few chopped chives on top. Beautiful and delicious. Serves 6 to 8.

(About 54 calories per serving-serving 8)
(About 72 calories per serving-serving 6)

Dilled Potato & Cucumber Soup

- 3   medium cucumbers, (about 1 pound), peeled and cut in half lengthwise. With a spoon, scrape out the seeds. Cut cucumbers into 1-inch chunks.

- 1/3   cup chopped chives
- 2   potatoes, peeled, cooked until tender, drained, (1/2 pound)
- 3   cups buttermilk
- 4   tablespoons lemon juice
- 1   teaspoon dried dill weed

- 4   teaspoons unflavored low-fat yogurt for garnish
  chives for garnish

In a food processor, puree together first 6 ingredients. Refrigerate until serving time. Serve in bowls with a spoonful of yogurt and a sprinkling of chives on top. Serves 6 to 8.

(About 72 calories per serving-serving 8)
(About 96 calories per serving-serving 6)

Salads & Dressings

From my notebook:

Vegetables are the backbone of salads. Using them raw, blanched or cooked provide an interesting variety of salads. Vegetables are high in dietary fiber and provide necessary vitamins and minerals. Use them generously.

Lots of interesting salads and dressings in this chapter with a wide range of calorie content. Cucumber salad at 19 calories provides a very generous serving that will amaze you. Asparagus Vinaigrette at 21 calories is a very lovely salad. These can be enjoyed often for they deliver a lot of pleasure for the few calories.

Many vegetables, raw and cooked, are included. Artichokes, leeks, red peppers, spinach, mushrooms, eggplant, cabbage, carrots, snow peas and many more are used throughout. These sometimes include Mozzarella, Parmesan or Feta cheese accompaniments. Remember "variety" when choosing your menus.

Middle Eastern Cracked Wheat Salad, White Bean Salad and Artichoke, Red Pepper & Potato Salad are very substantial and satisfying. Several cole slaws for picnics or barbecues are nice accompaniments.

Main course salads, excellent for lunch and beautiful on a buffet, include Chicken Salad with Cous Cous & Currants, very delicious and exciting. Pasta Salad with Chicken & Vegetables is one that uses a little pasta and lots of vegetables. Shrimp in Honey Yogurt Lemon Dressing is an appetizer salad or can be served for lunch.

Cucumber Sauce with Dill will sparkle a poached salmon. Lemon-Dill Yogurt, French Mustard or Basil Garlic Vinaigrettes will make any salad more beautiful.

Also included are some delicious sauces for dipping fresh vegetables...Tomato & Chile Salsa, Imperial Sauce Verte, exceedingly low in calories and very delicious. Enjoy these often. They are light and satisfying and nourishing.

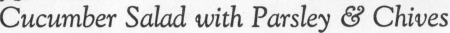

Cucumber Salad with Parsley & Chives

        2   large cucumbers, peeled, seeded (optional), and very thinly sliced.
              Can use the largest side of a 4-sided grater.
      1/4   cup chopped chives
        2   tablespoons finely chopped parsley
      1/3   cup seasoned rice vinegar
        1   tablespoon lemon juice
              white pepper to taste

In a bowl, toss together all the ingredients, cover and refrigerate. Can be prepared 2 hours before serving. Cucumbers will render a good deal of liquid and a little more vinegar can be added before serving. Serves 4.

(About 19 calories per serving)

Salad of Tomatoes, Onions & Feta Cheese

      1/2   large red onion, cut into thin slices
        2   tablespoons chopped parsley leaves
        1   tablespoon grated Parmesan cheese
        4   tablespoons rice vinegar
        1   tablespoon water

        3   large tomatoes, cut into 1/4-inch slices
        4   ounces feta cheese, crumbled

In a large bowl, toss together first 5 ingredients, cover bowl and refrigerate for several hours or overnight. Place tomatoes on a platter, top with onions and vinegar mixture and sprinkle top with feta cheese. Serves 6.

(About 72 calories per serving)

Tomato, Mushroom & Mozzarella Salad

        2   medium tomatoes, coarsely chopped
      1/4   pound part-skim Mozzarella cheese, grated
      1/2   pound mushrooms, sliced
      1/4   cup chopped green onions
        2   tablespoons chopped red onions
        2   tablespoons grated Parmesan cheese
        1   teaspoon oil
      1/4   cup rice vinegar
              pepper to taste

In a large bowl, toss together all the ingredients until nicely mixed. Cover bowl and refrigerate until ready to serve. Serves 8.

(About 71 calories per serving)

Note: - Can be prepared up to 4 hours before serving. Do not prepare 1 day earlier, as tomatoes will get mushy.

Pasta Salad with Chicken & Cooked Vegetables

This is another main course salad that is both satisfying and delicious. Adding extra vegetables does not increase the calories very much, so if you are using this as a main course for dinner, add more vegetables.

8   ounces spiral pasta, cooked al dente (tender but firm) and drained
2   chicken breasts, (about 4 ounces each), boned and skinned.
      Sprinkle with white pepper and garlic powder
1/2   cup chicken broth

2   bags (1 pound, each) mixed Del Sol Vegetables (carrot sticks, and
      broccoli and cauliflower florets), steamed al dente

1/2   cup chopped green onions
1/4   cup chopped parsley
4   tablespoons red wine vinegar
2   tablespoons lemon juice
2   teaspoons olive oil
      pepper to taste

Cook pasta in 1 gallon boiling water and drain. Poach the chicken breasts in broth until they are opaque, about 4 or 5 minutes. Do not overcook. Cut them into bite-size pieces, and reserve the broth. Steam vegetables. Before serving, combine pasta, chicken and broth, vegetables, and remaining ingredients in a large bowl and toss to blend. Add a little lemon juice to taste. Serve at once. Serves 8.

(About 190 calories per serving)

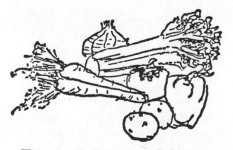

Raw Vegetable Salad

2   carrots, sliced or grated
2   large stalks celery, thinly sliced
1   red or green bell pepper, cut into thin slivers
3   cups lettuce, cut or torn into bite-size pieces
1   shallot
1/4   cup chopped green onions
6   tablespoons Lemon-Dill Yogurt Sauce

Stir together all the ingredients until blended. Serve at once. Serves 2.

(About 61 calories per serving)

Artichoke, Red Pepper & Potato Salad

This is one of the most beautiful salads. It is equally delicious. This can be prepared from scratch by steaming frozen artichokes, fresh red peppers and baby potatoes. I have prepared this dish both ways, and the raves have been about the same. It is certainly much easier using the marinated vegetables, so remember this dish on a night when you are running late. It is a hearty salad and served with broiled fish, it can be considered a full meal.

1	jar (6 ounces) marinated artichokes, drained and cut into fourths. Reserve the marinade.
4	marinated red peppers, cut into strips
1	can (1 pound) sliced potatoes, rinsed and drained
1/3	cup chopped green onions
1	tablespoon reserved artichoke marinade
4	tablespoons lemon juice

In a bowl, toss together first 4 ingredients until nicely mixed. Add the remaining ingredients and toss to blend. Cover bowl with plastic wrap and refrigerate until about 20 minutes before serving. Serve mildly chilled, but not straight from the refrigerator. Serves 6.

(About 78 calories per serving)

Spinach, Mushroom & Red Onion Salad

1	pound fresh spinach, stems removed. Wash spinach three times in a sinkful of water until every trace of sand is removed. Drain on paper towelling and tear into bite-size pieces.
1/2	pound mushrooms, stems removed, cleaned and thinly sliced
1/2	medium red onion, cut into very thin slices
1	tomato, peeled, seeded and chopped
2	shallots, minced
1/4	cup chopped chives
2	tablespoons red wine vinegar
2	tablespoons lemon juice
2	tablespoons water
1 1/2	teaspoons olive oil
2	teaspoons Dijon mustard

In a large bowl, toss together first 6 ingredients. Stir together remaining ingredients and toss into salad just before serving. Serves 4.

(About 74 calories per serving)

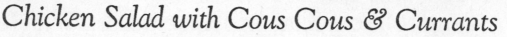

Chicken Salad with Cous Cous & Currants

This is a lovely fresh vegetable salad to serve for a buffet lunch. It also serves well for a light dinner. Add other fresh vegetables to your taste if you are planning this as a main course for dinner.

- 1 1/4 cups boiling water
- 1 cup pre-cooked cous cous

- 2 chicken breasts, boned and skinned, about 4 ounces each. Sprinkle with white pepper and garlic powder.
- 1/2 cup chicken broth

- 4 tomatoes, peeled, seeded and chopped
- 2 large cucumbers (about 1 pound), peeled and chopped
- 1/2 cup chopped green onions
- 1/4 cup dried black currants (about 2 ounces)
- 1/4 cup chopped parsley
- 4 tablespoons champagne vinegar
- 2 tablespoons lemon juice
- 1 teaspoon olive oil
  pepper to taste

In a saucepan, bring water to a boil. Stir in cous cous, stir and simmer for about 3 minutes. Remove from heat and continue stirring to help separate the grains. Poach the chicken breasts in broth until they are opaque, about 4 to 5 minutes. Do not overcook. Cut them into bite-size pieces. Before serving, in a large bowl, toss together all the ingredients, including the chicken broth. Add a little lemon juice if necessary and serve. Serves 8.

(About 169 calories per serving)

Carrot & Snow Pea Salad

- 1/2 pound carrots, peeled, sliced, and cooked until tender but firm
- 1/2 pound pea pods, steamed for 1 minute, until tender but firm
- 1/4 cup chopped green onions
- 1/2 cup (8 tablespoons) Imperial Sauce Verte

Toss together all the ingredients until nicely mixed. Serve at once. Serves 6.
(About 43 calories per serving)

Confetti Cole Slaw in Horseradish Vinaigrette

1   small head cabbage, a little under 1 pound, (cored and grated)
2   carrots, peeled and grated
1/3   chopped green onions
1/2   red bell pepper, chopped
1   teaspoon sugar
3   tablespoons vinegar

2   tablespoons prepared horseradish
1/4   cup buttermilk
1/4   cup low-fat mayonnaise
     salt and pepper to taste

In a large bowl, stir together first 6 ingredients and allow mixture to stand for 10 minutes. Stir together the remaining ingredients until blended and pour over cabbage mixture, tossing until everything is nicely combined. Cover bowl and refrigerate until ready to serve. Serves 8.
(About 44 calories per serving)

Note: -Can be prepared up to 4 hours earlier. Do not prepare 1 day earlier, as cabbage renders a good deal of liquid.

Eggplant Salad with Tomatoes & Cheese

1   medium eggplant (about 1 pound), peeled and cut into
     1/4-inch slices. Cut each slice into quarters.
2   cloves garlic, minced
1/2   cup chicken broth

3   medium tomatoes, peeled and coarsely chopped
1   cup grated low-fat Mozzarella cheese (4 ounces)
1/3   cup chopped green onions
4   tablespoons red wine vinegar
1/2   teaspoon dried dill weed
     pepper to taste

In a 9x13-inch baking pan, place eggplant and garlic and drizzle with broth. Cover pan tightly with foil and bake in a 350-degree oven for 30 minutes, or until eggplant is very soft.

In a large bowl, place the eggplant mixture, and the remaining ingredients and mix until nicely blended. (Eggplant will break into very small pieces.) Refrigerate for several hours to allow flavors to blend. Serve on a lovely platter, surrounded with thin slices of French bread. Nice to serve on a buffet or as a first course. Serve cold or at room temperature. Serves 8.
(About 69 calories per serving)

Marinated Red Pepper Salad

Marinated red peppers are sold in jars in a mild vinaigrette. They are packed in a little olive oil, but barely enough to mention. Leaving the fresh basil leaves whole, makes the dish especially attractive. These low-calorie peppers are nice to serve as an accompaniment to chicken or fish. They are also delicious as a topping on sandwiches...chicken, tuna, ham are all enhanced with the addition of these peppers.

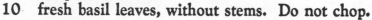

6	marinated red peppers, cut into wide strips
1/4	cup chopped green onions
2	cloves garlic, minced
2	tablespoons red wine vinegar
1	teaspoon olive oil
10	fresh basil leaves, without stems. Do not chop.

Combine all the ingredients in a glass bowl, cover with plastic wrap and store in the refrigerator. Serve on a bed of lettuce or on sandwiches. Serves 6

(About 30 calories per serving)

Tomato & Onion Salad with Basil Vinaigrette

4	tomatoes, cut into 1/4-inch slices
1	onion, sliced into very thin rings

Basil Vinaigrette:

1/2	cup seasoned rice vinegar
1	teaspoon Dijon mustard
1	teaspoon sweet basil flakes
1	clove garlic, minced
3	tablespoons chopped parsley (no stems)
4	tablespoons chopped chives
1	tablespoon grated Parmesan cheese
	black pepper to taste

In a 10 x 2-inch round dish, layer the tomatoes and onions. In a glass jar with a tight-fitting lid, shake together the remaining ingredients and pour over the tomatoes. Cover with plastic wrap and refrigerate for several hours before serving. Serves 4.

(About 43 calories per serving)

Eggplant & Tomato Salad with Lemon & Dill

Serve this as an hors d'oeurve or first course. It is basically low in calories so I would recommend serving it with thin slices of one of my flatbreads. Or serve on a bed of lettuce and omit the bread.

 2 medium eggplants, about 3/4 pound, each, peeled and thinly sliced
1/3 cup tomato juice

 2 medium onions, sliced
 2 cloves garlic, minced
 1 teaspoon olive oil

 2 cans (1 pound, each) stewed tomatoes, chopped and drained.
   Reserve juice for another use.
 3 tablespoons tomato paste

 4 tablespoons lemon juice
 3 tablespoons finely chopped parsley
1/2 teaspoon dried dill weed or more to taste
   pepper to taste

Place eggplant in a 9x13-inch baking pan and drizzle with tomato juice. Cover tightly with foil and bake in a 350-degree oven for 30 minutes, or until eggplant is soft.

Meanwhile, in a Dutch oven casserole, saute onions and garlic in oil, until onions are soft. Add the cooked eggplant. Stir in the tomatoes and tomato paste and simmer mixture for 20 minutes, uncovered. Stir in the remaining ingredients and heat through. Serves 12 as a first course.

(About 38 calories per serving)

Leeks & Tomatoes in Lemon Dressing

 4 leeks. Cut off roots and remove tough outer leaves. Trim off
   tops, leaving soft green leaves. Cut each leek in half
   lengthwise, wash thoroughly, removing every trace of sand.
   Now, cut into 1-inch pieces.
 1 can (1 pound) stewed tomatoes, chopped. Do not drain.
 4 tablespoons lemon juice
 1 teaspoon oil
   pepper to taste

1/4 cup chopped green onions

In a saucepan, place first 5 ingredients. With cover slightly ajar, simmer mixture until leeks are tender and soft. Place in a bowl, stir in green onions and cover bowl. Refrigerate until serving time. Serve as a first course on a bed of lettuce. Serves 6.

(About 48 calories per serving)

Tomatoes with Garlic Croutons & Parmesan

4   medium tomatoes, cut into 1/4-inch slices
1/4 cup garlic croutons crushed
1/4 cup chopped chives
2   tablespoons grated Parmesan cheese

2   tablespoons red wine vinegar
1   tablespoon water
1   teaspoon Italian Herb Seasoning flakes
1   teaspoon olive oil
     freshly ground black pepper

In a 10-inch round porcelain serving dish, lay tomato slices, overlapping, in a decorative fashion. Sprinkle with croutons, chives and Parmesan cheese. Stir together next 5 ingredients and drizzle evenly over all. Cover and refrigerate for several hours. Serves 6.

(About 38 calories per serving)

Low-Calorie Pineapple Cole Slaw

This is a lovely salad to serve on a buffet, for the colors are so inviting. Basically, it is a subtle sweet and sour dressing. Toss this shortly before serving, as it could render a good deal of liquid.

1   small head cabbage, grated, about 1 pound
6   medium carrots, grated, about 3 cups
1   red bell pepper, cored, seeded and chopped
1   cup chopped green onions

1   cup unsweetened crushed pineapple with juice
1/3 cup lemon juice, or more to taste
1/4 cup low-calorie mayonnaise

In a bowl, toss together first 4 ingredients. Shake together the remaining ingredients in a jar, with a tight-fitting lid, and pour over the vegetables. Toss until salad is nicely coated. Refrigerate until serving time. Serves 12.

(About 44 calories per serving)

Asparagus Vinaigrette with Cheese & Chives

1   pound asparagus. Trim off the tough bottoms and if the
      asparagus is thick-skinned, peel it with a vegetable peeler.
3   tablespoons chicken broth
3   tablespoons white wine vinegar

3   tablespoons chopped chives
2   tablespoons grated Parmesan cheese

In a large covered skillet, cook asparagus in broth and vinegar until asparagus is tender, about 4 to 5 minutes. Sprinkle with chives and cheese and refrigerate until serving time. Before serving sprinkle with a little parsley. A few toasted pine nuts are excellent but optional. Serves 4 to 6.

(About 21 calories per serving-serving 6)
(About 32 calories per serving-serving 4)

Shrimp in Honey Yogurt Lemon Dressing

This lovely dish serves well as an hors d'oeurve or small entree. Dressing can be prepared earlier in the day or 1 day earlier. Toss the shrimp in the dressing several hours before serving.

Honey Yogurt Lemon Dressing:

1   cup unflavored non-fat yogurt
1/4 cup lemon juice
1/4 cup honey
1   green onion
1/2 teaspoon dried dill weed

2   pounds small cooked shrimp

In a food processor, blend together first 5 ingredients until onion is pureed. Toss cooked shrimp with dressing and refrigerate for several hours. If serving as an hors d'oeurve, place shrimp on a bed of curly leaf lettuce and have cocktail forks close by.

If you are serving this as a small entree, then serve on a bed of lettuce in individual serving plates. Serves 8 as a small entree or 16 as an hors d'oeurve.

(About 75 calories per serving-serving 16)
(About 149 calories per serving-serving 8)

Middle Eastern Cracked Wheat Salad
with Tomatoes & Onions

1 1/2	cups cracked wheat (bulgur)
3	cups boiling water
3/4	cup chopped green onions
1/4	cup chopped parsley
2	tomatoes, chopped
1	large cucumber, peeled, seeded and chopped (8 ounces)
1/2	cup lemon juice
1	tablespoon olive oil
2	tablespoons chopped fresh mint (optional or to taste-I omit it.)
	salt and pepper to taste

In a large bowl, soak cracked wheat in boiling water for about 1 1/2 hours. Line a collander with double thicknesses of cheese cloth and thoroughly drain cracked wheat. In a large bowl, combine the cracked wheat with the remaining ingredients and toss until mixture is nicely mixed. Cover bowl and refrigerate until ready to serve. Serves 8.

(About 145 calories per serving)

White Bean Salad with Tomatoes & Scallions

1	can (15 ounces) Great Northern beans, rinsed and drained
1/2	cup sliced cherry tomatoes, seeded
1/4	cup minced red onions
1/3	cup minced green onions (scallions)
1	clove garlic, minced
1/4	cup seasoned rice vinegar
1	teaspoon olive oil
1	teaspoon Italian Herb Seasoning flakes
	pepper to taste

In a bowl, stir together all the ingredients, cover bowl and refrigerate for several hours or overnight, stirring from time to time. Nice salad to serve on a buffet or part of an antipasto. Serves 6.

(About 74 calories per serving)

Basil Pimiento Dressing

2   tablespoons pimiento strips, finely minced
3   tablespoons finely minced fresh basil leaves or
    3/4 teaspoon dried basil leaves
3   tablespoons lemon juice
1   clove garlic, minced
1/2 cup seasoned rice vinegar
    pepper to taste

In a glass jar, with a tight-fitting lid, shake all the ingredients. Refrigerate for several hours. This can be prepared in a food processor, but leave a little texture and do not puree. Yields 16 tablespoons.
(About 3 calories per tablespoon)

Cucumber Sauce with Dill & Chives for Poached Salmon

1   large cucumber, peeled, seeded and grated (8-ounces)
3   tablespoons seasoned rice vinegar
1/4 cup finely chopped chives
1/2 teaspoon dried dill weed
    white pepper to taste
1   cup unflavored non-fat yogurt

In a bowl, toss together all the ingredients until nicely mixed. Cover and refrigerate. Can be prepared 2 hours before serving. Yields 2 cups sauce.
(About 5 calories per tablespoon)

Lemon-Dill Yogurt Sauce

1   cup non-fat unflavored yogurt
2   tablespoons lemon juice
1/4 cup chopped chives
1   clove garlic minced
1   jar (2 ounces) finely chopped pimientos
1/2 teaspoon Dijon mustard
1/4 teaspoon dried dill weed

Stir together all the ingredients until blended. Serve with raw vegetables for dipping. Yields about 1 1/2 cups sauce.
(About 6 calories per tablespoon)

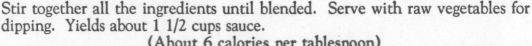

Imperial Sauce Verte

    2   cups non-fat unflavored yogurt
    4   tablespoons lemon juice
    1   shallot, coarsely chopped
  1/4   cup coarsely chopped green onions
    4   tablespoons chopped watercress (no stems)
    2   tablespoons chopped parsley (no stems)
  1/8   teaspoon dried mustard
         pepper to taste

  3/4   teaspoon dried dill weed
    1   package (10 ounces) frozen chopped spinach, defrosted. Place
         in a strainer and press until most of the liquid is removed.

In a food processor, blend together first 8 ingredients until mixture is very
finely chopped. Stir in the remaining ingredients until blended. Place in a
lovely footed bowl and surround with sliced fresh vegetables. Carrots, celery,
jicama, cucumbers, zucchini, etc. are all wonderful with this dip. Cut the
vegetables in various shapes and sizes; circles, sticks, curls, slices, on the
diagonal and the likes. Yields 3 cups sauce.

(About 7 calories per tablespoon)

Tomato & Chile Salsa
for Dipping with Fresh Vegetables

    1   can (1 pound) stewed tomatoes, very finely chopped. Do not drain.
  1/4   cup chopped green onions
    2   tablespoons minced red onion
    4   tablespoons chopped cilantro
    2   tablespoons chopped parsley
    1   clove garlic, minced
    2   tablespoons red wine vinegar (or more to taste)
    2   tablespoons lime juice
    1   can (4 ounces) diced green chiles
  1/4   teaspoon ground cumin
  1/4   teaspoon sugar
         pinch of cayenne
         salt to taste

In a quart-jar with a tight-fitting lid, shake together all the ingredients
until mixture is nicely blended. Refrigerate for several hours or overnight.
Serve with fresh vegetables that have been cut on the diagonal, so that the
sauce can be scooped up more easily. Yields 2 1/2 cups sauce.

(About 4 calories per tablespoon)

Basil Garlic Vinaigrette

- 2 tablespoons oil
- 2 tablespoons rice vinegar or champagne vinegar
- 2 tablespoons water
- 2 tablespoons lemon juice
- 1 teaspoon Dijon mustard
- 2 tablespoons chopped chives
- 1/2 teaspoon sweet basil flakes
- 1/8 teaspoon garlic powder
  - pinch cayenne pepper

In a glass jar with a tight-fitting lid, shake together all the ingredients until blended. Yields about 10 tablespoons dressing.

(About 27 calories per tablespoon)

French Mustard Vinaigrette

- 2 tablespoons olive oil
- 2 tablespoons lemon juice
- 2 tablespoons rice vinegar
- 3 tablespoons water
- 2 tablespoons minced chives
- 1 small shallot, finely minced, about 1 tablespoon
- 1 teaspoon Dijon mustard
- 1/2 teaspoon dried basil flakes
  - white pepper to taste
- 1 sprinkle cayenne pepper

In a glass jar, with a tight-fitting lid, place all the ingredients and shake until thoroughly blended. Allow flavors to blend for several hours in the refrigerator. Yields 3/4 cup.

(About 23 calories per tablespoon)

Yogurt Lemon Dressing or Dipping Sauce for Salads and Fresh Vegetables

- 1 cup non-fat yogurt
- 1 green onion, chopped
- 1/4 cup chopped cilantro
- 1 tablespoon lemon juice or more to taste
- 1 tablespoon vinegar or more to taste
- 1/8 teaspoon garlic powder
- 2 dashes Tabasco Sauce

In a blender or food processor, blend all the ingredients until mixture is very finely chopped. (Pureed is O.K., too.) Yields about 1 1/4 cups dressing.

(About 6 calories per tablespoon)

Fish & Shellfish

From my notebook:

Fish, chicken and vegetables are the most popular foods and recipes for these are the most abundant in this cookbook. In this chapter I have used low-fat fish more often than those with higher fat. As fish and chicken are being eaten more and more often by Americans, I have attempted to be as inventive as I could, to create interesting and exciting recipes that will appeal to all your senses.

Fish and shellfish are presented in many moods...Italian, Greek, French, Cajun, Chinese, Mediterranean, and many more. Range of calories is from the low 100's to the low 200's, except for the tuna steaks at 277, which is still within range.

Three very excellent chowders/stews, Costa del Sol Mediterranean Chowder, New Orleans Hot & Spicy Fish Stew and the very popular, always delicious, Bouillabaisse. These are very satisfying and low calorie. Two croustades are featured, that are beautiful with the stews, to dip into the delicious broth.

Fillets of Sole are presented in a variety of ways...Stuffed with Spinach & Cheese, with Sun-Dried Tomatoes & Pepper Sauce, with leeks, garlic, lemon, chives, spinach, yogurt, mushrooms, onions, artichokes and many other combinations, too numerous to mention.

Sea Bass with Salsa Español, or with Tomato, Currants & Pine Nuts will add interest and excitement to your meals.

A Chinese Whole Fish Steamed in the Oven, served with Fried Rice will surely satisfy a craving for Oriental food and still be low-fat and nourishing. Red Snapper Teriyaki with Ginger & Scallions is also in an Oriental mood.

Red Hot Shrimp Creole or Shrimp in a Red-Hot Garlic Sauce is very pleasurable. Shrimp, Barbecued or Greek-Style with Lemon & Feta add variety. Lobster with Chile Tomato Salsa and Scallops in Wine Sauce round out the recipes.

A few sauces to accompany fish that you might choose to broil and serve, include a Mexican Tomato Salsa, Tartar Sauce or a Honey Mustard Dill Sauce.

I hope these will help to make fish exciting and appealing.

Costa del Sol Mediterranean Chowder

Bouillabaisse, Cioppino and this Spanish chowder are all variations on a theme. By using different herbs and seasonings, the basic fish stew takes on a totally different character. Of course, fish and shellfish can be used in any amounts as there are no rules. Stew base can be prepared earlier in the day, or 1 day earlier, and stored in the refrigerator. Bring to a rolling boil and add the fish just before serving.

Stew Base:

1	large onion, chopped
6	cloves garlic, minced
3	shallots, minced
1/4	cup chopped green bell pepper
1/4	cup chopped red bell pepper
1	can (1 pound) stewed tomatoes chopped. Do not drain.
1 1/2	cups tomato juice
1	cup bottled clam juice
4	tablespoons tomato paste
1	tablespoon olive oil
1	sliver lemon peel
1	teaspoon ground turmeric (or more to taste)
1/2	teaspoon ground cumin
1/2	teaspoon oregano flakes
2	shakes cayenne pepper
	freshly ground black pepper to taste

1 1/2	pounds halibut, haddock or red snapper fillets, cut into 1-inch cubes (or shellfish of your choice)

In a Dutch oven casserole, place all the ingredients, except the fish and simmer mixture for 30 to 40 minutes, or until vegetables are soft. Raise heat and bring stew to a rolling boil, add the fish, and cook fish for about 4 or 5 minutes, or until fish becomes opaque. Do not overcook. Serve with Croustades of Olive Oil & Parmesan Cheese. Serves 6.

(About 156 calories per serving)

Croustades of Olive Oil & Parmesan Cheese:

12	thin slices French bread (1/2 ounce, each)
6	teaspoons olive oil
12	teaspoons chopped chives
6	teaspoons grated Parmesan cheese

Spread 1/2-teaspoon olive oil on each slice of French bread. Sprinkle with 1 teaspoon chopped chives and 1/2 teaspoon grated Parmesan. Place croustades under the broiler for about 1 minute to brown tops. Serves 6.

(About 130 calories per 2-slice serving)

New Orleans Hot & Spicy Fish Stew

As you probably know by now, I do not enjoy food that is overly hot, or overly anything (except delicious.) In all my recipes, I try to balance flavors and textures, so that there is a harmony with the ingredients. My husband, on the other hand, loves fiery dishes that catch in the throat and bring tears to his eyes. This dish is a compromise...quite hot for my taste, but mild for the initiated. Sauce can be prepared earlier in the day, or even 1 day earlier, and stored in the refrigerator. Cook the fish just before serving.

Hot & Spicy Sauce:
- 2   onions, chopped
- 6   cloves garlic, minced
- 1   medium green bell pepper, cut into strips
- 1   can (1 pound) stewed tomatoes, chopped. Do not drain.
- 1   can (8 ounces) tomato sauce
- 1   teaspoon, each, sweet basil flakes, thyme flakes, paprika and sugar
- 1/2   teaspoon freshly ground black pepper
- 1/8   teaspoon cayenne pepper (or more to taste)

- 2   pounds low-fat fish, (Sole, Halibut or Flounder), cut into 1 1/2-inch pieces

In a covered Dutch oven casserole, place all the ingredients, except the fish, and simmer mixture for 30 minutes, or until pepper is tender. Can be held at this point. Just before serving, bring sauce to a bubble, add the fish, and cook fish for 3 to 4 minutes, or until it becomes opaque. Do not overcook. Serve with Herbed Rice. Yields 6 to 8 servings.

      (About 167 calories per serving-serving 6)
      (About 125 calories per serving-serving 8)

Bouillabaisse

This hearty fish chowder is a rich and satisfying stew. The soup base can be prepared earlier in the day or even a day earlier, thus leaving the last 5-minute simmer just before serving. Sole, Flounder, Halibut are all lean low-fat fish and good choices. Do not overcook the fish. Cook only until fish becomes opaque, and not longer.

Soup Base:

2	large onions, minced
4	shallots, minced
6	cloves garlic, minced
3	carrots, grated
3	medium potatoes, cut into 1/2-inch dice
1	can (1 pound) stewed tomatoes, chopped. Do not drain.
3	cups tomato juice
1/2	cup clam juice
1	tablespoon parsley flakes
1	teaspoon thyme flakes
1	teaspoon sweet basil flakes
2	teaspoons sugar
1	teaspoon turmeric
	black pepper to taste
1/8	teaspoon cayenne pepper (or to taste)

In a Dutch oven casserole, combine all the ingredients, and with cover slightly ajar, simmer soup base for 20 to 25 minutes or until potatoes are tender. Can be held at this point stored in the refrigerator. Just before serving, bring soup to a rolling boil and add:

2	pounds low-fat fish fillets, cut into 1 1/2-inch pieces. Sea Bass, Red Snapper, Sole, Halibut, Flounder are all good choices.

Cook fish for about 5 minutes at a steady simmer, or until fish becomes opaque. Serve with Broiled Croustades with Cheese as an excellent accompaniment. Serves 8.

(About 175 calories per serving)

Broiled Croustades with Cheese:
Spread 1/3-inch slices of a crusty sourdough baguette (sometimes called flutes) with 1/3 teaspoon of olive oil. Sprinkle with 1/2 teaspoon of grated Parmesan cheese. Broil for a few seconds until tops are golden. (3 slices of bread equals 1-ounce.)

(About 42 calories per slice)

Fillets of Sole Stuffed with Spinach & Cheese

This recipe is a little more work, but worth every bit of extra time. As stuffing and topping ingredients can be assembled earlier in the day and stored in the refrigerator, rolling the fillets an hour before serving becomes no problem. Refrigerate rolled fillets until ready to bake just before serving. Bread crumbs can easily be made in a food processor.

> 6   fillets of sole, (about 1 1/2 pounds), sprinkled with garlic powder and white pepper to taste

Spinach & Cheese Stuffing:
- 1   package (10 ounces) frozen chopped spinach, defrosted and pressed in a strainer to drain excess moisture
- 1/2   cup low-fat Ricotta cheese
- 1/4   cup minced green onions
- 1   slice fresh whole wheat bread (1 ounce) made into crumbs
- 1/3   cup grated Parmesan cheese
- 1   egg white

Cheese Topping:
- 2   tablespoons fresh bread crumbs
- 2   tablespoons grated Parmesan cheese
- 3   tablespoons chopped chives
- 1   tablespoon melted butter

In a bowl, stir together stuffing ingredients until nicely blended. Divide stuffing into 6 parts. Place 1 part stuffing on the cut side of each fillet (on the widest part) and roll it up. Secure the seam with a wooden toothpick. Place the rolls, spiral side up and close together, in a 10-inch round baking pan.

Mix together Cheese Topping ingredients and sprinkle on top. Bake at 350-degrees for 15 minutes or until fish becomes opaque. Do not overbake. Broil for a few seconds to brown the top. Serve with fresh lemon wedges. Serves 6.
(About 190 calories per serving)

Sole with Sun-Dried Tomato & Pepper Sauce

This glamorous sauce is a far-cry from the usual bland, tasteless low-calorie sauces. It contains only 2 teaspoons of oil, but it is so deeply flavored with herbs and seasonings, you will never notice the reduced amount of oil.

Sun-Dried Tomato & Pepper Sauce:

1/3	cup chopped sun-dried tomatoes
1	sweet red bell pepper, chopped
4	shallots, minced
2	cloves garlic, minced
1/2	teaspoon sweet basil flakes
1/2	teaspoon Italian Herb Seasoning
1/4	cup bottled clam broth
2	teaspoons olive oil

1   1/2 pounds fillets of sole (halibut, red snapper or sea bass are also low-fat fish and can be substituted). Sprinkle with pepper, garlic powder and paprika.

In a saucepan, toss together first group of ingredients, cover pan and simmer mixture for 30 minutes, or until pepper is tender. Meanwhile, place fish in 1-layer in a 9x13-inch baking pan and bake at 350-degrees for 10 minutes or until fish becomes opaque and flakes easily with a fork. Do not overbake. Place sauce over the fish and heat through. Serves 6.

(About 125 calories per serving)

Sole with Garlic, Lemon & Chive Sauce

Garlic, butter, lemon and shallots add a good deal of taste and sparkle to the fish. This is an excellent sauce to serve on chicken and vegetables.

1   pound fillets of sole, sprinkle with white pepper, garlic powder and onion powder

4	teaspoons melted butter
1	shallot, minced
2	tablespoons lemon juice
1	clove garlic, minced
1	tablespoon minced parsley

Lay fish in 1-layer in an 8x12-inch baking pan. Stir together the remaining ingredients and spoon evenly over the fish. Broil fish, about 4-inches from the heat, for 3 minutes, or until fish becomes opaque. Careful not to overbake. Serves 4.

(About 128 calories per serving)

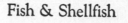

Fillets of Sole with Leeks & Tomato Sauce

Leeks, shallots, garlic and tomatoes add a beautiful bed of taste to the fish. The colors are also lovely and appetizing. Sauce can be prepared earlier in the day or even 1 day earlier and stored in the refrigerator. Bake the fish just before serving.

Leek & Tomato Sauce:

2	leeks, chopped. (Use only the white and about 1 1/2-inches of the soft green parts.)
4	shallots, thinly sliced
3	cloves garlic, minced
2	tomatoes, peeled, seeded and chopped (fresh or canned)
1/4	cup dry white wine
2	tablespoons lemon juice
1/2	teaspoon dried dill weed
1/8	teaspoon white pepper

2	pounds fillets of sole, sprinkled with white pepper and paprika

In a Dutch oven casserole, place all the ingredients, except the fish, cover pan and simmer mixture for 30 minutes, or until leeks are soft. Uncover pan and simmer sauce for 5 minutes, or until most of the liquid is evaporated. Can be held at this point in the refrigerator.

Just before serving, bake fish in one layer, in a 9x13-inch porcelain baking pan, at 350-degrees for about 8 to 10 minutes or until fish becomes opaque. Do not overbake. Heat the sauce and spoon it over the top. Serve with Steamed Baby Potatoes with Parsley & Dill. Yields 6 generous servings.

(About 152 calories per serving)

Mousse of Sole in Yogurt, Spinach & Chives

Looking for an extravagant, showy mold for a luncheon buffet, that will cheer the heart of the most stringent dieter? Well, here's one to consider. The yogurt imparts a tart creamy base, and the dill and lemon add a little depth.

1	pound fillets of Sole, sprinkled with white pepper and garlic powder
1/4	cup dry white wine
1/4	teaspoon dried dill weed
2	cups unflavored non-fat yogurt
1/2	cup coarsely chopped chives
1/2	teaspoon dried dill weed (or more to taste)
6	tablespoons lemon juice
1	package (10 ounces) frozen chopped spinach, defrosted and drained
2	tablespoons unflavored gelatin (2 packets)
1/3	cup water

More →

Mousse of Sole (Continued)

In a large skillet or Dutch oven casserole, simmer the fillets in wine and dill for about 5 minutes, or until fish becomes opaque and flakes easily with a fork. With a fork, flake the fish into very small pieces, and add fish and juices to a large bowl. Stir together next 4 ingredients and add to bowl. Stir in spinach until everything is nicely combined.

In a 1-cup metal measuring cup, soften gelatin in water. Place cup in a pan with simmering water until gelatin is liquefied. Quickly stir gelatin into fish mixture until blended.

Spoon mixture into a 8-cup fish mold and refrigerate until firm. Unmold onto a lovely platter and decorate with curly lettuce leaves and lemon slices sprinkled with parsley. Serves 6.

(About 129 calories per serving)

Sole Italienne with Red Pepper Tomato Sauce

Sole is a sweet, tender low-calorie fish, and one of my favorites. Here the sauce is sparkled with wine and herbs. The Red Pepper Tomato Sauce is also excellent over shellfish or pasta.

Red Pepper Tomato Sauce:
- 1 medium sweet red bell pepper, cut into strips
- 1 medium green bell pepper, cut into strips
- 1 can (1 pound) stewed tomatoes, drained and chopped. Reserve juice for another use.
- 1/2 cup chopped green onions
- 2 cloves garlic, minced
- 2 shallots, minced
- 1/3 cup dry white wine
- 2 tablespoons chopped parsley
- 2 tablespoons lemon juice
- 1/2 teaspoon oregano flakes
- 1/2 teaspoon sweet basil flakes
- 2 shakes cayenne pepper (or to taste)

- 1 pound fillets of sole
- 2 tablespoons grated Parmesan cheese

In a covered Dutch oven casserole, simmer sauce ingredients for 30 minutes, or until peppers are soft. Uncover pan and simmer sauce for another 5 minutes or until it is slightly reduced. Can be held at this point in the refrigerator, for several hours or overnight.

Before serving, place sauce in an 8x12-inch roasting pan and place fish on top. Sprinkle evenly with grated cheese. Broil fish, about 4-inches from the heat, until it becomes opaque. Depending on the thickness of the fillets, it should take about 2 minutes. Do not overcook. Serve fish on a bed of vegetables accompanied with Rice with Cheese & Chives. Serves 4.

(About 162 calories per serving)

Fillets of Sole in Artichoke & Tomato Sauce

This little dish assembles in minutes and is a lovely balance of flavors. The sauce can be prepared earlier in the day or 1 day earlier, stored in the refrigerator and heated before serving. Fish should be baked just before serving.

2 pounds fillets of sole. Sprinkle with white pepper, garlic powder and paprika. Brush lightly with unflavored yogurt and sprinkle with 1 tablespoon grated Parmesan cheese. (Halibut, Flounder or Sea Bass can be substituted.

Artichoke & Tomato Sauce:
1 jar (6 ounces) marinated artichoke hearts, rinsed, drained and chopped
2 medium tomatoes, peeled, seeded and chopped
2 shallots, minced
1/4 cup minced green onions
1 clove garlic, minced
2 tablespoons chopped parsley
2 tablespoons lemon juice
1/2 teaspoon sweet basil flakes
1/2 teaspoon oregano flakes
white pepper to taste

Place fish in one layer in a 12x16-inch baking pan and bake at 350-degrees for about 10 to 15 minutes, or until fish becomes opaque and flakes easily with a fork. Do not overbake.

Meanwhile, in a saucepan, combine all the sauce ingredients and simmer mixture, uncovered, for 10 minutes, or until sauce is slightly thickened. Spoon sauce over the fish and heat through. Serve with Cracked Wheat (also known as Bulgur or Kasha) with Mushrooms & Onions. Serves 6 to 8.

(About 163 calories per serving-serving 6)
(About 122 calories per serving-serving 8)

Sole Provencale with Tomatoes & Onions

Be certain that you do not overcook the fish to preserve its sweet flavor and tender texture.

2 pounds fillets of sole. Sprinkle generously with white pepper, garlic powder and paprika.

1 can (1 pound) stewed tomatoes, drained and chopped. Reserve juice for another use.

1/2 cup chopped green onions

4 tablespoons chopped parsley

4 tablespoons grated Parmesan cheese

6 thin slices lemon

In a 12x16-inch roasting pan, lay fillets in one layer. Now, scatter tomatoes, green onions, parsley and cheese evenly over the fish. Lay lemon slices on top. Bake at 350-degrees for 15 minutes, or until fish is opaque. Serve with vegetables on the top. Brown Rice with Mushrooms, Onion & Carrots is a lovely accompaniment. Yields 6 generous portions but could serve 8.

(About 151 calories per serving-serving 6)

(About 103 calories per serving-serving 8)

Brown Rice with Mushrooms, Onions & Carrots:

1/4 pound mushrooms, cleaned and sliced

1 onion, finely chopped

2 carrots, grated

1 teaspoon oil

pepper to taste

1 cup brown rice

1 1/4 cups chicken broth

1 cup water

1 teaspoon oil

pepper to taste

In a skillet, over low heat, cook together first 5 ingredients until vegetables are tender. Meanwhile in a covered saucepan, cook together the remaining ingredients until rice is tender and liquid is absorbed, about 35 minutes. Stir together rice and vegetables and heat through. Serves 6 to 8.

(About 147 calories per serving-serving 6)

(About 111 calories per serving-serving 8)

Tuna Steaks with Tomato Vinaigrette

Tuna with the flavors of Provence. The sauce is delicious, with tomato, pepper, onion and garlic sparkled in a mild vinaigrette. Tuna, as with most fish, can toughen with overcooking, so be especially careful. If you like tuna served medium rare, then broil just a few minutes on each side. The ingredients in Tomato Vinaigrette should be very finely chopped. Tuna, (576 calories per pound) can be substituted with a less fatty fish, such as halibut (336 calories per pound).

Tomato Vinaigrette:
- 1   teaspoon sweet basil flakes
- 1   tablespoon olive oil
- 2   cloves garlic, minced
- 2   shallots, minced
- 1   tablespoon minced parsley leaves
- 1   can (1 pound) stewed tomatoes, drained and finely chopped
- 2   tablespoons red wine vinegar
- 2   tablespoons lemon juice

- 4   tuna steaks, (6 ounces, each), brushed with a little oil and sprinkled with white pepper

In a saucepan, heat together vinaigrette ingredients for 10 minutes, or until shallots are softened. (This sauce can be served warm or slightly chilled, not hot or cold.) Broil tuna, about 4 minutes on each side, or until steaks are barely cooked through. (If you enjoy tuna undercooked, then watch carefully for your degree of doneness.) Divide sauce on 4 plates and place tuna on top. Serves 4.

(About 277 calories per serving-using tuna)
(About 187 calories per serving-using halibut)

Fillets of Sole in Lemon Dill Cream Sauce

The sauce is delicate and subtle with just a faint hint of lemon and dill. Serve it with Brown Rice with Carrots & Onions or simply with steamed baby potatoes.

Lemon Dill Cream Sauce:
- 1/2   pound mushrooms
- 6   shallots, minced
- 1   teaspoon butter

- 1/4   cup dry white wine
- 1/4   cup clam juice

- 2   tablespoons lemon juice, or more to taste
- 1/4   cup unflavored non-fat yogurt
- 1/4   cup half and half cream
- 1/4   teaspoon dried dill weed
-    white pepper to taste

More →

Sole in Lemon Dill Cream Sauce (Continued)

Fish:
1 1/2 pounds fillets of sole, sprinkle with garlic powder and white
      pepper

In a saucepan, cook together first 3 ingredients, until mushrooms are tender and liquid rendered is evaporated. Add the wine and clam juice, and cook over high heat until it is partly evaporated (about 1/4 cup should remain.) Stir together next 5 ingredients, add to sauce, and heat through, over low heat.

Place fish into a 9x13-inch baking pan and pour sauce over the top. Bake in a 350-degree oven for about 10 minutes, or just until fish becomes opaque. Do not overcook. Serves 6.

(About 140 calories per serving)

Note: - Sauce can be prepared earlier in the day and stored in the refrigerator. Pour over fish just before baking.

Sea Bass in Salsa Español

Turmeric and cumin give this sauce a spicy Spanish flavor. It can be used with most fish and shellfish. Flat fish can be laid over the sauce and broiled for a few minutes.

Salsa Español:
1   can (7 ounces) diced green chiles
1   can (1 pound) stewed tomatoes, chopped and drained. Reserve
      juice for another use.
1   medium onion, sliced into thin rings
4   cloves garlic, minced
2   tablespoons lemon juice
3   tablespoons raisins
1   teaspoon turmeric (or more to taste)
1/2 teaspoon cumin powder
1   tablespoon minced cilantro
2   sprinkles cayenne

2   pounds sea bass fillets. (Halibut, haddock or pollack can be
      substituted.)

In a saucepan, simmer together sauce ingredients until onions are soft. Place fish in a 12x16-inch baking pan and spoon sauce on top. Bake at 350-degrees for 10 to 12 minutes or until fish becomes opaque. (If using a flat fish like sole or halibut, then cooking time can be less.) Serve with steamed baby potatoes or steamed rice. Serves 8.

(About 143 calories per serving)

Sea Bass with Tomato, Currants & Pine Nuts

Currants and pine nuts add an exotic touch to the Sea Bass and the tomatoes, garlic and lemon add a Spanish touch. I originally created this recipe for Mackerel, but as it is an oily fish, I opted for the less fatty Sea Bass. Four ounces of Sea Bass contain 107 calories, while four ounces of Mackerel contain 217 calories.

2	small onions, finely chopped
4	cloves garlic, minced
1	teaspoon oil

2	medium tomatoes, peeled, seeded and chopped (fresh or canned)
1/2	teaspoon sugar
4	tablespoons dried black currants
2	tablespoons lemon juice
2	sprinkles cayenne pepper

1 1/2	pounds fillets of sea bass
1	ounce toasted pine nuts (about 3 tablespoons), optional

In a saucepan, cook together first 3 ingredients until onions are soft. Stir in the next 5 ingredients and simmer sauce for 10 minutes, uncovered. Place fish in a 9x13-inch baking pan and bake at 325-degrees for about 15 minutes, or until fish is opaque and flakes easily with a fork. Sprinkle top with pine nuts before serving. Serve with Herbed Orzo with Tomatoes & Onions. Serves 6.

(About 177 calories per serving-with pine nuts)

Bass with Mushrooms, Tomatoes & Leeks

3/4	pound mushrooms, thinly sliced
1	tomato, peeled, seeded and finely chopped
1	leek, white part and 1-inch of the tender green part, thoroughly washed and very thinly sliced
1/4	cup dry white wine
1	tablespoon olive oil
2	tablespoons lemon juice
1	tablespoon minced parsley leaves

1 1/2	pounds striped bass fillets. Sprinkle with white pepper, garlic powder and paprika.

In a covered saucepan, simmer together first 7 ingredients, until leek is soft, about 25 minutes. Uncover pan and simmer until most of the liquid has evaporated. (Serve sauce warm or slightly chilled, not hot or cold.) Broil striped bass for about 1 or 2 minutes on each side until it is opaque. Place fish on a plate and surround with sauce. Serves 6.

(About 161 calories per serving)

Sea Bass Persillade with Yogurt & Tomatoes

A persillade is a savory parsley and crumb coating that adds a good deal of flavor to meat, poultry or fish. It is especially good in this recipe, as it adds an enormous amount of flavor to the Sea Bass and the tomato slices. The whole wheat bread crumbs are easily prepared in a food processor and add a nutty flavor.

1   pound fillets of sea bass, cut into 4 ounce portions, sprinkled with garlic powder and white pepper. Brush each top with 1 teaspoon unflavored non-fat yogurt.
2   medium tomatoes, peeled, seeded and sliced

Persillade:
1   slice fresh whole wheat bread (1 ounce) made into crumbs
2   tablespoons grated Parmesan cheese
2   tablespoons chopped parsley
1/3 cup minced green onions
2   cloves garlic, minced
3   tablespoons lemon juice

Place fish and tomatoes in 1 layer in a 9x13-inch baking pan. Stir together the Persillade ingredients until blended and sprinkle crumb mixture over the fillets and tomatoes. Bake at 350-degrees for 15 minutes, or until fish becomes opaque. Broil for 1 minute to brown top. Serves 4.

(About 159 calories per serving)

Sea Bass with Low-Calorie Basil Sauce

Pesto is a popular sauce, but made with olive oil, butter or cream, it can be heavy-duty calorically. This sauce is richly flavored with basil, thickened with a few walnuts, and nicely balanced with garlic and cheese. As the sea bass is a thick fillet, sprinkle it more generously with seasonings.

1   pound fillets of sea bass (4 ounces, each), sprinkle with garlic powder, onion powder and white pepper

1/4 cup minced fresh parsley
1/4 cup minced fresh basil
1   tablespoon melted butter
2   tablespoons grated Parmesan cheese
2   cloves garlic, minced
1/4 cup grated walnuts (use a nut grater), (1-ounce)
2   tablespoons lemon juice

Place fillets in 1-layer in an 8x12-inch baking pan. Stir together the remaining ingredients and spread over the fish. Bake in a 350-degree oven for 15 to 20 minutes, or until fish becomes opaque. Brown tops for a few seconds under the broiler. Serve with Green Beans with Tomatoes and Green Rice. Serves 4.

(About 191 calories per serving)

Chinese Whole Fish Steamed In Oven

If salt is not a problem, then use the dark soy sauce which adds a good deal of flavor to this dish. Each pound of whole fish yields about 1/2 pound filleted fish. It is good to know, if you don't own a steamer, that fish wrapped in foil steams in the oven.

   1   whole red snapper or sea bass, (3-pounds), thoroughly cleaned and
         scaled. Rinse in cold water and pat dry.
   2   tablespoons low-sodium soy sauce

1/4   cup chopped green onions
1/4   cup cilantro leaves (without the stems)
   2   tablespoons low-sodium soy sauce
   4   thin slices ginger root, cut into slivers
   1   tablespoon sesame oil
   1   tablespoon peanut oil

Cut a piece of heavy-duty foil, large enough to completely seal the fish and lay it on a baking sheet. Place fish on foil and drizzle with soy sauce. Wrap fish in foil, folding the edges, 2 or 3 times, to thoroughly seal. Bake at 350-degrees for about 15 minutes, or about 10 minutes for each inch of thickness.

Meanwhile, in a saucepan, heat together remaining ingredients. To serve, remove foil and discard juices. Place fish on a serving platter and drizzle the green onion and oil mixture over all. To cut, run a knife along the upper side of the backbone, releasing the top fillet. Remove the bone. Serve with a little of the green onion and oil mixture on top. Fried Rice with Green Onions is a nice accompaniment. Serves 6.

(About 160 calories per serving)

Red Snapper Teriyaki with Ginger & Scallions

1 1/2   pounds red snapper fillets (cut into 1-inch chunks)

1/4   cup low-sodium soy sauce
   2   teaspoons honey
   1   tablespoon rice vinegar
1/4   cup chopped green onions (scallions)
   2   thin slices ginger root, cut into slivers
         white pepper to taste

Toss fish with remaining ingredients in a 9x13-inch baking pan and broil, 4-inches from the heat, and turning once, until fish becomes opaque. Do not overcook. Serve with Fried Rice with Green Onions. Serves 6.

(About 121 calories per serving)

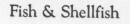

Red Snapper Sesame with Ginger & Scallions

Very Oriental in mood, this is a delicious low-calorie dish. Sauce can be prepared earlier in the day and heated before serving. Scallions should be tender but firm. Sesame seeds can be toasted in a 350-degree oven until just beginning to take on color. Make a large batch and store them in the refrigerator.

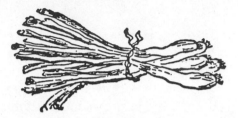

3/4	cup chopped green onions (scallions)
2	shallots, minced
2	teaspoons olive oil
4	tablespoons seasoned rice vinegar
2	tablespoons lime juice
1	tablespoon low-sodium soy sauce
1	tablespoon minced cilantro leaves
1/4	teaspoon powdered ginger
	white pepper to taste
1 1/2	pounds red snapper fillets, sprinkled with pepper and garlic powder
2	teaspoons toasted sesame seeds

In a skillet, over high heat, saute onions and shallots in oil, for 2 minutes, stirring. Add the next 6 ingredients and heat through. Broil fish for 1 or 2 minutes on each side, or until cooked through. Do not overcook. Place fish on a plate, drizzle with a little sauce, and sprinkle with toasted sesame seeds. Serves 6.

(About 132 calories per serving)

Fillets of Red Snapper with Crumb Topping

1 1/2	pounds red snapper fillets, sprinkled with garlic powder
1	cup fresh bread crumbs (2 slices pulsed in food processor)
1/3	cup chopped chives
2	tablespoons minced parsley leaves
1/2	teaspoon sweet basil flakes
1/2	teaspoon thyme flakes
	white pepper to taste
2	tablespoons lemon juice
1/4	cup bottled clam juice
1	tablespoon olive oil (optional)

In a 9x13-inch baking pan, place fish in 1 layer. In a bowl, toss together remaining ingredients until nicely blended. Sprinkle topping evenly over the fish and bake at 350-degrees for about 20 to 25 minutes, or until fish is opaque. Broil for a few seconds to brown crumbs. Serve with Baked Baby Potatoes with Onions. Serves 6.

(About 156 calories per serving)

Cajun Shrimp in Red Hot Garlic Clam Sauce

This spicy hot sauce adds good solid taste to fish and shellfish. It is exceedingly low in calories, yet gives a bland fish rich and opulent flavor. This is a nice sauce to serve over pasta.

Red Hot Garlic Clam Sauce:

6	shallots, minced
6	cloves garlic, minced
1	tablespoon butter
1/4	cup tomato sauce
1	can (7 ounces) chopped clams, do not drain
1	tablespoon lemon juice
1/4	teaspoon sugar
1	teaspoon paprika
1/2	teaspoon dried basil flakes
1/2	teaspoon oregano
1/4	teaspoon cayenne pepper (or to taste-this amount makes it HOT)
1/2	teaspoon black pepper
1 1/2	pounds medium raw shrimp, shelled and deveined

In a large skillet, saute shallots and garlic in butter until shallots are soft, but not browned. Add the next 9 ingredients, and simmer sauce over low heat for 5 minutes, or until it is slightly reduced and thickened. Raise heat to medium, add shrimp and cook, tossing and turning until shrimp become opaque. (Please do not overcook, or shrimp will become tough and rubbery.) Serve with Rice with Lemon & Chives. Serves 6.

(About 148 calories per serving)

Red Hot Baby Shrimp Creole

The deep flavor of the red hot tomato sauce, makes this dish especially satisfying. The sauce is full of all manner of good things and highly seasoned with shallots, garlic and onions. Serve on a bed of plain steamed or boiled rice. While it appears to be hefty in the number of ingredients, 8 of the ingredients are herbs and spices. This dish is truly a cinch to prepare. And best of all, soup base can be prepared early in the day or 1 day before serving, leaving the simple task of heating the shrimp minutes before dinner.

Red Hot Creole Sauce:

1	teaspoon oil
8	shallots, minced
1	stalk celery, minced
1	onion, chopped
1	small green bell pepper, chopped
1	small sweet red bell pepper, chopped
6	cloves garlic, minced
1/4	cup minced parsley
1	can (1 pound) stewed tomatoes, chopped. Do not drain.
4	tablespoons tomato paste
1/4	cup white wine
2	tablespoons lemon juice
1	teaspoon, each, sweet basil flakes, thyme flakes and chili powder
1/4	teaspoon, each, black pepper and powdered cloves
1/8	teaspoon cayenne

1 1/2   pounds baby shrimp, shelled and deveined

In a Dutch oven casserole, place first group of ingredients and simmer mixture, with cover slightly ajar, for 30 minutes, or until vegetables are soft. Add the shrimp and cook until just opaque. Serve on a bed of steamed rice. Serves 6.

(About 166 calories per serving)

Shrimp in a Honey Barbecue Sauce

This amount of sauce is not very generous…doubling the recipe would be tastier. But if calories are a main consideration, this will flavor the shrimp just enough. As this dish is the essence of simplicity, no need to prepare any part of it in advance.

1	pound raw shrimp (about 20 to the pound), peeled and deveined
1/4	cup ranch-style barbecue sauce. (This is a little hotter than the regular barbecue sauce…or add a little cayenne to the regular sauce.)
1	tablespoon honey
1	teaspoon lemon juice
1	clove garlic, minced

Toss together all the ingredients until nicely mixed. Place in a 10-inch round baking pan, and broil, 4-inches from the heat, turning once, until shrimp become opaque, about 3 minutes on each side. Serves 4.

(About 128 calories per serving)

Shrimp Greco with Lemon & Feta Cheese

Tomatoes, lemon, olives and feta cheese add a wonderful excitement to the shrimp. Sauce base can be prepared earlier in the day, or 1 day earlier, and stored in the refrigerator. Heat the sauce and broil shrimp just before serving.

Sauce Base:

- 1 can (1 pound) stewed tomatoes, chopped and drained. Reserve juice.
- 1/2 cup chopped red onions
- 6 black Greek olives, pitted and sliced
- 4 tablespoons lemon juice
- 1 tablespoon minced parsley
- 1/2 teaspoon, each, dried thyme flakes and sweet basil flakes
- 1 shake cayenne pepper
  white pepper to taste

- 1 pound raw shrimp, shelled and deveined
- 1 tablespoon olive oil
- 3 cloves garlic, minced

- 1/4 cup crumbled feta cheese (2 ounces)

In an uncovered saucepan, simmer together sauce ingredients until onions are soft, adding just a little of the reserved tomato juice as needed. You want the sauce to be concentrated and not soupy.

In a 10-inch round baking pan, toss together shrimp, olive oil and garlic until nicely mixed. Lay shrimp in one layer and broil, 4-inches from the heat, until shrimp turn pink and become opaque. Do not overcook. Spread hot sauce over the shrimp and sprinkle top with feta cheese. Broil for another few seconds to soften cheese and slightly brown top. Serve with Toasted Fideos or another fine noodle. Serves 4.

(About 214 calories per serving)

Lobster with Chile Tomato Salsa & Garlic Cheese Crumbs

- 1 1/2 pounds cooked lobster meat, cut into chunks
- 2 tablespoons lemon juice

Chile Tomato Salsa:

- 1/2 cup minced green onions
- 2 medium tomatoes, peeled, seeded, chopped and drained
- 1 can (4 ounces) diced green chiles
- 2 tablespoons chopped cilantro
- 2 tablespoons lemon juice

More →

Lobster with Chile Tomato Salsa (Continued)

Garlic Cheese Crumbs:
- 3 tablespoons cracker crumbs
- 3 tablespoons grated Parmesan cheese
- 2 tablespoons minced parsley
- 1 clove garlic, minced

In a 10-inch round porcelain baker, toss lobster with lemon juice and spread evenly. Stir together salsa ingredients and place over the lobster. Toss together crumb mixture and sprinkle over the salsa. Bake in a 350-degree oven for 15 to 20 minutes or until heated through. Do not overbake. Serve with Pink Orzo with Tomatoes & Onions. Serves 6.

(About 146 calories per serving)

The Best Herbed Scampi with Leeks, Shallots & Lemon Garlic Sauce

This delicious dish has a rich, deep flavor that belies its low calories. As sauce can be prepared earlier in the day or 1 day earlier, this is a good dish to plan on a night when you know you will run late. Shrimp should be broiled just before serving.

Leek, Shallot & Lemon Garlic Sauce:
- 1 teaspoon olive oil
- 1 leek (white part and about 1 1/2-inches of the tender green part), cut in half, washed thoroughly and cut into very thin slices
- 4 cloves garlic, minced
- 2 shallots, minced
- 4 tablespoons lemon juice
- 2 tablespoons minced parsley
- 1/2 teaspoon oregano flakes
- 1/2 teaspoon sweet basil flakes
- 1/2 teaspoon paprika
- 1/8 teaspoon cayenne pepper (or to taste)

In a saucepan, toss together all the ingredients, cover pan, and simmer mixture for 20 minutes, stirring from time to time, until vegetables are soft and most of the liquid rendered is absorbed. (Don't let it get too dry.) Can be held at this point stored in the refrigerator.

Just before serving, toss sauce with:
- 1 pound medium raw shrimp, peeled and deveined

Place shrimp and sauce in one layer in a 10-inch round broiling pan and broil (about 4-inches from the heat) for 5 to 6 minutes, turning once, until shrimp become opaque. Do not overcook. Serve with Potatoes Roasted with Garlic. Serves 4.

(About 128 calories per serving)

Scallops in Wine Sauce

Here is another simple sauce to serve over fish and shellfish. It is especially easy to prepare, using dried spices and seasonings. Of course, fresh is always better than dried, but there are times, when the clock is unforgiving, we're awfully glad to have the choice.

2	teaspoons butter
2	tablespoons lemon juice
1/4	teaspoon, each, onion powder and garlic powder
1/2	teaspoon paprika
1/4	teaspoon, each, sweet basil flakes and oregano flakes
2	teaspoons minced parsley
1/2	cup white wine

1 1/2   pounds bay scallops. (If using sea scallops, slice in thirds.)

4	teaspoons dried bread crumbs
4	teaspoons grated Parmesan cheese

In a skillet, simmer first group of ingredients until wine is reduced to 1/4 cup. Add the scallops and cook, tossing and turning, over medium heat until scallops become opaque. Do not overcook. Divide scallops between 4 individual au gratin dishes and sprinkle with mixture of crumbs and cheese. Brown under the broiler for 1 minute. Serve with Rice with Mushrooms. Serves 6.

(About 125 calories per serving)

Scallops & Mushrooms in Herb & Wine Sauce

1	tablespoon butter
1/2	pound mushrooms, sliced
4	cloves garlic, minced
2	shallots, minced
2	tablespoons chopped green onions

1/2	cup dry white wine
1/2	teaspoon paprika
1/2	teaspoon, each, sweet basil and oregano flakes
1	tablespoon minced parsley
2	tablespoons lemon juice
2	shakes cayenne pepper

1	pound bay scallops
1	tablespoon, each, grated Parmesan cheese and dried bread crumbs

In a skillet, heat butter. Add next 4 ingredients and cook until liquid rendered has evaporated. Add the next 6 ingredients and simmer mixture until wine is almost evaporated. Raise heat, add the scallops and quickly cook, tossing and turning until scallops are opaque. Do not overcook. Sprinkle mixture of cheese and crumbs on top and broil for a few seconds to brown the top. Serve with Emerald Rice with Parsley & Chives. Serves 4.

(About 168 calories per serving)

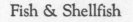

Mexican Tomato Salsa for Fish or Shellfish

1   can (1 pound) stewed tomatoes, chopped and drained.
      Reserve juice for another use.
1   can (4 ounces) diced green chiles
1/3 cup minced green onions
1   tablespoon red wine vinegar
1   tablespoon minced cilantro

In a bowl, stir together all the ingredients until blended. Yields about 1 1/2 cups salsa.

(About 6 calories per tablespoon)

Honey Mustard Dill Sauce for Fish & Shellfish

1   cup non-fat cottage cheese
1   tablespoon lemon juice
2   teaspoons Dijon mustard
1   tablespoon honey
1/2 teaspoon dried dill weed

In a food processor, puree cottage cheese until smooth as sour cream. Blend in the remaining ingredients. Yields 1 cup sauce.

(About 13 calories per tablespoon)

Tartar Sauce for Fish & Shellfish

1   cup unflavored non-fat yogurt
3   tablespoons sweet pickled relish
1   green onion, minced
1   tablespoon lemon juice
1/2 teaspoon dill weed

Stir together all the ingredients until blended. Yields 1 1/4 cups sauce.

(About 8 calories per tablespoon)

Poultry

From my notebook:

As I mentioned earlier, chicken and fish are being chosen by more and more Americans, as the main course for dinner. For this reason, the recipes in the chicken and fish chapters are the most abundant. More than 40 recipes for chicken appear in this chapter, plus a few accompaniments.

The range of calories are from around 200 to 300. I am particularly excited about the scope of the recipes and their low-calorie range. There are too many recipes to single out so, I'll mention a few family favorites and great party choices. Many can be used for both...just serve the dish on a silver platter.

Plum-Glazed Teriyaki Chicken is a real family treat. Chicken Parmesan in Light Tomato Sauce is an old favorite and still a good family dish. Chicken Paella is truly delicious and isn't really high in calories as it includes the rice.

Chicken with an international flair include Caribbean Chicken, Kung Pao Chicken, Moroccan Chicken with Cous Cous, Chicken Italienne, Chicken Enchiladas, Chicken Indienne with Yogurt & Lemon, Chicken Romano, Chicken Dijonnaise, Mexican Chicken with Tomatoes & Chiles, Chicken Normandy with Apples & Wine.

On the home front, Country Chicken with Potatoes & Carrots, Chicken Baroness with Artichokes & Mushrooms, Chicken Creole in Hot Pepper Tomato Sauce, Chicken with Apples & Honey Ginger Sauce, Chicken Breasts with Herb Stuffing, Old-Fashioned Chicken Stew, Hot & Spicy Cajun Chicken Wings. I could go on, but you get the idea.

Here you will find certain accompaniments that could have been placed in other chapters. They are included here so that you could keep the main course and its accompaniment together. Potato & Onion Cake is perfect with Chicken with Red Cabbage & Cranberries...As is Dirty Rice with Hot & Spicy Cajun Wings...and Moroccan Chicken with Cous Cous & Chick Peas is a marriage made in heaven.

Chicken with Mushrooms in a Delicate Champagne Sauce is a poem of flavors and recommended for a dinner party. Your guests will love it...as they will you.

The Rich Basting Mixture is nice for turkey or chicken. It adds intense flavor to the meat.

Remember the motto...Keep it Light...Keep it Varied...

Plum-Glazed Teriyaki Chicken

The is perhaps one of the easiest methods to prepare chicken, and is, also, one of the very best. The glaze turns a deep, rich color and fried rice is a lovely accompaniment.

1   fryer chicken, (about 2 1/2 pounds) cut into serving pieces.
     Sprinkle with pepper, garlic and onion powders. Place in a
     roasting pan and baste with 2 tablespoons teriyaki marinade.
     (Teriyaki marinade can be purchased in any market.)

Plum Glaze:
2   tablespoons plum jam
2   tablespoons ketchup
1   tablespoon vinegar
1   teaspoon brown sugar

Bake chicken at 325-degrees for 50 minutes. Heat together glaze ingredients, until blended, about 3 minutes. Baste chicken with Plum Glaze and continue baking for 20 minutes, or until chicken is tender and glaze is browned. Excellent with fried rice. Serves 4.

(About 241 calories per serving)

Chicken in Honey Lemon Yogurt Sauce

Substituting yogurt for the cream and sour cream, trims this exotic curry dish to slimming proportions, but it is still truly delicious.

4   chicken breast halves, skinned, boned and flattened slightly,
     (about 4 ounces, each). Sprinkle with white pepper, garlic and
     onion powders.

Honey Lemon Yogurt Sauce:
4   tablespoons lemon juice
1/4   cup minced onion
1   medium apple, peeled, cored and grated
2   teaspoons honey
1   tablespoon curry powder
1/3   cup chopped chives
       white pepper to taste

1   cup unflavored non-fat yogurt

Bake chicken at 350-degrees for about 20 minutes, or until chicken becomes opaque. Do not overbake. In a saucepan, simmer together next 7 ingredients until onion and apple are soft. Stir in yogurt and heat through. When chicken is finished baking, pour sauce over and heat through. Serve with Spiced Peaches and rice. Serves 4.

(About 258 calories per serving)

Chicken Parmesan in Light Tomato Sauce

This is a low-calorie version of an old favorite. The herbed sauce is light and fresh, and the chicken is baked, eliminating frying in oil. The bread crumbs and cheese make a delicious crust. Using only the egg white reduces the cholesterol.

Seasoned Bread Crumbs:
- 1/4 cup dry bread crumbs
- 2 tablespoons grated Parmesan cheese
- 1/4 teaspoon, each garlic and onion powders
  white pepper to taste

- 6 chicken breast halves, skinned, boned and flattened slightly, (about 4 ounces, each)
- 1 egg white, beaten with 2 teaspoons water

Toss together bread crumbs, cheese, garlic and onion powders and pepper until blended. Dip chicken in beaten egg white and sprinkle with crumb mixture. Place chicken on a non-stick baking pan and bake at 350-degrees for 15 to 20 minutes, or until chicken is cooked through. Do not overbake or chicken will toughen. Serve with a little Light Tomato Sauce spooned on top. Pass the rest of the sauce at the table with linguini (or any pasta) as a nice accompaniment. Serves 6.

Light Tomato Sauce:
- 1 can (1 pound) stewed tomatoes, finely chopped do not drain
- 4 tablespoons tomato paste
- 1 clove garlic, minced
- 1 carrot, grated
- 1 small onion, grated
- 1/2 teaspoon each, sweet basil and Italian Herb Seasoning flakes
  pepper to taste

In a saucepan, simmer together all the ingredients for 15 minutes. (All the ingredients can be grated together in a food processor, saving a good deal of time. Blend until carrots and onions are very finely chopped, but not pureed.)

(About 254 calories per serving)

Chicken in Dill & Wine Sauce

Using whole chickens is fine if you are planning a casual dinner with family or friends. But this dish does take on a more festive look with the use of boned chicken breasts. In this instance, figure 1/2 chicken breast for each portion, about 4 ounces, each.

    2   fryer chicken (about 2 1/2 pounds, each) cut into fourths.
        Sprinkle with pepper and garlic powder.

Dill & Wine Sauce:

     1   small onion, minced
     3   shallots, minced
     2   cloves garlic, minced
    1/2 cup chicken broth

    1/4 cup dry white wine

    1/2 cup chicken broth
    1/2 teaspoon dried dill weed (or more to taste)
     1   teaspoon lemon juice (or more to taste)
         white pepper to taste

In a 12x16-inch roasting pan, place chicken in one layer and bake at 350-degrees for about 1 hour and 10 minutes, or until chicken is tender. Meanwhile, make the sauce. In a saucepan, cook together first 4 ingredients until the onion is very soft. Add wine and simmer sauce for 10 minutes. Blend the mixture in a food processor and puree until smooth.

Return mixture to saucepan and add the remaining ingredients. Simmer sauce for 5 minutes. Place chicken on a lovely platter and spoon a little sauce on top. Sprinkle top with finely chopped chives and garnish with bouquets of parsley. Serves 8.

(About 217 calories per serving-using whole chickens)
(About 209 calories per serving-using chicken breasts)

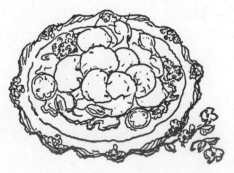

Chicken Paella with Tomatoes & Chiles

This lovely dish with the flavors of Valencia, is trimmed down in calories, but still maintains high flavor and taste.

1	fryer chicken (about 2 1/2 pounds) cut into small serving pieces. Sprinkle generously with pepper, garlic and onion powders, turmeric and cumin.
3	tablespoons chicken broth
1	tablespoon oil
1	large onion, chopped
3	cloves garlic, minced
3	shallots, minced
2	tomatoes, peeled, seeded and chopped
1	can (4 ounces) diced green chiles
3/4	cup rice
1 1/2	cups chicken broth
1 1/2	teaspoons ground turmeric (or more to taste)
1/2	teaspoon ground cumin (or more to taste)
	pepper to taste
1	package (10 ounces) frozen peas

In a 9x13-inch baking pan, place chicken and drizzle with broth. Bake at 350-degrees for 1 hour 10 minutes, basting with the juices in the pan.

Meanwhile, in a Dutch oven casserole, saute together next 4 ingredients until onions are soft. Stir in the tomatoes, chiles and rice. Stir in the broth, turmeric, cumin and pepper. Lower heat, cover pan and simmer mixture for 30 minutes, or until rice is tender and liquid is absorbed. Add the peas and the chicken and continue cooking for 5 minutes, or until heated through. Yields 6 generous servings.

(About 305 calories per serving)

Chicken with Red Cabbage, Apples & Cranberries

This is a complex dish in a German mood. The sweet and sour red cabbage is enriched with the flavors of cranberries and apples. The perfect accompaniment would be a potato cake (like potato pancakes, but easier to prepare.) Dumplings would be another delicious accompaniment.

6   chicken breast halves, skinned and boned (4 ounces, each). Sprinkle with pepper, paprika, garlic and onion powders.

1   jar (1 pound) sweet and sour red cabbage
1/2   cup cranberries, fresh or frozen
1   apple, peeled, cored and grated
1   tablespoon sugar (or to taste)
2   teaspoons vinegar

Lay chicken in one layer in a 9x13-inch baking pan. Bake at 350-degrees for 15 to 20 minutes, or until chicken is opaque. Do not overbake.

In a saucepan, simmer together the remaining ingredients until cranberries are popped, about 8 minutes. Lay cabbage mixture on a platter and top with baked chicken breasts. Serve with Potato & Onion Cake. Serves 6.

(About 255 calories per serving)

Potato & Onion Cake:
1   teaspoon oil

4   medium potatoes, peeled and grated (1 pound)
1   small onion, grated
1/2   of a beaten egg
1/4   cup dried bread crumbs
    pinch of salt

Oil a 10x3-inch round non-stick baking dish. Stir together the remaining ingredients and spread evenly in prepared pan. Bake in a 350-degree oven for about 45 to 50 minutes or until potatoes are tender and top is crusty and brown. Serves 6.

(About 96 calories per serving)

Caribbean Chicken with Apricots &
Brown Rice with Onions & Cinnamon

This is a spicy, colorful dish just brimming with taste. The chicken is juicy and tender with the apricots adding a touch of sweetness and tartness.

    1   fryer chicken (about 2 1/2 pounds) cut into serving pieces.
         Sprinkle with pepper, garlic and onion powders.
    1/2 cup chicken broth

Caribbean Sauce:
    1/4 cup chopped dried apricots
    1   tablespoon yellow raisins
    2   tablespoons dried currants
    1   tablespoon grated orange peel
    1/4 cup orange juice or apricot nectar
    2   teaspoons honey
    1/2 teaspoon ground ginger

In a 9x13-inch baking pan, bake chicken with the chicken broth at 350-degrees for 55 minutes, basting, now and again, with some of the juices in the pan. Heat the sauce ingredients, pour it over the chicken and continue baking for 15 minutes, or until chicken is tender. Place chicken and sauce on a platter and serve with Brown Rice with Onions & Cinnamon. Serves 4.
(About 269 calories per serving)

Brown Rice with Onions & Cinnamon:
    1   onion, chopped
    1   teaspoon butter
    1   cup chicken broth
    1/2 cup long grain brown rice
    1/4 teaspoon cinnamon

In a saucepan, saute onion in butter until onion is transparent. Stir in the broth, brown rice and cinnamon, cover pan, and simmer mixture for 35 minutes, or until rice is tender, and liquid is absorbed. Serves 4.
(About 106 calories per serving)

Kung Pao Chicken with Peanuts

This is a slimmed-down version of an Oriental favorite. Normally, it is a very spicy dish, so if you have a fiery palate, increase the amount of red pepper flakes. Small, dried red chiles (sometimes referred to as "red devils") are traditional, but they are very hot, indeed. They can be used in this dish, but use them sparingly, and remove them before serving. They are very hot and will diminish the sensitivity of a palate, and, of course, should not be eaten.

6	chicken breast halves (4 ounces, each) skinned, boned and cut into 1/2-inch cubes
3/4	cup green onions sliced on the diagonal
2	cloves garlic, minced
1/2	teaspoon red pepper flakes (more or less to taste)
	pinch of salt
	pepper to taste
1	tablespoon low-sodium soy sauce
1	tablespoon cornstarch
1/2	teaspoon ground ginger
3/4	cup rich chicken broth
1	tablespoon oil
1/4	cup chopped peanuts

In a bowl, toss together the first 6 ingredients until blended. In another bowl, stir together next 4 ingredients until blended.

In a wok or skillet, heat oil over high heat until sizzling hot. (Oil must be very hot or chicken will toughen up.) Add chicken mixture, all at once, tossing and turning until chicken becomes opaque, about 1 to 2 minutes. Add the next group of ingredients, and continue cooking, over high heat, until sauce thickens slightly, about 1 to 2 minutes. Stir in peanuts. Serve with steamed rice. Serves 6.

(About 262 calories per serving)
(1/2 cup steamed rice, about 110 calories)

Moroccan Chicken with
Chick Peas, Raisins & Cous Cous

This is a glamorous way to serve chicken and fun to serve as a casual dinner with family and friends. It can be prepared earlier in the day and stored in the refrigerator until serving. The cous cous can also be prepared earlier, but be careful when reheating. To prevent scorching add a few drops of water before heating. Please note, 1-ounce of uncooked cous cous will yield 1/2 cup cooked cous cous.

1   fryer chicken (about 2 1/2 pounds) cut into serving pieces.
      Sprinkle with pepper, garlic and onion powders.

Moroccan Sauce:
   1/2   cup chicken broth
   1   can (1 pound) stewed tomatoes, chopped and drained. Reserve
      juice for another use.
   1   onion, minced
   6   cloves garlic, minced
1 1/2   teaspoons turmeric (or more to taste)
   1/2   teaspoon ground cumin (or more to taste)
   1/8   cup raisins or currants or a mixture of both, packed
   2   sprinkles cayenne pepper

Cous Cous with Chick Peas:
   1/2   cup medium-grained pre-cooked cous cous
   1/2   cup chicken broth
   1/4   cup canned chick peas, rinsed and thoroughly drained

Bake chicken at 350-degrees for 30 minutes, basting with some of the juices accumulating in the pan. Meanwhile, in a covered Dutch oven casserole, cook together the sauce ingredients for 20 minutes. Lay partly-cooked chicken into the sauce, cover pan, and continue cooking chicken for 30 minutes or until tender.

Meanwhile, prepare the cous cous. Place cous cous in a small saucepan. Bring chicken broth to a boil, and pour over the cous cous, stirring until mixture is nicely blended. Cover pan, cook over low heat for 1 minute, and allow to stand for 5 minutes. Liquid should be absorbed. Stir in chick peas and heat through. Toss cous cous with a fork to fluff it up. Serves 4.
    (About 263 calories per serving for the chicken)
    (About 118 calories per serving for the cous cous)

Country Chicken with Potatoes & Carrots

This is my recipe for "Country Pot Roast", adapted for chicken. (It appeared in my first cookbook, "The Joy of Eating" .) It's a delicious, homey dish, just right for an informal dinner with family and friends.

1   fryer chicken (2 1/2 pounds) cut into small serving pieces.
      Sprinkle generously with pepper, garlic and onion powders.
1   large onion, chopped
6   medium carrots, cut into 2-inch slices
3   medium potatoes, peeled and cut into 1-inch slices

1   cup chicken broth
2   tablespoons ketchup
1   tablespoon brown sugar
    pepper to taste

In a 9x13-inch baking pan, lay chicken in one layer. Scatter onion, carrots and potatoes evenly around the chicken. Stir together the remaining ingredients and pour it evenly over all.

Cover pan tightly with foil and bake in a 350-degree oven for 1-hour. Remove foil and continue baking for 15 minutes, or until chicken and vegetables are tender. Yields 6 servings.

(About 215 calories per serving)

Old Fashioned Chicken Stew

This is a nice dish to consider for an informal Sunday night dinner with family or friends. A cold wintry night would be the perfect setting.

1   fryer chicken (about 2 1/2 pounds) cut into serving pieces.
      Sprinkle with pepper, garlic and onion powders and paprika.

2 1/2   cups chicken broth
1   can (1 pound) stewed tomatoes, chopped. Do not drain.
2   medium potatoes, cut into 1/2-inch thick slices
4   large carrots, cut on the diagonal into 1/2-inch slices
2   stalks celery, thinly sliced
1   large onion, chopped
4   shallots, minced
4   cloves garlic, minced
1/2   teaspoon dried thyme flakes
    pepper to taste

Place chicken in a baking pan and bake in a 350-degree oven for 40 minutes. Meanwhile, in a Dutch oven casserole, place all the remaining ingredients and simmer mixture for 30 minutes. Add the chicken to the Dutch oven, and continue cooking stew until chicken and vegetables are tender. Serves 6.

(About 216 calories per serving)

Chicken Italienne in Red Pepper Tomato Sauce

The flavor of this sauce is rich and deep and in no way tastes like a diet dish, which, indeed, it is. The angel hair pasta is the perfect accompaniment.

Red Pepper Tomato Sauce:
- 1 small red bell pepper, stemmed, seeded and cut into slivers
- 1 small onion, finely chopped
- 2 cloves garlic, minced
- 1 can (1 pound) stewed tomatoes, chopped. Do not drain.
- 4 tablespoons tomato paste
- 1/4 cup finely chopped sun-dried tomatoes (optional, but awfully good)
- 1 teaspoon olive oil
- 1 teaspoon Italian Herb Seasoning flakes
  pepper to taste
- 2 shakes cayenne pepper

Crusty Chicken:
- 6 chicken breast halves, skinned and boned, and flattened slightly, (about 4 ounces, each). Sprinkle with pepper, garlic and onion powders and paprika.
- 2 tablespoons bread crumbs
- 2 tablespoons grated Parmesan cheese
- 2 teaspoons olive oil

Combine all the sauce ingredients in a Dutch oven casserole. Cover pan and simmer mixture for 20 minutes, uncover pan and continue cooking for 25 minutes, or until vegetables are very tender and sauce has thickened.

Meanwhile, in a flat dish, mix crumbs and cheese and sprinkle it evenly on both sides of the chicken. Lay chicken in a 10x3-inch round baking pan and drizzle oil over the top. Bake at 350-degrees for 15 to 20 minutes, or until chicken is just cooked through. Do not overbake.

Place chicken on a serving platter and spoon a little sauce on top. Serve additional sauce with angel hair pasta as an accompaniment. Serves 6.
(About 279 calories per serving-for the chicken)
(About 110 calories per serving-for the angel hair pasta)

To make Angel Hair Pasta:
Place 6 ounces of angel hair pasta (or other pasta of your choice) in 3 quarts of rapidly boiling water. Bubble for 3 to 4 minutes or until pasta is tender but firm. Serves 6.

Chicken & Mixed Vegetable Stir-Fry

This recipe uses the technique of stir-frying. Instead of copious amounts of oil, a little oil is paired with chicken broth, which adds a good deal of flavor to the dish and reduces the calories markedly. The main point to keep in mind is to be certain wok or large skillet is kept very hot. As with all recipes, especially stir-fries, have everything ready before you begin.

1   pound boned chicken breasts, cut into thin strips. Place in a bowl
    and sprinkle with garlic powder and pepper. Toss with
    1 tablespoon low-sodium soy sauce.
1   teaspoon oil

Vegetables:
2   teaspoons oil
1/4 pound snow peas, tips trimmed
1/2 pound broccoli florets
1/2 pound mushrooms sliced
1   small red bell pepper, cored and seeded and cut into strips
1   onion, cut in half lengthwise, and thinly sliced
2   cloves garlic, minced

Sauce:
1/2 cup rich chicken broth or 2 teaspoons chicken-seasoned stock base
    mixed with 1/2 cup water
1   tablespoon cornstarch
1   tablespoon low-sodium soy sauce
1/2 teaspoon ground ginger
2   teaspoons vinegar
1/2 teaspoon sugar
    pepper to taste

To prepare the chicken: Heat 1 teaspoon oil in a wok, over high heat, until wok is sizzling hot. Add the chicken and quickly toss and turn until chicken is opaque, about 1 minute. Remove chicken from wok with a slotted spoon.

To prepare the vegetables: Continue over high heat. (No need to wash the pan.) Heat 2 teaspoons oil until very hot. Add the vegetables and cook, tossing and turning, until vegetables are almost tender, about 4 minutes. Add chicken to wok.

Stir together sauce ingredients, and add to wok, tossing and turning until sauce thickens about 3 minutes. Serve with steamed rice. Serves 6.
(About 198 calories per serving)
(About 110 calories per 1/2 cup steamed rice)

Chicken with Tomatoes, Cabbage & Onions

Even those who don't love cabbage will like this dish. The cabbage, flavored with tomatoes, onion, garlic and sparkled with lemon is simply delicious. The bread crumbs mixed with the cheese adds flavor and texture. However, this can be omitted and the dish will be 15 calories less.

1	small head cabbage, shredded (about 1 pound)
1	can (1 pound) stewed tomatoes, chopped. Do not drain.
1	medium onion, chopped
2	cloves garlic, minced
1	cup chicken broth
4	tablespoons lemon juice
1	teaspoon sugar
	pepper to taste

1	fryer chicken, (about 2 1/2 pounds) cut into serving pieces. Sprinkle with pepper, paprika, garlic and onion powders.

4	tablespoons toasted fresh bread crumbs (1/2 slice bread)
1	tablespoon grated Parmesan cheese

In a covered Dutch oven casserole, simmer together first group of ingredients for 30 minutes, or until cabbage is almost tender. Meanwhile, bake chicken at 350-degrees for 40 minutes. Spread cabbage mixture around the chicken and continue to bake for 30 minutes, or until chicken is tender.

Combine toasted bread crumbs and Parmesan cheese. When ready to serve, place chicken on a platter and surround with cabbage. Sprinkle cabbage with crumb/cheese mixture (optional). Do this just before serving or crumbs will get soggy. Serves 4.
> (About 287 calories per serving-using cheese/crumb mixture)
> (About 272 calories per serving-without cheese/crumb mixture)

To toast fresh bread crumbs:
Place white or egg bread slices in the container of food processor and process until fine crumbs form. Place crumbs in a thin layer in a baking pan, and bake at 350-degrees until crumbs are dried and crisp, turning now and again. Store unused crumbs in a freezer bag in the freezer. These can also be used to coat chicken or fish. 1 slice of bread (1 ounce) will yield about 1/2 cup of crumbs.

Enchiladas with Chicken, Chiles & Cheese
in Spicy Tomato Salsa

If you are looking for a fresh and interesting way to serve leftover chicken or turkey, this is a good dish to consider. It is a lovely medley of flavors, color and texture. Don't be discouraged by the number of ingredients. If you look carefully, you will note that the only work in this recipe is to chop green onion, garlic and cilantro.

Filling:

3/4	pound cooked chicken or turkey breast, cut into small dice
1/2	7-ounce can diced green chiles. (Reserve 1/2 for the sauce.)
1/2	cup chopped green onions
1/2	1-pound can stewed tomatoes, drained and chopped. (Reserve 1/2 for the sauce. Reserve juice for sauce.)
2	tablespoons chopped cilantro
1	teaspoon ground turmeric (or more to taste)
1/2	teaspoon ground cumin
1/2	teaspoon oregano flakes
	dash cayenne pepper

Spicy Tomato Salsa:

1/2	can diced green chiles (from above)
1/2	can stewed tomatoes and juice (from above)
2	garlic cloves, minced
1/3	cup chopped green onions
2	tablespoons chopped cilantro
2	tablespoons lemon juice
1/2	teaspoon ground cumin
	dash cayenne pepper or to taste

To Assemble:

8	6-inch corn tortillas (1 ounce, each)
1/4	cup unflavored non-fat yogurt
2	tablespoons finely chopped green onions

In a bowl, toss together all the filling ingredients until nicely mixed. In a saucepan, stir together all the Salsa ingredients and heat for 5 minutes.

To Assemble: Wrap tortillas in foil and heat in a 325-degree oven for 4 minutes to soften. Place 1/8 chicken filling on each tortilla, roll it up and place seam side down and in one layer in a 9x13-inch baking pan. Pour sauce over the top. Bake at 350-degrees for about 20 minutes, or until heated through. Stir together the yogurt and green onions. Serve with 2 teaspoons yogurt mixture over each tortilla. Yields 8 filled tortillas and serves 4 or 8.

(About 325 calories per serving-serving 4)
(About 163 calories per filled tortilla-serving 8)

Hot & Spicy Cajun Chicken Wings

This dish takes its inspiration from our own fabulous New Orleans. Skinned chicken breasts are lower in calories than chicken wings and can be substituted. It is included with wings for the sake of variety. Removing the skin from the chicken wings will lower the calories. If using boned and skinned chicken breasts, they should weigh 4 ounces, each, and should be baked for 10 minutes and then basted for 10 minutes.

12   chicken wings, tips removed, and cut at the joint (1 1/2 pounds).
      Sprinkle with white pepper, paprika, garlic and onion powders.
1/3   cup chicken broth

Cajun Seasoning:
   1/4   cup ketchup
    1   tablespoon spicy brown mustard
    2   teaspoons sugar
   1/2   teapoon, each, garlic powder, cumin and paprika
   1/8   teaspoon cayenne pepper (or more to taste)

Bake chicken wings in chicken broth at 350-degrees for 35 minutes, basting, now and again, with the juices in the pan. Stir together the seasoning ingredients and baste chicken with this mixture. Continue baking and basting, until wings are tender, about 30 minutes. Serve with Dirty Rice or brown rice. Serves 4.

(About 265 calories per serving-using chicken wings)
(About 224 calories per serving-using chicken breasts)

Note: -Dirty Rice, a traditional New Orleans accompaniment, is made with bits of chicken livers, chicken gizzards, pork and vegetables. This version is only made with vegetables, keeping the fat and cholesterol count low.

Dirty Rice:
    1   medium onion, chopped
    1   medium carrot, grated
   1/2   medium green bell pepper, slivered
   1/2   medium red bell pepper, slivered
    2   cloves garlic, minced
    1   teaspoon oil
   1/2   teaspoon each pepper, paprika and cumin
    2   sprinkles cayenne pepper, or more to taste

   1/2   cup long-grain rice
    1   cup chicken broth

In a covered saucepan, cook together first group of ingredients until vegetables are soft. Stir in the rice and broth, cover pan and simmer mixture for 30 to 35 minutes, or until rice is tender and liquid is absorbed. Serves 4.

(About 118 calories per serving)

Chicken Breasts Stuffed with Spinach & Cheese with Emerald Cream Sauce

3   whole chicken breasts, boned, skinned and cut into halves, (about 4 ounces, each). Remove the fillet strips and reserve these for the stuffing. Flatten each breast slightly and sprinkle with garlic powder.

1/4   cup chicken broth

Spinach & Cheese Stuffing:

6   fillet strips, from above, ground in food processor

6   tablespoons frozen chopped spinach, thoroughly drained. Reserve remaining spinach, (from a 10-ounce package), for the sauce.

1/4   cup low-fat Ricotta cheese

2   tablespoons grated Parmesan cheese

3   tablespoons chopped chives

2   tablespoons fresh bread crumbs

1/4   teaspoon ground poultry seasoning

     pepper to taste

Prepare chicken breasts. Combine all the stuffing ingredients until blended. Divide stuffing between 6 half-breasts, roll and secure with a toothpick. Place breasts in one layer in an 8x12-inch baking pan, drizzle with broth and sprinkle lightly with Cheese Topping.

Bake in a 350-degree oven for about 30 minutes, basting now and again with the juices in the pan, until chicken is cooked through. Do not overbake. Serve with a spoonful of Emerald Cream Sauce on top. Serves 6.

Emerald Cream Sauce:

     Reserved Spinach from above, drained

1/2   cup chicken broth

4   tablespoons chopped chives

1   tablespoon lemon juice

3   tablespoons half and half cream

Heat together all the ingredients, stirring until blended. Yields 1 cup sauce.

Cheese Topping: Toss together 1 tablespoon grated Parmesan cheese and 1 tablespoon bread crumbs until blended.

(About 249 calories per serving)

Chicken Breasts with Mushrooms, Red Peppers and Sun-Dried Tomatoes

This is a lovely balance of flavors and truly delicious in the full sense of the word. It is also a caloric bargain when you consider the rich and wonderful ingredients. Angel hair pasta is the perfect accompaniment.

Red Pepper & Sun-Dried Tomato Sauce:
- 1 pound mushrooms, thinly sliced
- 1 red bell pepper, cut into 1/4-inch strips
- 4 shallots, minced, about 4 tablespoons
- 2 cloves garlic, minced
- 1 teaspoon olive oil

- 1/4 cup white wine
- 1/4 cup chicken broth
- 1/2 cup chopped sun-dried tomatoes
- 2 tablespoons lemon juice
- 1/4 teaspoon, each, sweet basil flakes and oregano flakes
- 2 sprinkles cayenne pepper

Chicken:
- 3 whole chicken breasts, skinned, boned and halved, about 4 ounces, each. Sprinkle lightly with garlic powder, onion powder and pepper.

In a covered skillet, over medium-high heat, cook together first 5 ingredients until vegetables are soft, about 10 minutes. Add the wine and cook over high heat until wine has evaporated, about 3 minutes. Add the remaining ingredients and simmer sauce for 3 minutes.

In a 9x13-inch baking pan, place chicken breasts and bake at 350-degrees for 10 minutes. Pour sauce evenly over the chicken and bake for an additional 5 minutes or until heated through. Serve chicken and sauce on a bed of angel hair pasta. Serves 6.

(About 247 calories per serving)

To make angel hair pasta:
Place 6 ounces of angel hair pasta in 2-quarts of rapidly boiling water, and cook at a rolling boil for 2 minutes, or until tender but firm, for fresh pasta. Dried pasta will take 2 or 3 minutes longer. Serves 6.

(About 110 calories per serving)

Chicken Indienne with Yogurt & Lemon

If you are looking for an interesting and original way to prepare chicken breasts, this is a good dish to consider. Basically simple and quick to prepare, it is also a good choice on an evening when you are running late.

Yogurt & Lemon Sauce:
- 1 apple, peeled, cored and thinly sliced
- 2 tablespoons raisins
- 2 tablespoons lemon juice
- 1 tablespoon honey
- 2 teaspoons curry powder

- 1 cup unflavored non-fat yogurt
- 2 tablespoons chopped chives

Chicken Breasts:
- 3 whole chicken breasts, halved, skinned and boned, about 4 ounces, each. Sprinkle lightly with garlic powder, onion powder and pepper.

In a saucepan, simmer together first 5 ingredients for about 15 minutes, or until apples are tender. Stir in yogurt and chives.

In a 9x13-inch baking pan, place chicken breasts and bake at 350-degrees for 10 minutes. Pour the sauce over the chicken breasts and bake for another 5 minutes, or until the breasts are just cooked through. Do not overbake or breasts will get tough and rubbery.

Serve on a bed of rice with additional chives and 2 teaspoons of chopped peanuts as an optional accompaniment (add 36 calories). Serves 6.

(About 244 calories per serving)

To prepare rice using Cold Method:
In a saucepan, stir together 1 cup rice, 2 cups chicken broth, 1 teaspoon oil, 1 tablespoon chopped chives and a few sprinkles of white pepper. Cover pan and simmer rice for 30 minutes or until liquid is absorbed and rice is tender. Serves 6.

(About 128 calories per serving)

Note:- As the rice takes longest to prepare, start it first. Start the sauce, and place chicken in oven at the last. In this manner, everything will be ready to serve at the same time. Enjoy!

Chicken Breasts Stuffed with Mushrooms in a Delicate Champagne Sauce

3 whole chicken breasts, boned, skinned and halved (about 4 ounces, each). Remove the fillet strips and reserve these for the stuffing. Flatten each breast slightly and sprinkle with garlic powder and white pepper.

Mushroom Stuffing:
1/4 pound medium mushrooms, thinly sliced
2 tablespoons finely minced shallots
1 clove garlic, minced
1 teaspoon oil

1/4 teaspoon dried dill weed
6 fillet strips, from above, coarsely chopped
1/2 cup chicken broth, or more as needed

Prepare chicken breasts. In a skillet, saute mushrooms, shallots and garlic in oil until all the liquid rendered is absorbed. Add the dill and chicken and cook for 2 or 3 minutes, or until chicken is opaque. Finely chop chicken and mushroom mixture in food processor.

Divide stuffing between 6 half-breasts, roll and secure with a toothpick. Place breasts in one layer in an 8x12-inch baking pan and drizzle with the broth. Bake at 350-degrees, basting now and again for about 40 minutes, or until chicken is cooked through and tender. Do not overbake. Serve with a spoonful of Champagne Sauce on top. Serves 6.

Champagne Sauce:
1/2 cup chicken broth
1/4 cup champagne or semi-dry white wine
2 tablespoons lemon juice
1/2 teaspoon dried dill weed
1/8 teaspoon garlic powder
pinch of white pepper

1/4 cup Low-Calorie Creme Fraiche
2 tablespoons chopped chives (or more to taste)

In a saucepan, simmer together first 6 ingredients for about 10 minutes, or until sauce is reduced to 1/2 cup. Stir in the Creme Fraiche and chives and heat through. Yields 3/4 cup sauce.
        (About 234 calories per serving with sauce)

To make Low Calorie Creme Fraiche: Stir together 2 tablespoons half and half and 2 tablespoons half and half sour cream, until blended. Allow to stand at room temperature for 1 hour, and then refrigerate until adding to sauce. Yields 1/4 cup (20 calories per tablespoon).

Chicken Breasts with Herbed Stuffing in Dilled Mushroom Cream Sauce

When you are planning a special dinner, this is a lovely dish to consider. Tender chicken breasts, filled with a savory herb stuffing and topped with a light creamy dill sauce will never allow you or your guests to feel deprived.

Herbed Stuffing:

4	slices fresh whole wheat bread, crumbled
3	tablespoons grated onion
1/3	teaspoon paprika
1/3	teaspoon ground poultry seasoning
1/4	teaspoon ground sage
	white pepper to taste
1/2	cup rich chicken broth

8	chicken breast halves, boned, skinned and gently flattened. Sprinkle lightly with white pepper, garlic powder and paprika.
1	tablespoon whole wheat pastry flour
1/2	cup chicken broth

Toss together first 6 stuffing ingredients and add only enough chicken broth to hold stuffing together. Divide stuffing into 8 parts. Place 1 part stuffing on each chicken breast, roll and secure with toothpicks. Dust stuffed breasts lightly with flour.

Place 1/2 cup chicken broth in a 9x13-inch baking pan, and place breasts on top, in one layer. Bake at 325-degrees for about 45 minutes, basting from time to time with the juices in the pan. Serve with a spoonful of Dilled Mushroom Cream Sauce on top. Serve with broccoli, sprinkled with lemon, and whole spiced peaches. Very delicious! Serves 8.
(About 241 calories per serving)

Dilled Mushroom Cream Sauce:

1/4	cup finely minced onion
1/4	pound mushrooms, thinly sliced
1	teaspoon butter
2	teaspoons flour
1/2	cup half and half

2	tablespoons chopped chives
1/4	teaspoon dried dill weed
1 1/2	tablespoons lemon juice
	white pepper to taste

In a skillet, saute onion and mushrooms in butter until onions are soft. Add flour, and cook, stirring for 2 minutes. Stir in the half and half and cook, over low heat, stirring until sauce thickens slightly. Stir in the seasonings. Yields 1 cup sauce. (About 34 calories per 2 tablespoons sauce)

Chicken in Tomato Vinaigrette Sauce

These simple, everyday ingredients produce a delectable meal. The flavor of the sauce is light and delicate and sparkled with wine and herbs.

2   fryer chickens (about 2 1/2 pounds) cut into fourths.
    Sprinkle with garlic and onion powders and paprika.

1   can (1 pound) stewed tomatoes, chopped. Do not drain.
3   tablespoons tomato paste
1   medium onion, chopped
2   shallots, minced
3   cloves garlic, minced
3   tablespoons dry white wine
3   tablespoons vinegar
1   teaspoon sugar
1   teaspoon Italian Herb Seasoning
    dash cayenne pepper
    freshly ground black pepper to taste

Place chicken in a 12x16-inch baking pan and bake at 325-degrees for 40 minutes. Meanwhile, in a saucepan, simmer together the remaining ingredients for 30 minutes. Pour the tomato mixture evenly over the chicken and continue baking for 30 minutes, or until chicken is tender. Serve with Pink Orzo. Serves 8.

(About 230 calories per serving)

Chicken with Honey Mustard Dill Sauce

The combination of honey, mustard and dill adds a marvelous sparkle to the unflavored yogurt. Sauce can be prepared earlier in the day and heated before serving.

4   chicken breast halves, skinned and boned (about 4, ounces each)
    Sprinkle with pepper, garlic and onion powders.
1   teaspoon oil

Honey Mustard Dill Sauce:
1   teaspoon butter
2   tablespoons finely chopped shallots
1/4   cup dry white wine

1/2   cup unflavored non-fat yogurt
1   tablespoon lemon juice
1   teaspoon Dijon mustard
1   teaspoon cornstarch
2   teaspoons honey
1/2   teaspoon dried dill weed

More →

Chicken with Honey Mustard Dill Sauce (Continued)

Place chicken in 10-inch round roasting pan and drizzle with oil. Bake at 350-degrees for 15 to 20 minutes or until chicken is opaque. Do not overbake or chicken will toughen up.

Meanwhile, in a saucepan, saute shallots in butter until shallots are limp. Add the wine and cook until wine has evaporated. Stir together the remaining ingredients until blended and add to saucepan. Simmer mixture, stirring, until heated through. Pour sauce over chicken and reheat in oven until heated through. Do not overheat. Serve with rice made with chicken broth. Serves 4.

(About 252 calories per serving)

To make rice:
In a saucepan, stir together 1 1/2 cups chicken broth, and 3/4 cup rice. Cover pan and simmer mixture for 30 minutes, or until rice is tender and liquid is absorbed. Yields 2 1/4 cups cooked rice and serves 4.

(About 137 calories per serving)

Baked Chicken Breasts in
Tomato Artichoke Sauce & Angel Hair Pasta

This is especially easy to prepare and can be made, literally, in minutes. The sauce is light and delicious and very flavorful. Sauce can be prepared earlier in the day and stored in the refrigerator. Bake chicken before serving.

- 4 whole chicken breasts, skinned, boned and cut into halves (about 4 ounces, each). Sprinkle with garlic powder and paprika.

- 1 can (1 pound) stewed tomatoes, chopped. Do not drain.
- 1 jar (6 ounces) marinated artichoke hearts, drained and chopped
- 1 clove garlic, minced
- 1 teaspoon sugar
- 1 tablespoon lemon juice (or a little more to taste)
  pinch of red pepper and white pepper to taste

Bake chicken breasts, in 1 layer, at 350-degrees for 20 minutes, or until breasts are cooked through. Do not overbake. Meanwhile, in a saucepan, heat together the remaining ingredients and simmer mixture for 10 minutes. Pour sauce over the chicken breasts and bake for another 5 minutes. Serve on a bed of angel hair pasta, cooked al dente. Serves 8.

(About 230 calories per serving)

To prepare Angel Hair Pasta: Bring 2 quarts water to a boil. Add 8 ounces of angel hair pasta and cook until pasta is tender, but firm, about 3 to 4 minutes. Drain. (About 110 calories per serving)

Chicken Romano
with Sweet Red Peppers & Garlic

This simple little dish has a good deal of solid character. Tender, succulent chicken breasts, in a medley of red and green bell peppers, strongly accented with garlic and served with angel hair pasta is truly delicious. A few sprinklings of grated Parmesan cheese is lovely.

> 3   boneless chicken breasts, skinned, boned and cut into halves (about 4 ounces, each) sprinkled lightly with garlic powder, onion powder and pepper
>
> 2   red bell peppers, seeded and cut into 1-inch strips
> 1   green bell pepper, seeded and cut into 1-inch strips
> 4   garlic cloves, minced
> 2   sun-dried tomatoes, chopped
> 1/2   cup chicken broth
> 1   teaspoon olive oil
>   pinch of cayenne and black pepper to taste
>
> 2   tablespoons grated Parmesan cheese

In a 9x13-inch baking pan, bake chicken breasts at 325-degrees for 20 minutes. Allow to cool and cut into 1-inch chunks.

While chicken is baking, simmer together the next 7 ingredients in a covered Dutch oven casserole, for about 15 minutes, or until peppers are tender. Uncover pan and simmer for 5 minutes to evaporate some of the juices. Add the chicken and juices to the casserole, and heat through. (Do not overheat at this point or chicken will toughen.) Serve over a bed of angel hair pasta. Rice is good, too. Sprinkle with grated cheese before serving. Serves 6.
(About 230 calories per serving)

Chicken Dijonnaise with
Mushroom, Pepper & Tomato Sauce

This is a delicious dish to serve for informal dinners with family and friends. The sauce is keen and spicy and is filled with all manner of good things. Sauce can be prepared earlier in the day and stored in the refrigerator. Served on a bed of orzo...Delicious!

> 2   fryer chickens, (about 2 1/2 pounds, each), cut into serving pieces. Brush chicken with 2 tablespoons Dijon mustard and sprinkle with pepper and garlic powder.
> 1/2   cup chicken broth

More →

Chicken Dijonnaise (Continued)

In a 12x16-inch pan, place chicken and drizzle with broth. Bake in a 350-degree oven for about 40 minutes. Pour Mushroom, Pepper & Tomato Sauce over the top and continue baking for about 30 to 35 minutes, or until chicken is tender. Serve chicken and vegetables on a bed of orzo. Serves 8.

Mushroom, Pepper & Tomato Sauce:

1/2	pound mushrooms, sliced
2	medium onions, chopped
4	cloves garlic, minced
1	medium red bell pepper, cut into strips
1	medium green bell pepper, cut into strips
1	can (1 pound) stewed tomatoes, finely chopped. Do not drain.
1	tablespoon paprika
1/8	teaspoon cayenne pepper (or more to taste)

In a covered skillet, simmer together all the ingredients until vegetables are tender.

(About 238 calories per serving)

Chicken with Yogurt, Lemon & Garlic Sauce

This little dish substitutes yogurt for cream or creme fraiche. It is highly seasoned with turmeric and cumin. The chives and pimientos add good color and interest.

4	chicken breast halves, skinned and boned (about 4 ounces, each). Sprinkle with pepper, garlic and onion powders.
1/2	cup chicken broth

Yogurt, Lemon & Garlic Sauce:

1/2	cup chicken broth
1/2	small onion, chopped
2	tablespoons lemon juice
2	cloves garlic, minced
1	teaspoon turmeric
1/2	teaspoon ground cumin
3/4	cup non-fat yogurt
1	tablespoon flour
1	jar (2 ounces) slivered pimientos
1/4	cup chopped chives

In a 10-inch round baking pan, place chicken and broth and bake at 350-degrees for 15 to 20 minutes, or until chicken becomes opaque. Do not overbake or chicken will toughen up.

In a covered saucepan, simmer together first 6 sauce ingredients until onions are soft. Stir together yogurt and flour, and stir it into the sauce mixture, cooking and stirring until sauce thickens slightly. Stir in pimientos and chives. Pour sauce over the chicken and heat through. Serve with baby boiled potatoes or rice. Serves 4.

(About 246 calories per serving)

Chicken New Orleans with Apricots & Pecans

The thin coating of mustard adds a lovely balance to the sweetness of the apricots. This is a very tasty dish and quite low in calories, considering the use of apricots, butter and pecans.

6   chicken breast halves, skinned, boned and flattened slightly (4 ounces, each). Spread with a very thin coating of Dijon mustard and sprinkle with garlic powder.
2   shallots, minced and stirred with 2 teaspoons melted butter or oil

Apricot & Pecan Sauce:
   4   ounces dried apricots, chopped
1/2   cup orange juice
   2   teaspoons sugar
   2   teaspoons bourbon
   2   tablespoons finely chopped toasted pecans

Lay chicken in one layer in a 9x13-inch baking pan. Brush with shallot/butter mixture. Bake in a 350-degree oven for 15 to 20 minutes, or until chicken becomes opaque. Do not overbake.

Meanwhile, simmer together apricots, orange juice, sugar and bourbon for 10 minutes, or until apricots are soft. (Careful not to scorch the apricots.) Arrange chicken on a platter, and surround with Apricot Sauce. Sprinkle chopped pecans over all. Serves 6.
(About 290 calories per serving)

Chicken with Carrots, Apples & Prunes

This is a homey and delectable dish, great to serve for informal dinners with family and friends. It is also an attractive dish with its medley of fruits and vegetables. Above all, it is a delicious blend of flavors.

2   fryer chickens (about 2 1/2 pounds, each) cut into fourths. Sprinkle with pepper and garlic powder.

1/4   cup dry white wine
   1   cup chicken broth
   1   medium apple, peeled, cored and thinly sliced
   2   onions, finely chopped
   4   carrots, peeled and sliced
   6   pitted prunes, coarsely chopped
   4   medium potatoes, (4 ounces, each), peeled and sliced
   1   teaspoon each, paprika, orange peel, thyme flakes
      pepper to taste

More →

Chicken with Carrots, Apples & Prunes (Continued)

In a 12x16-inch baking pan, lay chicken in one layer. Stir together the remaining ingredients and place evenly around the chicken. Cover pan with foil and bake at 350-degrees for 40 minutes. Remove foil and continue baking until chicken and vegetables are tender, about 30 minutes. Remove skin from chicken and serve on a large platter, surrounded with the vegetables and fruit. Serves 8.

(About 293 calories per serving)

Chicken in Mushroom Wine Sauce

This is a nice herby sauce that is richly flavored with onions and shallots. A tablespoon or 2 of low-fat half and half cream, stirred in just before serving adds a few calories and a bit of depth to the sauce. However, it is lovely, as is.

- 4 chicken breast halves, skinned, boned and flattened slightly (4 ounces, each). Sprinkle generously with pepper, garlic and onion powders and a faint sprinkling of flour.
- 2 teaspoons oil

Mushroom Wine Sauce:
- 1 teaspoon butter (for flavor, optional)
- 3 shallots, minced
- 2 cloves garlic, minced
- 1 small onion, minced
- 1/2 pound mushrooms, cleaned and sliced
- 1/4 cup semi-dry white wine

- 1/2 cup rich chicken broth
- 2 teaspoons cornstarch
- 1 teaspoon Italian Herb Seasoning
- 1 tablespoon chopped parsley

Lay chicken in one layer in a 10x3-inch round baking pan and drizzle with oil. Bake at 350-degrees for 15 to 20 minutes, or until chicken becomes opaque. Do not overbake.

Meanwhile, make the sauce. In an uncovered saucepan, place first 6 ingredients and simmer mixture for about 10 minutes, or until onions are very soft. Stir together the next 4 ingredients and add to the saucepan, cooking and stirring for 4 to 5 minutes, or until sauce thickens slightly. Pour sauce over chicken and heat through. Serve with brown rice. Serves 4.

(About 270 calories per serving-with butter)
(About 262 calories per serving-without butter)

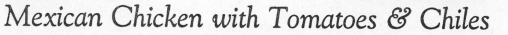

Mexican Chicken with Tomatoes & Chiles

This simple little dish is a special delight of flavor and color. Golden roasted chicken in a mosaic of tomatoes and chiles and sparkled with cumin, red pepper and garlic is a lavish dish...and very low calorie, too. It has a "bite", but is not very hot. Add a little cayenne if you you like it hot.

2   fryer chickens (about 2 1/2 pounds, each) cut into serving pieces. Sprinkle lightly with garlic powder, ground cumin, cayenne pepper and chili powder.

1   can (1 pound) stewed tomatoes, chopped. Do not drain.
1   can (4 ounces) diced green chiles
1/3   cup chopped green onions
1   tablespoon chili powder
1/4   teaspoon ground cumin
2   sprinkles cayenne pepper
2   tablespoons rice vinegar

In a 12x16-inch baking pan, place chicken in one layer. Bake in a 350-degree oven for 45 minutes, basting from time to time, with the juices that formed in the pan. Stir together the remaining ingredients and spoon sauce evenly over the chicken and continue baking for 25 minutes or until chicken is tender. Serve with Pink Rice and Green Peas. Serves 8.
(About 219 calories per serving)

Note: - Entire dish can be prepared earlier in the day but shorten baking time by 10 minutes. Store in the refrigerator and reheat before serving.

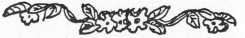

Chicken Smothered in Honey Onions

This is for those who love liver smothered in onions. But liver is high in cholesterol, so this low cholesterol chicken version is a nice substitution. As in most of the recipes in this chapter, the chicken is defatted by baking it separately, and then removing it from the baking pan. Bulgur (cracked wheat) is a nice balance with its nut-like flavor and chewy texture. This yields 4 generous portions and could be stretched to serve 6.

1   fryer chicken (about 2 1/2 pounds), cut into serving pieces. Sprinkle with pepper, garlic and onion powders.

1   teaspoon butter
4   small onions, sliced
1   tablespoon honey
1   tablespoon brown sugar
1   teaspoon vinegar
1/2   cup chicken broth

More →

Chicken Smothered in Honey Onions (Continued)

Bake chicken in one layer in a 350-degree oven for 1 hour. Meanwhile, in a large Dutch oven casserole, melt the butter and stir in the onions, honey, sugar and broth. Cover pan and over low heat, cook the onions, until they are very soft and beginning to turn amber, about 30 minutes.

Place the chicken in the Dutch oven, and continue to cook, over low heat, for 10 to 15 minutes, or until chicken is tender. Serve chicken covered with onions. Bulgur with Mushrooms is a lovely accompaniment. Serves 4.

(About 259 calories per serving)

To make Bulgur with Mushrooms:
In a saucepan, saute 3/4 cup bulgur in 1 teaspoon oil, tossing and turning for 3 minutes. Add 1 1/2 cups chicken broth, cover pan and simmer mixture for 15 to 20 minutes or until bulgur is tender. Meanwhile in a skillet, cook 1/2 cup sliced mushrooms with 1 tablespoon chicken broth, until mushrooms are tender. Add to bulgur and stir through. Serves 4.

(About 138 calories per serving)

Rock Cornish Hens with Mushrooms, Carrots & Onions

This dish relies heavily on the fresh garden flavors of carrots, onions, mushrooms, garlic and shallots. It is a homey dish, exceedingly tasty and a good choice for an informal dinner with family and friends. Brown Rice with Leeks rounds out the garden feeling and is an excellent accompaniment. This is higher calorically than any other dish in this book, and it is included for comparison. Substituting 4-ounces of chicken white meat for the hens will reduce each serving by 161 calories.

3	Rock Cornish Hens (about 1 pound, each), split in half. Sprinkle with garlic powder, onion powder, paprika and pepper.
1/2	cup chicken broth

1/2	pound mushrooms, sliced
6	shallots, minced
6	cloves garlic, minced
1/2	pound frozen baby white onions, peeled
1	pound bag, whole baby carrots
1/2	cup chicken broth

In a 9x13-inch roasting pan, bake hens at 350-degrees, for 45 minutes, basting from time to time with the juices forming in the pan.

Meanwhile in a Dutch oven casserole, cook together the remaining ingredients until carrots and onions are tender. Place vegetables around the hens and continue baking for 20 minutes or until hens are tender. Serves 6.

(About 417 calories per serving-using hens)
(About 256 calories per serving-using chicken)

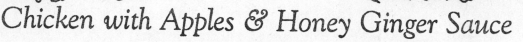

Chicken with Apples & Honey Ginger Sauce

Not sweet, not sour, but fruity and tart is this quite delicious chicken dish. Sparkled with yogurt and honey and flavored with apples and lemon, this is a nice dish to consider for a Sunday night dinner with family and friends. Do not boil the sauce, or it will curdle. Simply heat it through before serving.

2 fryer chickens (about 2 1/2 pounds each) cut into serving pieces. Sprinkle with pepper and garlic powder.

2 medium apples, peeled, cored and grated
1/2 cup unflavored yogurt
1/2 cup apple juice
2 tablespoons lemon juice
1 tablespoon honey
1/2 teaspoon curry powder
1/4 teaspoon ground ginger
1/4 cup yellow raisins (optional)

In a 12x16-inch baking pan, lay chicken in 1 layer. Bake in a 350-degree oven for about 1 hour and 5 minutes or until chicken is tender.

Meanwhile in a saucepan, cook apples for about 15 minutes or until apples are softened. Stir in the remaining ingredients and heat through. Do not allow to boil. Remove the skin and place chicken on a lovely platter. Drizzle sauce on top. Serve with a simple pilaf. Serves 8.

(About 241 calories per serving without raisins)
(About 256 calories per serving with raisins)

Normandy Chicken with Apples & Wine

This little gem is an adaptation of a classic dish from Normandy. Traditionally, cream is added to the sauce after baking. If you wish to sparkle the sauce then add 2 to 4 tablespoons half and half to the finished dish.

1 fryer chicken (2 1/2 pounds), cut into small serving pieces. Sprinkle with pepper, garlic and onion powders.
1 medium apple, peeled, cored and very thinly sliced
1 onion, finely chopped
3 carrots, thinly sliced
2 cloves garlic, minced

1/4 cup white wine
1 cup apple juice
1 teaspoon honey

4 tablespoons half and half cream (optional)

More →

Normandy Chicken with Apples & Wine (Continued)

In a 9x13-inch baking pan, spread chicken in one layer. Scatter apples, onions, carrots and garlic evenly around chicken. Stir together the next 3 ingredients and pour evenly over all. Cover pan tightly with foil and bake at 350-degrees for 1 hour. Remove foil and continue baking for 15 minutes, or until chicken is lightly browned and vegetables are tender.

Remove chicken from the pan and place on serving platter. (At this time, stir the optional cream into the apple and vegetable sauce.) Spoon sauce over the chicken and serve. Serves 4.

(About 282 calories per serving-without half and half)
(About 302 calories per serving-using half and half)

Chicken Creole in Hot Pepper Tomato Sauce

It is no small wonder that Creole cooking is so popular today. While this dish will not blister your palate, it is not for the faint of heart either. Of course, if you like it more peppery, add a pinch extra of cayenne. Go easy, though, to avoid an overpowering taste.

Hot Pepper Tomato Sauce:
1	can (1 pound) stewed tomatoes, finely chopped
3	tablespoons tomato paste
2	onions, finely chopped
1	red bell pepper, cut into thin strips
1	green bell pepper, cut into thin strips
6	cloves garlic, minced
2	tablespoons lemon juice
1/2	teaspoon paprika
1/2	teaspoon sweet basil flakes
1/2	teaspoon thyme flakes
1/8	teaspoon cayenne pepper
1/8	teaspoon white pepper

6   chicken breasts halves, skinned and boned, about 4 ounces, each.
     Sprinkle with garlic powder, onion powder and paprika.

In a Dutch oven casserole place all the sauce ingredients and simmer sauce for 30 minutes or until onions and peppers are softened. (If you are preparing Pink Rice and Mushrooms, reserve 2 tablespoons for the rice.)

In a 9x13-inch pan, place chicken breasts and bake at 350-degrees for 10 minutes. Pour sauce over the breasts and bake for an additional 5 minutes, or until entire dish is heated through. Do not overcook at this point, or breasts will toughen up. Serve with Pink Rice and Mushrooms. Serves 6.
(About 239 calories per serving)

Chicken with Mushrooms & Onions in Burgundy Wine

This is an epicurean delight and a caloric bargain. It is the French Coq au Vin slimmed down in calories, but still very high in taste and pleasure. This serves beautifully in a 9x13-inch porcelain baking dish, and is lovely for a casual dinner with family and friends.

2   fryer chickens (about 2 1/2 pounds, each) cut into serving pieces
1   pound small white onions, peeled and left whole
1/2   cup chicken broth
     garlic powder, paprika and white pepper to taste

1/2   pound mushrooms, cleaned and sliced
6   carrots, thinly sliced
3   shallots, minced
3   cloves garlic, minced
1   teaspoon oil

2   tablespoons Cognac
1/2   cup Burgundy wine

1/2   cup chicken broth
2   tablespoons tomato paste
1   teaspoon Bovril (beef extract)
1   teaspoon thyme flakes
     white pepper to taste

In a 12x16-inch baking pan, place chicken and onions in 1 layer. Pour broth over the chicken and sprinkle with garlic powder, paprika and pepper. Bake in a 350-degree oven for 40 minutes, basting now and again with the juices in the pan.

Meanwhile, in a large skillet, cook together the next 5 ingredients until the vegetables are tender and liquid rendered is absorbed. Heat the Cognac in a brandy warmer, ignite and gently pour it over the vegetables. When the flames subside, add the wine and simmer mixture until wine is reduced by 1/2. Stir in the remaining ingredients and simmer sauce for 10 minutes.

Pour sauce over the chicken and continue baking for 30 minutes, or until chicken is tender. Serve with Brown Rice with Chives. Serves 8.
(About 274 calories per serving)

Chicken Baroness
with Artichokes & Mushrooms

One of my techniques to seal in the juices and avoid the need to brown poultry in fat, is to prebake the chicken and then sauce it. This defats the chicken and saves a good number of calories.

2   fryer chickens (about 2 1/2 pounds, each), cut into quarters and sprinkled with pepper, garlic powder and paprika

Artichoke & Mushroom Sauce:

1   teaspoon olive oil
4   cloves garlic, minced
4   shallots, minced
1/2   pound mushrooms, thinly sliced

1/4   cup dry white wine

1   can (1 pound 12 ounces) crushed tomatoes in tomato puree. Reserve 2 tablespoons for the rice.
1   jar (6 ounces) marinated artichoke hearts, drained and chopped
1/2   teaspoon each, dried thyme, sweet basil flakes and sugar pepper to taste
2   sprinkles cayenne pepper or to taste

In a 12x16-inch pan, place chicken in 1 layer and bake at 350-degrees for 50 minutes. Meanwhile, in a Dutch oven casserole, saute together garlic, onion and mushrooms, in oil, until most of the liquid is evaporated. Add the wine and continue cooking until the wine is almost evaporated. Add the remaining ingredients and simmer sauce for 10 minutes.

Place chicken in a clean pan, and pour sauce over the chicken and continue baking for 20 minutes, or until chicken is tender. Serve with Pink Rice with Chives & Parsley as a lovely accompaniment. Serves 8.
(About 275 calories per serving)

Rich Basting Mixture for Chicken or Turkey

This is a benign mixture of seasonings and spices for basting chicken or turkey. Calories are negligible and need not be calculated. The amounts listed below are adequate for a 20-pound turkey. Use 1/4 the quantity for a 2 1/2-pound chicken.

1   cup chicken broth
1   teaspoon garlic powder
1   teaspoon onion powder
2   teaspoons paprika

In a jar with a tight-fitting lid, stir together all the ingredients. With a brush, scooping up the seasonings if they settle to the bottom and baste turkey or chicken. Yields about 1 cup basting mixture.

Meats

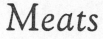

From my notebook...

Sad to say, meats are not as popular as they once were. But it is suggested that they be eaten sparingly. So I have been sparing with the recipes. There is much controversy about the benefits of meat...and at this point, with the Surgeon General's Recommendations, it would seem wise to use beef in small quantitites and trimmed of all separable fat.

The Paupiettes of Beef is a grand dish for a dinner party. It uses only 2 ounces of beef per roll, is filled with a savory stuffing and served with a lovely Mushroom Sauce. The Paupiettes are cooked very quickly and they are tender and succulent. It's a good choice for a beef dish as the quantity of beef is low.

German-Style Beef is like a Sauerbraten. Who doesn't love Hungarian Goulash or Irish Stew with Mashed Potatoes? Beef and Red Peppers is a nice combination. In all these instances, the amount of beef is kept low and the dish rounded out with vegetables or other accompaniments.

Some really delicious lamb recipes...Moroccan Lamb Dumplings with Cous Cous is filled with vegetables and a little lamb. Leg of Lamb with Lemon, Garlic & Rosemary is just lovely. Lamb Indienne is Indian in character and flavored with garlic and yogurt.

Two pork recipes, one with Baked Apples and the other with Red Cabbage & Apples both use small amounts of pork.

There are more veal recipes, only because it is tender and succulent and cooks more quickly. Veal shanks in Tomato Wine Sauce is a delicious Osso Bucco. Veal with Roasted Leeks & Carrots is somewhat innocent with its large amounts of vegetables. Veal Dumplings in Light Tomato Sauce is very flavorful and a good way to stretch the veal...as is the Veal Pate with Spinach & Tomato Sauce. Paupiettes of Veal use very little meat like the Paupiettes of Beef. They are quite different in taste and flavor as these are filled with apple stuffing.

If meats are not your preference at this time, then skip this chapter. But I do recommend meats, perhaps sparingly, but not to be eliminated altogether. Remember Moderation...and Common Sense is the key.

Sweet & Sour Boiled Beef & Cabbage

1   pound round steak, cut into cubes, remove every trace of fat
2   medium onions, chopped
1   teaspoon oil

1   can (1 pound) stewed tomatoes, chopped
1 1/4 cups beef broth
1   head cabbage (about 1 pound), shredded
1   can (8 ounces) tomato sauce
3   tablespoons lemon juice
1   teaspoon sugar
    pepper to taste

In a Dutch oven casserole, saute together first 3 ingredients until meat loses its pinkness. Add the remaining ingredients, cover pan, and simmer mixture for about 1 1/2 hours, or until meat is tender. Serve with Brown Rice with Pimiento & Parsley. Serves 6.

(About 212 calories per serving)

Oven-Baked Stew with Carrots & Potatoes

1 1/4 pounds round steak, trimmed of fat, and cut into 3/4-inch cubes
4   medium potatoes, peeled and cut into 1-inch slices (about 1 pound)
8   large carrots, cut into 1-inch thick slices

6   cloves garlic, minced
2   onions, chopped
1 1/4 cups beef broth
1   can (1 pound) stewed tomatoes, chopped. Do not drain.
1   can (8 ounces) tomato sauce
1   tablespoon vinegar
1   teaspoon sugar
    pinch of salt and black pepper to taste

In a 9x13-inch baking pan, place meat, potatoes and carrots. Stir together the remaining ingredients and pour evenly over all. Cover pan tightly with foil and bake in a 350-degree oven for about 2 hours or until meat is tender. Allow to cool and remove every trace of fat. Reheat in a 350-degree oven, covered loosely with foil, until heated through. Serves 6.

(About 302 calories per serving-serving 6)

Note: -Can be prepared one day earlier and stored in the refrigerator. Reheat as described above.

Paupiettes de Boeuf in Mushroom Wine Sauce

This is an impressive little dish that serves well for the most discriminating dinner party. Succulent, tender beef rolls, filled with a savory, herb stuffing and served with a delicious mushroom sauce is truly manna from your kitchen.

12   slices Spencer steaks. (Ask your butcher to slice these from the small end, not more than 1/4-inch thick, and to remove every trace of fat.) Total should weigh about 1 1/2 pounds or 2-ounces each slice. Sprinkle lightly with garlic powder.
1   tablespoon Seasoned Flour

Savory Herbed Stuffing:
12   slices fresh white bread, cubed
6   tablespoons chopped chives
2   tablespoons grated onion
1/2   teaspoon paprika
1/2   teaspoon poultry seasoning
    salt and white pepper to taste

1   cup extra-rich chicken broth (about)

Preheat oven to 350-degrees. In a bowl toss together stuffing ingredients. Slowly add the chicken broth, adding only enough to allow stuffing to hold together. Do not allow it to get soggy.

Place 1 heaping tablespoon stuffing on the end of each steak, roll it up, and fasten it with a toothpick. Dust very lightly with Seasoned Flour. Place in one layer in a 9x13-inch baking pan and bake at 350-degrees for about 10 minutes, or until meat loses its pinkness. Do not overcook. (These steaks are exceedingly tender.) Serve with Mushroom Wine Sauce. Serves 12.

Mushroom Wine Sauce: Saute 1/2 pound sliced mushrooms, 2 cloves mashed garlic, and 1 finely chopped shallot in 1 teaspoon butter, until mushrooms are tender. Add 1/4 cup dry white wine and simmer mixture until wine has evaporated. Add 1 cup canned beef broth, 1 teaspoon Bovril, 1 tablespoon Sauce Robert, 1 tablespoon each chopped chives and parsley, and pepper to taste. Simmer sauce for 3 minutes. (Can be prepared 1 day earlier and stored in the refrigerator. Heat before serving.) Yields 1 1/4 cups sauce.
(About 232 calories per serving)

Seasoned Flour: Combine in a plastic bag and shake until blended, 1 cup flour; 2 teaspoons garlic powder; 1 tablespoon paprika; 1/2 teaspoon pepper; 4 sprinkles cayenne pepper; 1/4 cup grated Parmesan cheese. Store unused flour in the refrigerator. Can also be used on fish or chicken.
(About 25 calories per tablespoon)

German-Style Sweet & Sour Potted Beef

- 2 pounds boneless chuck, trimmed of all separable fat and cut into 3/4-inch cubes. Sprinkle with garlic and onion powders, and pepper.
- 2 onions, chopped
- 4 carrots, sliced
- 4 cloves garlic, minced
- 1/2 cup dry red wine
- 1 1/2 cups beef broth
- 1/4 red wine vinegar
- 1 tablespoon brown sugar
- 1 bay leaf
- 6 peppercorns
- 1/8 teaspoon ground cloves

Toss all the ingredients in a bowl and refrigerate for several hours or overnight. Place all the ingredients in a covered Dutch oven casserole and bring mixture to a boil. Lower heat and simmer stew for about 2 hours or until meat is tender. Skim off any trace of fat. If you want to thicken gravy, add 2 to 3 tablespoons of ginger snap cookie crumbs. Serve on a bed of Noodles with Poppy Seeds. Serves 8.

(About 215 calories per serving)

Old-Fashioned Hungarian Goulash

- 2 onions, chopped
- 3 cloves garlic, minced
- 4 medium carrots, grated
- 1/4 cup dry white wine
- 1/4 cup tomato sauce
- 1 1/4 cups beef broth
- 2 tablespoons paprika

- 2 pounds boneless chuck, trimmed of all separable fat, and cut into 3/4-inch cubes. Toss with 2 tablespoons Dijon mustard. Sprinkle with garlic and onion powders and pepper.

In a covered Dutch oven casserole, place first group of ingredients and bring mixture to a boil. Add the meat, cover pan, lower heat and simmer mixture for about 2 hours or until meat is tender. Serve with Noodles with Poppy Seeds. Serves 8.

(About 202 calories per serving)

Noodles with Poppy Seeds:
Toss together 8-ounces wide noodles, cooked in boiling water until tender, with 1/4 cup beef broth, 4 tablespoons low-fat sour cream, 1 tablespoon lemon juice and 2 teaspoons poppy seeds. Serves 8.

(About 116 calories per serving)

Beef with Peppers & Onions

2 onions, coarsely chopped
1 teaspoon olive oil

4 roasted red peppers, (from a 1-pound jar) cut into slivers
2 tomatoes, peeled, seeded and chopped
2 tablespoons chopped parsley

1 pound sirloin steak, all visible fat removed, cut into strips
1 teaspoon olive oil
 pinch of salt and black pepper to taste

In a Dutch oven casserole, saute onions in olive oil until onions are soft. Add the next 3 ingredients and cook sauce for 10 minutes over low heat.

Meanwhile, in a skillet, over high heat, saute steak in olive oil until meat loses its pinkness. Do not overcook. Season to taste. Add meat to Dutch oven and heat through. Do not overcook at this point or meat will toughen. Serve with Brown Rice & Lentils with Onions. Serves 4 to 6.
(About 206 calories per serving-serving 6)
(About 308 calories per serving-serving 4)

Irish Beef Stew with Mashed Potatoes

2 pounds boneless chuck, trimmed of all separable fat, and cut into
  3/4-inch cubes
2 onions, chopped
8 medium carrots, cut into 1-inch pieces
2 teaspoons oil

1/2 cup beer
1 1/2 cups beef broth
1 teaspoon Bovril meat extract
1 teaspoon sugar
1/2 teaspoon mustard

In a Dutch oven casserole, cook together first 4 ingredients until onions are transparent. Stir in the remaining ingredients and bring mixture to a boil. Reduce heat and simmer stew for about 2 hours or until meat is tender. Serve with Old-Fashioned Mashed Potatoes. Serves 8.
(About 218 calories per serving)

More ➔

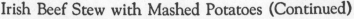

Irish Beef Stew with Mashed Potatoes (Continued)

Old-Fashioned Mashed Potatoes:

2	pounds potatoes, peeled and sliced
1/4	teaspoon onion powder
1/4	cup milk
1	tablespoon unsalted butter

Cook potatoes in boiling water until tender and drain. Mash potatoes and add the remaining ingredients, stirring until fluffy. Serves 8.

(About 107 calories per serving)

Beef & Red Peppers Romano with Cheese

The beauty of this dish is that it can be prepared in minutes using the tender sirloin cut. After the beef is cooked, heat the sauce and serve at once. You do not want to cook the beef in the sauce or it will toughen up. A tender cut of veal can be substituted for the beef.

4	red peppers, cut into 1/2-inch strips
1/2	pound mushrooms, sliced
2	onions, cut into rings
1	can (1 pound) stewed tomatoes
1	can (8 ounces) tomato sauce
1/2	cup beef broth
2	tablespoons parsley
1	teaspoon Italian Herb Seasoning
1	teaspoon sweet basil flakes
1	tablespoon olive oil
3	cloves garlic, minced
1 1/2	pounds sirloin steak, trimmed of all separable fat and cut into 1/4-inch slices. Cut each slice into 2-inch strips.
16	teaspoons grated Parmesan cheese

In a Dutch oven casserole, simmer together first group of ingredients for 30 to 40 minutes, or until peppers are tender. (This can be done earlier in the day.) Just before serving, heat oil in a skillet until it is very hot, but not brown. Add the garlic and the meat and cook and stir, tossing, until meat loses its pinkness. Add the meat to the hot sauce and serve with Pink Rice or Orzo or pasta. Sprinkle each serving with 2 teaspoons grated cheese. Serves 8.

(About 254 calories per serving with cheese)

Moroccan Lamb Dumplings in
Apple, Raisin & Vegetable Cous Cous

1   pound extra-lean ground lamb (or turkey)
1   medium onion, grated
3   cloves garlic, minced
1   egg
1/2   cup fresh bread crumbs (1 slice bread whisked in a food processor)
      black pepper to taste

In a bowl, mix together all the ingredients and form into 3/4-inch balls. Flatten them slightly and place, in one layer, on a 9x13-inch baking pan. Bake at 350-degrees for 10 to 15 minutes or until dumplings are cooked through. Place dumplings in Apple, Raisin & Vegetable Sauce and continue cooking at a simmer until heated through. Serve over a bed of Cous Cous. Yields 16 dumplings and serves 8.

Apple, Raisin & Vegetable Sauce:
2   onions, chopped
2   cloves garlic, minced
1   teaspoon oil

1   can (1 pound) stewed tomatoes, chopped. Do not drain.
1 1/4 cups beef broth
6   medium carrots, peeled and thinly sliced
1   pound zucchini, sliced. (Do not peel.)
1   apple, peeled, cored and thinly sliced
1   tablespoon brown sugar
1   teaspoon turmeric
1   teaspoon curry powder
1/4   teaspoon crushed red pepper flakes
1/4   cup raisins
      black pepper to taste

In a Dutch oven casserole, saute onions and garlic in oil until onions are transparent. Add the remaining ingredients and simmer mixture, with cover slightly ajar, for about 30 minutes, or until vegetables are tender.
      (About 231 calories per serving using ground lamb)
      (About 202 calories per serving using ground turkey)

To make Cous Cous:
In a saucepan, bring 1 1/4 cups chicken broth to boil. Stir in 1 cup pre-cooked (sometimes called "quick-cooking") medium-grain cous cous, stir and simmer for about 3 minutes. Remove from heat and continue stirring to help separate the grains. Heat through to serve. Serves 8.
      (About 104 calories per serving)

Leg of Lamb with Lemon, Garlic & Rosemary

1   lean, leg of lamb, defatted, boned and butterflied, about 3 pounds

2   tablespoons lemon juice
2   tablespoons vinegar
1   tablespoon olive oil
6   cloves garlic, minced
1/2   cup non-fat unflavored yogurt
1   teaspoon dried whole rosemary
1/4   teaspoon pepper

Ask your butcher to bone, butterfly and trim all separable fat from the leg of lamb. Combine the remaining ingredients and brush over the entire surface of the lamb. Place meat in a roasting pan and allow to stand at room temperature for 1 hour. Insert a meat thermometer in the thickest part of the meat and roast, uncovered, in a 325-degree oven until meat thermometer registers 150-degrees for medium-rare or 160-degrees for medium, about 1 3/4 hours. To serve, cut into slices across the grain. Serves 10.

(About 270 calories per serving)

Lamb Indienne with Garlic & Yogurt

By changing a few seasonings of the above recipe, the lamb takes on a totally different character.

1   lean leg of lamb, defatted, boned and butterflied, about 3 pounds

1/2   cup non-fat unflavored yogurt
3   cloves garlic, minced
2   teaspoons ground turmeric
1   teaspoon ground cumin
2   tablespoons lemon juice
1/4   teaspoon dried red pepper flakes

Ask your butcher to bone, butterfly and trim all fat from the leg of lamb. Place lamb in a roasting pan. Combine the remaining ingredients and brush over the surface of the lamb and allow to stand at room temperature for 1 hour. Insert a meat thermometer in the thickest part of the meat, and roast at 350-degrees, uncovered, for about 1 3/4 hours or until the meat thermometer registers 150-degrees for medium-rare or 160-degrees for medium. To serve, cut into slices across the grain. Serves 10.

(About 257 calories per serving)

Honey Glazed Pork Roast with Baked Apples

1 loin of pork (about 4 pounds). Ask butcher to remove the chine bone and all separable fat. Sprinkle with garlic and onion powders, and pepper.

4 apples, peeled, cored and cut into halves
1/2 cup apple juice

2 tablespoons honey
2 teaspoons Dijon mustard
2 tablespoons lemon juice

Place roast in a roasting pan, bone side down and insert meat thermometer in thickest part of meat (not touching bone). Roast at 350-degrees for about 1 3/4 hours. Remove from pan and place in a clean baking pan. (This will remove every trace of fat.) Place apples around roast and drizzle with apple juice. Combine the remaining ingredients and brush top of roast. Continue baking until meat thermometer registers 175-degrees, apples are tender and pork is glazed, about 45 minutes. Carve meat into 8 servings. Serve with the apples and Sweet and Sour Red Cabbage or Potato & Onion Cake. Serves 8.

(About 295 calories per serving)

Pork with Red Cabbage & Apples

2 onions, finely chopped
1 head red cabbage (about 1 pound), shredded
2 apples, peeled, cored and grated
1 cup apple juice
3 tablespoons lemon juice
1 teaspoon sugar

1 1/2 pounds boneless pork, trimmed of all separable fat and cut into 3/4-inch cubes. Sprinkle with garlic and onion powders and pepper.

Place first 6 ingredients in a Dutch oven casserole and bring to a boil. Add the meat, cover pan, lower heat, and simmer mixture until meat is tender, about 2 hours. (Time will depend on cut of meat you are using.) Serve with Potato & Onion cake. Serves 8.

(About 290 calories per serving)

Veal Shanks in Tomato Wine Sauce

4   pounds veal shanks (also called shinbones). Ask your butcher to saw them into 3-inch pieces. Sprinkle with garlic and onion powders, and pepper.

2   onions, sliced into rings

1   can (1 pound) stewed tomatoes, chopped. Do not drain.

4   tablespoons tomato paste

1/2   cup white wine

1/2   cup beef broth

2   teaspoons beef seasoned stock base

3   carrots, grated

4   cloves garlic, minced

1 1/2   teaspoons Italian Herb Seasoning

Place veal in a 9x13-inch baking pan, marrow side up. Combine the remaining ingredients and pour over the veal. Cover pan tightly with foil and bake at 350-degrees for about 2 hours, or until veal is tender. Sauce will be thick and delicious. Serve with Pink Orzo as a delicious accompaniment. Serves 6.

(About 302 calories per serving)

Veal with Roasted Leeks and Carrots

The beauty of this dish rests with the large attractive cuts of vegetables, surrounding the succulent veal. Broiling the entire dish at the end adds an attractive splash of color. Note that no oil is added.

2   pounds extra-lean boneless veal, cut from the leg and into 1-inch cubes and sprinkled with pepper

3   leeks, (white and tender green parts), cut in half lengthwise and thoroughly washed

6   carrots, peeled and cut in half

3   medium potatoes, peeled and cut in half, 3/4 pound

3   onions, peeled and cut in fourths

12   cloves garlic, peeled and left whole

12   shallots, peeled and left whole

1 1/2   cups chicken broth

1/2   cup dry white wine

2   teaspoons dried dill weed or 2 tablespoons fresh dill

In a 12x16-inch pan, place the veal. Lay the vegetables around the veal and top with broth, wine and dill. Cover pan with foil and bake at 350-degrees for 45 minutes. Uncover pan and continue baking for about 20 minutes or until veal is tender. Place under a broiler for a few minutes to brown the meat and vegetables. Serve the veal surrounded with vegetables. Serves 8.

(About 299 calories per serving)

Veal Dumplings in Light Tomato Sauce

1   pound lean ground veal
1   small onion, grated. (Must be grated on a 4-sided grater or in a food processor. Do not use chopped onions for this dish or they have to be sauteed separately.)
1   clove garlic, minced
2   slices egg bread, soaked in water and squeezed dry
1   egg, beaten
1   tablespoon chopped parsley
     pepper to taste

In a large bowl, mix together all the ingredients until nicely blended. Shape meat into 12 balls and flatten them slightly to form dumplings. Broil meat about 1 minute on each side to lightly brown. Place dumplings in Light Tomato Sauce and simmer for 5 minutes. Serve on a bed of Pink Orzo with Tomatoes & Onions. Serves 4 to 6.

Light Tomato Sauce:
4   canned Italian tomatoes, with 1/3 cup broth, chopped
1   tablespoon tomato paste
1/4 teaspoon sweet basil flakes
1/4 teaspoon oregano flakes
1   teaspoon dried onion flakes

Stir together all the ingredients in a 12-inch skillet and simmer sauce for 5 minutes. Add the dumplings and simmer for another 5 minutes.

(About 197 calories per serving-serving 6)
(About 296 calories per serving-serving 4)

Veal Italienne with Onions, Carrots & Tomatoes

2   pounds extra-lean veal, cut from the leg, into 1-inch cubes. Sprinkle with pepper, garlic powder and paprika.

1   onion, chopped
3   carrots, grated
1   can (1 pound) stewed tomatoes, chopped. Do not drain.
4   tablespoons tomato paste
2   cloves garlic, minced
1   teaspoon grated lemon peel
1/2 cup rich chicken broth
1/2 cup dry white wine
1   teaspoon chicken stock base
1   teaspoon sugar
1   teaspoon Italian Herb Seasoning
2   sprinkles cayenne pepper

More →

Veal Italienne with Onions (Continued)

In a 9x13-inch baking pan, place veal. Stir together remaining ingredients and pour over veal. Cover pan tightly with foil and bake at 350-degrees for about 1 1/2 to 2 hours or until veal is tender. Serve on a bed of linguini or with Pink Orzo with Tomatoes & Onions or Brown Rice with Mushrooms. Serves 8.

(About 249 calories per serving)

Note: -Best made earlier in the day or a day earlier and stored in the refrigerator to allow flavors to blend. Reheat in a 350-degree oven until heated through.

Veal & Vegetable Pate
with Spinach & Tomato Sauce

This little pate is practically a complete meal as it contains meat, eggs, vegetables and bread. It is delicious served warm, yet equally good when sliced cold and served in a sandwich with an interesting bread.

    2   carrots, peeled and cut into 1-inch chunks
    1   medium red pepper, cored, seeded and cut into fourths
    1   medium onion, peeled and cut into fourths
    2   sprigs parsley, stems removed
    1   egg

    1   pound lean ground veal
    1   slice bread (1 ounce) made into crumbs
    1   package (10 ounces) frozen chopped spinach, defrosted and
          thoroughly drained
        pinch of garlic powder and pepper to taste

    1/2 cup tomato sauce

In a food processor, blend first 5 ingredients until vegetables are finely chopped. In a large bowl, mix together chopped vegetables and next 4 ingredients until blended. Pat mixture into a 9x5-inch loaf pan and pour tomato sauce on top. Bake in a 350-degree oven for 1 hour, or until meat is cooked through. Serve with Orzo with Tomatoes & Onions as a delicious accompaniment. Serves 6.

(About 184 calories per serving)

Veal Roast Persillade
with Garlic, Tomato & Wine Sauce

A persillade is basically a parsley, garlic and crumb mixture that is pressed on the meat for deep flavor. It adds depth and distinction to a dish. This can be prepared with a less expensive veal, cut from the shoulder. In this case, follow the above instructions, but cover pan tightly with foil and bake for about 2 hours or until veal is tender.

1	boneless veal roast, from the leg, (about 3 pounds), defatted, rolled and tied. Sprinkle with garlic and onion powders, and pepper.
1/4	cup chopped parsley
6	cloves garlic, minced
2	tablespoons grated Parmesan cheese
3	tablespoons lemon juice
1/2	cup herb seasoned stuffing mix
1	teaspoon sweet basil flakes

Place roast in a 9x13-inch baking pan. Combine the remaining ingredients in a food processor and blend until finely minced. Pat mixture on top of the roast. Place Garlic, Tomato & Wine Sauce around the meat and roast at 325-degrees for 1 hour and 15 minutes, or until meat is tender. Remove strings, carve meat into 1/4-inch slices and serve with 1/2 cup of cooked pasta. Sauce is delicious and does not need to be thickened. Serves 10.

Garlic, Tomato & Wine Sauce:
2	onions, finely chopped
2	carrots, grated
2	cloves garlic, minced
1	can (1 pound) stewed tomatoes, chopped. Do not drain.
3	tablespoons tomato paste
1/2	cup dry white wine
1	teaspoon Italian Herb Seasoning

Stir together all the ingredients until blended.

(About 292 calories per serving)

Paupiettes of Veal Filled with Apple Stuffing

This is a lovely party dish that is elegant in taste and appearance. Use the optional Apple Cream Sauce for grand occasions. The veal is delicious served natural so the choice of a spoonful of sauce is personal.

Apple Stuffing:

2	apples, peeled, cored and grated
1	onion, chopped
3	shallots, minced
2	cloves garlic, minced
1	teaspoon butter
1/2	teaspoon poultry seasoning
	white pepper to taste

1 1/2 cups fresh bread crumbs
chicken broth

8 veal scallops, (about 3 ounces, each), sprinkled with garlic and onion powders and white pepper

2 teaspoons butter

In a skillet, saute together first 7 ingredients until the onions are soft. Add the crumbs and stir until nicely mixed. Some juice will have accumulated from the apples. Add a little chicken broth, if necessary so that the stuffing is moist and holds together. Divide the stuffing between the 8 veal scallops, roll and skewer with a toothpick.

Heat butter in a large skillet and saute veal rolls just until meat loses its pinkness. Do not overcook. Place veal on a lovely platter and serve with Spiced Peaches and fresh broccoli. A spoonful of Apple Cream Sauce is a festive addition. Serves 8.

(About 218 calories per serving)

Apple Cream Sauce:

2 apples, peeled, cored and grated
1/2 cup orange juice
2 teaspoons cinnamon sugar

1/4 cup half and half cream

In a covered saucepan, over low heat, cook together first 3 ingredients until apples are soft. Add the cream and heat through. Yields about 1 cup sauce.

(About 32 calories per 2 tablespoons sauce)

Noodles, Rice & Grains

From my notebook:

In this chapter you will find some delicious accompaniments to the main course. These will give you a good variety to choose from. Aside from rice, brown rice and noodles, you will find cracked wheat (bulgur), egg barley, lentils, pastina and orzo.

Brown Rice is paired with Pimiento & Parsley, Lentils & Onions, Scallions & Peppers, Leeks & Onions...all exciting and pleasurable.

Rice, prepared with Onions, Peppers & Peas, or with Onions & Pine Nuts, or Fried with Green Onions, will add sparkle to meals. Pink Rice, Lemon Rice, Emerald Rice, Herbed Rice all are delicious and far more satisfying than plain rice. Rice with Mushrooms, Cheese & Chives, or with Lemon & Chives are all interesting and imaginative.

Cracked Wheat with Mushrooms & Onions is a nice family dish. Bulgur with Lemon, Currants & Pine Nuts would be a better choice for dinner with friends, (unless your children are very adventuresome).

Pastina creates a good deal of excitement at meals. Served with Fresh Tomatoes & Basil, a real treat. Toasted Fideos are a pure joy to serve and everybody loves them.

And last, but certainly not least, orzo, a rice-shaped pasta, that everybody just raves about everytime I serve it. It is especially delicious with Mushrooms & Onions or with Tomatoes & Onions. Orzo comes in 3 sizes. The smallest size is good for certain brothy soups...the largest is the size I used in all the recipes throughout this cookbook. It is exciting in appearance and character and doesn't look like rice. I find the shape good for soups, also.

Brown Rice with Pimiento & Parsley

1 1/3 cups brown rice
2 2/3 cups chicken broth
  1 jar (2 ounces) slivered pimientos
  2 tablespoons chopped parsley
      pepper to taste
  1 teaspoon olive oil

In a saucepan, stir together all the ingredients, cover pan and simmer rice for about 30 to 35 minutes or until rice is tender and liquid is absorbed. Serves 8.

(About 129 calories per serving)

Brown Rice & Lentils with Onions

1/2 cup brown rice
1/2 cup lentils, picked over for foreign particles
  2 cups beef broth
  2 tablespoons dried chopped onions
      pepper to taste
  1 teaspoon oil

In a saucepan, stir together all the ingredients, cover pan, and simmer mixture for 40 minutes, or until lentils are tender. Serves 6.
(About 122 calories per serving)

Confetti Brown Rice with Scallions & Red & Green Peppers

  1 cup brown rice
2 1/4 cups chicken broth
  1 teaspoon oil
  1 teaspoon low-sodium soy sauce

1/2 cup finely chopped green bell pepper
1/2 cup finely chopped sweet red bell pepper
1/4 cup finely chopped green onion
  1 teaspoon oil

In a covered saucepan simmer together first 4 ingredients for about 35 minutes, or until rice is tender and liquid is absorbed. Meanwhile in a skillet, saute together next 4 ingredients, for about 10 minutes, stirring, until vegetables are tender. Toss vegetables with rice and heat through. Serves 6.

(About 144 calories per serving)

Cracked Wheat with Mushrooms & Onions

Kasha (bulgur) is an interesting accompaniment to homey dishes like roast chicken or brisket. I particularly like it made with a medley of vegetables. Carrots add a touch of color and sweetness, but aren't mandatory. Same with pimientos. If you don't have them handy, omit them.

1	cup cracked wheat (also called "bulgur")
2	teaspoons oil
1 1/4	cups beef broth
3/4	cup water
	black pepper to taste
1	onion, chopped
1/4	pound mushrooms, sliced
1/4	cup grated carrots (optional)
1/4	cup beef broth
1	tablespoon chopped parsley
1	jar (2 ounces) sliced pimientos (optional)

In a saucepan, cook cracked wheat in oil, stirring now and again, for 2 minutes. Carefully (it could splatter), add the broth, water and seasoning, cover pan, lower heat, and simmer mixture for about 15 minutes, or until liquid is absorbed.

Meanwhile, in another covered saucepan, cook together next 4 ingredients until onion is soft and mushrooms are tender. Uncover pan and cook for another few minutes or until all the juices have evaporated. Toss vegetable mixture into cracked wheat and heat through. Serve with chopped parsley and sliced pimientos on top. Serves 6.

(About 134 calories per serving)

Brown Rice with Leeks & Onions
(*Stove Top Method*)

1   leek, tough green parts removed, thoroughly washed to remove
      every trace of sand and finely chopped
1   small onion, minced
2   cups chicken broth
1   teaspoon oil

1   cup brown rice
      salt and pepper to taste

In a covered saucepan, simmer together first 4 ingredients, until leek is soft. Add the rice and seasonings, cover pan, and simmer mixture for about 30 minutes, or until rice is tender and liquid is absorbed. Serves 6.

(About 136 calories per serving)

Brown Rice with Leeks & Onions
(*Oven-Method*)

1   leek, tough upper green leaves removed, chopped and thoroughly
      cleaned of every grain of sand
1   small onion, chopped
1/2   cup chicken broth

1   cup brown rice
1 3/4   cups chicken broth
1   teaspoon oil
      pepper to taste

This is an alternate method of preparing this dish. In a covered oven casserole, cook together first 3 ingredients, on top of stove, until vegetables are soft. Add the remaining ingredients, cover casserole and bake mixture for about 1 hour in a 350-degree oven, or until rice is tender and liquid is absorbed. Serves 6.

(About 139 calories per serving)

Toasted Egg Barley with Onion & Mushrooms

        1   medium onion, minced
      1/2   pound mushrooms, sliced
        1   teaspoon oil

        1   package (7 ounces) toasted egg barley
        2   cups chicken broth
             salt and pepper to taste

In a covered saucepan, cook together onion and mushrooms in oil until vegetables are soft. Stir in the remaining ingredients, cover pan, and simmer mixture until barley is tender and liquid is absorbed, about 30 minutes. Serves 8.

(About 120 calories per serving)

Note: *This can be prepared in the oven in an 8x3-inch round baking pan that is securely sealed with foil. In this instance, bake for about 45 minutes.*

Lentils with Tomatoes, Carrots & Onions

Lentils are a healthy and delicious accompaniment to an informal dinner with family and friends. This dish is especially delicious served with roast chicken or veal. If you are left with a little extra broth, then drain it off. This is not a soup, but an accompaniment to dinner. I do recommend, however, that you serve it in a separate, small bowl.

        1   cup lentils, washed and picked over for any foreign matter
        3   carrots, peeled and thinly sliced
        2   cloves garlic, minced
        1   large onion, minced
        2   shallots, minced
        1   can (1 pound) stewed tomatoes, chopped. Do not drain.
        3   cups rich chicken broth
        1   teaspoon olive oil
             pepper to taste

In a Dutch oven casserole, stir together all the ingredients, cover pan and simmer mixture for 45 minutes to 1 hour, or until lentils are tender and most of the broth is absorbed. Serve with roast chicken. Serves 6.

(About 159 calories per serving)

Toasted Fideos

Rather than browning the vermicelli in oil, these are toasted in the oven, thus reducing the amount of oil markedly. These are super delicious and such a nice choice with chicken or beef. Use the appropriate broth when serving with chicken or beef.

1	package (8 ounces) fideo coils (also known as vermicelli coils) crushed slightly
1 1/4	cups beef broth or chicken broth
1	teaspoon oil
3/4	cup water
	pepper to taste

Toast fideos in a 350-degree oven for 8 minutes, or until it is golden brown. Careful, that it does not burn. Set aside.

In a saucepan, combine the remaining ingredients and bring mixture to a boil. Add toasted fideos, cover pan and reduce to low heat. Simmer mixture for about 10 minutes, or until fideos are tender and liquid is absorbed. Toss with a fork to separate fideos and serve 6 to 8.

(About 157 calories per serving-serving 6)
(About 118 calories per serving-serving 8)

Fideos with Mushrooms & Onions:
To the above recipe, add to cooked fideos, 1/4 pound sliced mushrooms and 1 small chopped onion, sauteed until tender, in 1 teaspoon oil. (Add 15 calories per serving.)

Fideos with Tomato:
To the basic recipe, before cooking, stir in 1 small chopped tomato (seeded and peeled). (Add 4 calories per serving.)

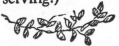

Bulgur with Lemon, Currants & Pine Nuts

1	cup bulgur (also called "cracked wheat")
1	teaspoon oil
1 1/4	cups chicken broth
1/2	cup water
3	tablespoons lemon juice
	black pepper to taste
1/2	cup chopped green onions
3	tablespoons dried black currants
3	tablespoons pine nuts (about 1 ounce)

In a saucepan, cook cracked wheat in oil, stirring now and again, for 2 minutes. Carefully (it could splatter), add the next 4 ingredients, cover pan, lower heat and simmer mixture for about 15 minutes, or until liquid is absorbed. Stir in remaining ingredients and serve with roast lamb. Serves 6.

(About 156 calories per serving)

Confetti Rice with Onions, Peppers & Peas

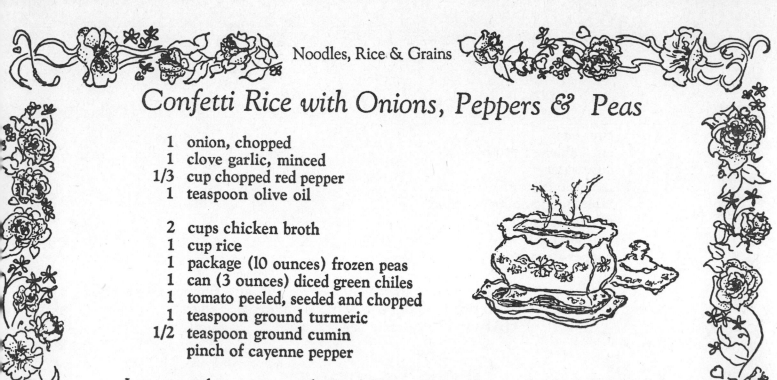

1   onion, chopped
1   clove garlic, minced
1/3   cup chopped red pepper
1   teaspoon olive oil

2   cups chicken broth
1   cup rice
1   package (10 ounces) frozen peas
1   can (3 ounces) diced green chiles
1   tomato peeled, seeded and chopped
1   teaspoon ground turmeric
1/2   teaspoon ground cumin
      pinch of cayenne pepper

In a covered saucepan, cook together first 4 ingredients until onions are soft. Stir in the remaining ingredients, cover pan and simmer mixture until rice is tender and liquid is absorbed. Serves 8.

(About 131 calories per serving)

Lemon Rice with Onions & Pine Nuts

1   onion, chopped
1   teaspoon oil

2   cups chicken broth
1   cup rice
2   tablespoons lemon juice
    white pepper to taste

2   tablespoons toasted pine nuts
1   tablespoon grated Parmesan Cheese
4   tablespoons chopped chives

In a covered saucepan, saute onion in oil until onion is soft. Add the next 4 ingredients, cover pan and simmer mixture until rice is tender and liquid is absorbed. Just before serving, stir in the pine nuts, cheese and chives. Serves 6.

(About 148 calories per serving)

Note: - Rice can be prepared earlier in the day, and reheated before serving. Do not stir in pine nuts, cheese or chives until just before serving. Pine nuts can get soggy, and cheese will make rice sticky if added earlier.

Pink Rice with Chives & Parsley

1 1/2 cups rice
2 cups chicken broth
1 cup water
2 tablespoons tomato sauce
2 tablespoons chopped chives
2 tablespoons chopped parsley
1 teaspoon oil
   pepper to taste

In a saucepan, stir together all the ingredients, cover pan and simmer mixture for about 30 minutes, or until rice is tender and liquid is absorbed. Serves 8.
(About 138 calories per serving)

Rice with Lemon & Chives

1 cup rice
1 teaspoon olive oil
2 cups chicken broth
2 teaspoons grated lemon peel
1/4 cup minced chives

In a saucepan, stir together all the ingredients, cover pan, and simmer mixture for about 30 minutes, or until rice is tender and liquid is absorbed. Fluff rice with a fork and serve. Serves 6.
(About 129 calories per serving)

Pink Rice and Mushrooms

1 cup rice
1 can (10 1/2 ounces) chicken broth
3/4 cup water
2 tablespoons tomato sauce
   pepper to taste

1/2 pound mushrooms
1 teaspoon oil

In a saucepan, stir together first 4 ingredients and simmer mixture for about 30 minutes, or until rice is tender and liquid is absorbed. Meanwhile, saute mushrooms in oil until mushrooms are tender and liquid is evaporated. Toss mushrooms into rice, heat through and serve. Serves 6.
(About 135 calories per serving)

Fried Rice with Green Onions

    1   cup rice
    1   teaspoon oil
1 1/4   cups beef broth
  3/4   cup water
    1   tablespoon low-sodium soy sauce

In a saucepan, saute rice in oil, until rice is just beginning to take on color. Carefully stir in the remaining ingredients, cover pan, and simmer rice over low heat, until it is tender and liquid is absorbed. When rice is cooked, add:

  1/3   cup minced green onions
    6   water chestnuts, minced (optional)

Heat through, fluff rice with a fork and serve 6.
        (About 128 calories per serving)

Herbed Rice

  3/4   cup rice
1 1/2   cups chicken broth
    1   teaspoon oil
  1/4   teaspoon each, sweet basil flakes, thyme flakes and paprika
    2   shakes cayenne pepper (or to taste)

In a saucepan, stir together all the ingredients, cover pan and simmer mixture for about 30 minutes, or until rice is tender and liquid is absorbed. Fluff rice with a fork and serve. Serves 5
        (About 117 calories per serving)

Lemon Rice with Leeks & Herbs

    1   cup rice
    2   cups chicken broth
    2   tablespoons lemon juice
    1   teaspoon oil

    1   leek, (white and 1-inch of the tender green parts) cut into thin
         slices
    2   shallots, minced
    1   clove garlic, minced
    1   tablespoon minced parsley
  1/2   teaspoon thyme flakes
    1   teaspoon oil

In a covered saucepan, simmer together first 4 ingredients for 30 minutes, or until rice is tender and liquid is absorbed. Meanwhile, in a skillet, saute together the remaining ingredients for 20 minutes, or until leeks are soft. Toss together rice and vegetables and heat through. Serves 6.
        (About 143 calories per serving)

Rice with Cheese & Chives

- 1/2   cup rice
- 1   teaspoon olive oil
- 1   cup chicken broth

- 1/4   cup coarsely chopped chives
- 4   teaspoons grated Parmesan cheese

In a saucepan, stir together all the ingredients, cover pan and simmer mixture for about 30 minutes, or until rice is tender and liquid is absorbed. Fluff rice with a fork and place on a serving platter. Sprinkle top with chives and grated Parmesan. Serves 4.

(About 110 calories per serving)

Emerald Rice with Parsley & Chives

- 1   cup rice
- 2   cups chicken broth
- 1   teaspoon oil
    white pepper to taste

- 1/4   cup minced chives
- 2   tablespoons minced parsley

In a covered saucepan, simmer together first 4 ingredients, until rice is tender and liquid is absorbed. Stir in chives and parsley and heat through. Serves 6.

(About 129 calories per serving)

Rice with Mushrooms

- 1   cup rice
- 2   cups chicken broth
- 1   teaspoon oil

- 1/2   pound mushrooms
- 1   teaspoon butter

In a saucepan, stir together rice, broth and oil, cover pan and simmer mixture for 30 minutes, or until rice is tender and liquid is absorbed. Meanwhile, cook mushrooms in butter, until mushrooms are tender and most of the liquid rendered is evaporated. Stir mushrooms into the cooked rice. Serves 6.

(About 144 calories per serving)

Pastina with Fresh Tomato & Basil Sauce

Pastinas are little dots of pasta that are an interesting starch accompaniment to a meal. Here, I pair it with fresh tomatoes and basil...truly delicious. Serve with roast veal or chicken.

> 3   tomatoes, peeled, seeded and chopped
> 1   teaspoon olive oil
> 1   teaspoon sweet basil flakes (or 1 tablespoon fresh basil)
> 1/4   cup chopped chives
>   pinch of cayenne
>
> 8   ounces pastina

In a skillet, cook together first 5 ingredients until liquid is absorbed and tomatoes are soft, about 10 minutes.

Cook the pastina in 2-quarts of rapidly boiling water, until tender, about 10 minutes. Drain thoroughly in a large strainer, or a collander with very small holes, or your pastina will disappear down the drain. Stir pastina into tomato sauce, heat through and serve at once. Serves 6 to 8.

(About 126 calories per serving-serving 8)
(About 168 calories per serving-serving 6)

Toasted Orzo with Mushrooms & Onions

Orzo is a rice-shaped pasta that comes in 3 sizes. For this recipe, I hope you can find the largest size. It is more dramatic in appearance and texture, and adds excitement to the meal. When you serve this dish get ready for applause.

> 1   cup orzo
> 2   teaspoons oil
> 2   cups chicken broth
>
> 1/2   pound mushrooms, thinly sliced
> 1   small onion, minced
> 1   teaspoon oil

In a 9x13-inch baking pan, lay orzo evenly. Bake at 350-degrees for 7 to 8 minutes or until orzo is just beginning to take on color. In a saucepan, place orzo with oil and chicken broth, cover pan, and simmer mixture until orzo is tender and liquid is absorbed.

Meanwhile, saute together mushrooms and onions in oil, until onions are tender and liquid rendered is evaporated. Add this to the cooked orzo, mix well and heat through. Serves 6.

(About 157 calories per serving)

Pink Orzo with Tomatoes & Onions

I love orzo and so do my family and friends. Whenever I serve it, everybody seems to enjoy and relish every bite. It is versatile, in that it can be combined with an infinite number of vegetables or meat.

1 cup orzo (rice-shaped pasta). This comes in various sizes.
    I prefer the large size (about 1/4-inch long) in this recipe.
1 tablespoon oil

1 1/4 cups chicken broth
1 cup water
    pinch of salt (optional) and pepper to taste

1 small onion, chopped
2 cloves garlic, minced
2 tomatoes, peeled, seeded and chopped (fresh or canned)
1 teaspoon oil

In a saucepan, saute orzo in oil until just beginning to take on color. Add the next 3 ingredients, cover pan and simmer mixture for about 40 minutes, or until orzo is tender and liquid is absorbed.

Meanwhile, in a covered saucepan, cook together the remaining ingredients until onion is soft. Toss together cooked orzo and tomato mixture until blended. Heat through before serving. Serves 6.

(About 159 calories per serving)

Note: - By preparing the orzo and sauce separately, you avoid the risk of getting the orzo sticky and pasty.

Important Note: Orzo needs to be toasted or browned in oil before cooking. In the preceding recipe, you will find instructions for browning in the oven. In the above recipe, instructions are given for browning in a little oil. Thought I should point this out to you.

Vegetables

From my notebook:

Vegetables are the third of the triumvirate, and I have included numerous recipes for all occasions. You'll find here vegetable accompaniments to dinner, and more substantial vegetable casseroles that will serve well for lunch or snacks.

Vegetables are virtuous...period. They are relatively low in calories, filled with vitamins and minerals and dietary fiber, and should add quite a bit of excitement to a meal.

At least, that is what I tried to do. You really don't need me for a recipe for steamed vegetables with a squeeze of lemon. I find the simplest way of preparing vegetables is to prepare them with a flavorful broth and then add a little Hollandaise, herbs, spices, seasonings or whatever.

The recipes I have included here are more complex in flavor and texture. Why? Well, because that is the essence of variety and interest. There is always room for plain steamed vegetables. But achieving satisfaction and pleasure sometimes requires a little more creativity.

Here you will find a host of vegetables, paired with an abundance of flavors and tastes...Green Beans with Parsley Sauce, Broccoli with Garlic & Shallots, Brussel Sprouts with Lemon Chive Sauce, Honey & Butter Glazed Carrots.

Often they are prepared with a combination of vegetables...Green Beans with Tomatoes & Onions. Artichokes, with Mushrooms and Cheese or with Potatoes & Green Onions, both very low in calories and delicious. Sweet & Sour Red Cabbage with Apples & Currants, Baked Eggplant with Tomatoes & Ricotta, Roasted Red Pepper & Onion Cake, Spinach Pate with Onions, Peppers & Carrots...great vegetable recipes that aren't silent partners to a meal, but stand alone quite well.

Often they are the essence of simplicity, but with a special touch...Potatoes Roasted with Garlic, Country Baked Potatoes, Sweet Potatoes with Sugar & Spice, Broiled Tomatoes with Garlic Cheese Crumbs, Broiled Mixed Vegetable Platter, Steamed Baby Potatoes with Parsley & Dill, and the like.

Some of the recipes serve as more substantial accompaniments...Frittata of Broccoli, Ramekins of Zucchini, Baked Eggplant with Tomatoes & Ricotta and are good lunch choices, also. So, here they are, and enjoy, to your heart's content.

Artichokes & Mushrooms with Cheese

    1   pound mushrooms, sliced
    1   onion, minced
    2   shallots, minced
    4   cloves garlic, minced
  1/4   cup chicken broth
    1   package (10 ounces) frozen artichoke hearts
         pepper to taste

  1/4   cup half and half cream
  1/4   cup chopped chives
    1   tablespoon lemon juice

    1   tablespoon grated Parmesan cheese

In a covered saucepan, cook together first 7 ingredients until onion is soft. Remove cover, and cook over higher heat, until liquid is absorbed. Stir in the next 3 ingredients and cook for 2 to 3 minutes to heat through. Place in a lovely casserole and sprinkle top with cheese before serving. Nice to serve with beef or veal. Serves 8.

(About 48 calories per serving)

Artichokes & Potatoes with Green Onions

Instead of browning the vegetables in large quantities of oil, broiling them with a little butter produces a similar effect, with a saving of 400 calories. The small amount of butter adds a good deal of flavor.

    2   packages (10 ounces, each) frozen artichoke hearts
  1/2   pound baby red-skinned potatoes, peeled or unpeeled

    6   green onions, cut into 1-inch lengths
    1   tablespoon butter, melted
    1   teaspoon dried rosemary

Cook the artichokes in boiling water for 5 to 7 minutes or until tender and drain. Cook the potatoes in boiling water for 12 to 15 minutes or until tender and drain. Cut the artichokes and potatoes in quarters and place them in a bowl. Add the remaining ingredients and toss together until nicely mixed.

Place vegetable mixture in 1 layer in a broiler pan and broil, 4-inches from the heat, turning until nicely browned on all sides. Serves 8.

(About 68 calories per serving)

Asparagus in Lemon Chive Sauce
with Garlic Crumbs

2 packages (10 ounces, each) frozen asparagus spears, cooked in
1/2 cup water for 5 minutes and drained.

1/2 cup unflavored non-fat yogurt
2 tablespoons low-calorie and low-cholesterol mayonnaise
1 1/2 tablespoons lemon juice
1/2 teaspoon grated lemon zest (yellow part of the peel)
4 tablespoons chopped chives
pinch of salt

2 tablespoons crumbled garlic croutons
1 tablespoon grated Parmesan cheese

In a pretty porcelain baker, lay drained asparagus. Stir together the next 6 ingredients until blended and spoon mixture over the asparagus. Sprinkle top with garlic crumbs and grated Parmesan. Heat in a 350-degree oven until heated through, but do not allow to boil. Brown under the broiler for 1 minute until golden. Serves 8.
(About 41 calories per serving)

Note: - Entire dish can be assembled earlier in the day (except for sprinkling the crumbs, which should be done just before heating). Store in the refrigerator and heat before serving.

Asparagus with Lemon, Garlic & Cheese

2 packages (10 ounces, each) frozen asparagus, cooked in
1/2 cup water for 5 minutes, and drained.

2 tablespoons low-calorie, low-cholesterol mayonnaise
4 tablespoons chopped chives
2 teaspoons lemon juice
2 tablespoons bread crumbs
2 tablespoons grated Parmesan cheese
1 teaspoon melted butter

Arrange cooked asparagus in a porcelain baking dish. Brush asparagus with mayonnaise, sprinkle with chives and drizzle with lemon. Sprinkle with bread crumbs and Parmesan. Drizzle top with melted butter.

Bake in a 350-degree oven until heated through. Broil for a few seconds to brown the crumbs and then serve immediately. Serves 8.
(About 43 calories per serving)

Note: - Entire dish can be assembled earlier in the day and brought to room temperature before heating.

Green Beans with Tomatoes & Onions

1 pound fresh green beans, ends snapped
1 can (1 pound) stewed tomatoes, chopped. Do not drain.
1 small onion, chopped
1 teaspoon chicken seasoned stock base
1 clove garlic, minced
2 tablespoons lemon juice
  black pepper to taste

In a Dutch oven casserole, lay green beans. Stir together the remaining ingredients and pour over the beans. Cover pan and simmer mixture for 20 to 25 minutes or until green beans are tender. Do not overcook. Serves 6.
(About 46 calories per serving)

Green Beans with Parsley Sauce

1/2 cup chicken broth
1/4 cup dry white wine
4 shallots minced
3 cloves garlic, minced
1/4 cup minced parsley leaves
  white pepper to taste

1 pound green beans, ends snapped off

In a Dutch oven casserole, simmer first 6 ingredients until shallots are softened, about 5 minutes. Add the green beans, cover pan and cook green beans until tender, about 8 minutes. If sauce appears soupy, remove green beans and cook sauce over high heat until reduced to 1/3 cup. Serve with meat, chicken or fish. Serves 6.
(About 35 calories per serving)

Lima Beans with Onions & Tomatoes

Lima beans are high in calories, so use this recipe instead of pasta, potatoes or rice.

1 packages (10 ounces) frozen lima beans
1 small onion, minced
2 medium tomatoes, peeled, seeded and chopped
2 tablespoons lemon juice
  pepper to taste

In a saucepan, stir together all the ingredients. Cover pan and simmer mixture until onion is soft and beans are tender, about 20 minutes. Serves 6.
(About 79 calories per serving)

Broth-Fried Broccoli with Ginger

1   pound broccoli. Remove the 2-inches of the tough bottoms. Cut off the florets from the stalk. With a vegetable peeler, peel the stalk and cut it on the diagonal into 1/4-inch thick slices.

2   cloves garlic, minced

2   tablespoons low-sodium soy sauce

1/2   teaspoon finely minced ginger

1   teaspoon oil

2   tablespoons chicken broth

In a bowl, toss together first 4 ingredients. In a large skillet, over high heat, heat the oil and broth until sizzling hot. Add the broccoli mixture, and toss and turn for 3 minutes. Cover pan and cook until broccoli is tender, about 3 minutes longer. Serves 4.

(About 35 calories per serving)

Broccoli with Garlic & Shallot Cream Sauce

The broccoli and sauce can be prepared earlier in the day. Heat before serving and stir in the yogurt at the end to avoid curdling.

2   packages (10 ounces, each) broccoli spears

1/2   cup chicken broth

3   cloves garlic, minced

3   shallots, minced

1   teaspoon butter

1   tablespoon lemon juice

1/4   cup dry white wine

2   tablespoons unflavored non-fat yogurt

In a Dutch oven casserole, lay broccoli spears and cook in chicken broth for about 4 to 5 minutes or until broccoli is tender. Remove broccoli from pan. Add the next 5 ingredients to the pan and simmer sauce for 10 to 12 minutes, or until shallots are tender and sauce is reduced to 1/2. Remove from heat and stir in the yogurt. Pour over the hot broccoli and serve. Serves 8.

(About 39 calories per serving)

Frittata of Broccoli, Mushrooms & Tomatoes

- 2 packages (10 ounces, each) frozen chopped broccoli, defrosted
- 2 medium tomatoes, peeled, seeded and chopped
- 1/2 pound mushrooms, sliced
- 1/2 cup chopped green onions
- 2 tablespoons grated Parmesan cheese
- 2 eggs beaten
- 1/4 cup cracker crumbs
- 1/2 teaspoon Italian Herb Seasoning

In a large bowl, mix together all the ingredients until nicely blended. Place in an oiled 8x12-inch porcelain baker and bake at 350-degrees for about 40 minutes, or until casserole is set and top is browned. Serves 6 for lunch or 12 as an accompaniment to dinner.

(About 49 calories per serving-serving 12)
(About 97 calories per serving-serving 6)

Brussel Sprouts with Lemon Chive Sauce

- 2 packages (10 ounces, each) frozen Brussel sprouts
- 1/2 cup chicken broth
- 4 tablespoons lemon juice
- 1/4 teaspoon thyme flakes
- 2 tablespoons minced parsley leaves
-   white pepper to taste

- 2 tablespoons half and half cream
- 4 tablespoons minced chives

In a saucepan, simmer together first group of ingredients until sprouts are tender, about 5 minutes. Remove sprouts with a slotted spoon, add the cream and cook down the broth mixture until it is reduced by half. Return sprouts to the sauce and heat through. Sprinkle with chopped chives at serving time. Serves 6.

(About 60 calories per serving)

Brussel Sprouts with Mushrooms & Shallots

2 packages (10 ounces, each) frozen Brussel sprouts
1/2 cup chicken broth

1/4 pound mushrooms, sliced
3 shallots, minced
2 cloves garlic, minced
1/4 cup chicken broth
1/2 teaspoon Italian Herb Seasoning
1 tablespoon minced parsley

In a saucepan, cook sprouts in chicken broth until they are tender and drain. In a skillet, cook together remaining ingredients until mushrooms are tender and all the liquid rendered is evaporated. Combine sprouts and mushroom mixture and heat through. Serves 6.

(About 59 calories per serving)

Pureed Carrots with Cinnamon

This is a beautiful dish to serve for a dinner party. It can be prepared earlier in the day and heated before serving. Serve with veal or chicken.

1 pound carrots, peeled and sliced. Cook in boiling water for about 15 minutes or until soft. Thoroughly drain and pat dry with paper towelling.

1/2 teaspoon cinnamon
1 teaspoon sugar
3 eggs
1/2 cup low-fat milk

Line the bottoms of 6 individual ramekins with parchment paper. (This will make for easy removal.) Puree carrots in food processor. Beat together the remaining ingredients and add to carrots and pulse for 2 or 3 seconds until blended.

Divide mixture between the 6 prepared ramekins and place in a baking pan with boiling water coming halfway up the sides. Bake at 350-degrees for about 30 to 40 minutes or until mold is firm. Remove from pan and allow to set for 2 or 3 minutes. Run a knife around the edge, and invert on a plate, remove paper and allow some of the liquid rendered to drain. Place onto a porcelain server. Can be held at this point. Before serving, heat in a 350-degree oven for 10 to 12 minutes. Plant a small parsley leaf on top. Serves 6.

(About 79 calories per serving)

Carrot & Potato Cake

Carrots and potatoes are paired with onions and cheese and it is very good, indeed. This is excellent to serve with roast meats, chicken or broiled fish.

- 1 pound carrots, peeled and grated
- 2 medium potatoes, peeled and grated. Allow to stand in a bowl of cold water until ready to use and then drain. Dry on paper towelling.
- 2 medium onions, grated
- 2 eggs, beaten
- 1/4 cup cracker crumbs
- 1/4 cup grated Parmesan cheese
  salt and pepper to taste

In a large bowl, stir together all the ingredients until everything is nicely mixed. Spread evenly in a 9x13-inch non-stick baking pan and bake at 350-degrees for 40 to 50 minutes or until top is golden brown. Run a knife around the edge, cut into servings, remove from pan and serve. Serves 10.

(About 74 calories per serving)

Honey & Butter Glazed Carrots with Parsley

- 1 pound baby carrots, steamed over boiling water until tender, about 5 minutes. Refresh under cold water.

- 2 teaspoons butter
- 1 teaspoon honey
- 1 tablespoon chopped parsley
  pinch of salt (optional)

In a large skillet, place all the ingredients and cook, over low heat, tossing and turning until carrots are nicely coated. Carrots will render a little liquid, so, cook until the liquid is evaporated and carrots appear glazed. Serves 6.

(About 41 calories per serving)

Celery in Lemon Dill Sauce

Celery is one of the many ignored vegetables. It is used as an accompaniment to stuffings or soups, but it is not often served alone. It is so low in calories that it is a good vegetable to consider serving when a little dessert is around the bend.

1	large bunch celery (1 pound). Remove leaves, scrub the stalks, and cut on the diagonal into 1/2-inch thick slices.
1/2	cup chicken broth
2	tablespoons dry white wine
2	tablespoons lemon juice
3	shallots, minced
1	clove garlic, minced
1/2	teaspoon dried dill weed

In a Dutch oven casserole, with cover slightly ajar, simmer together all the ingredients until celery is tender, about 7 to 10 minutes. Serves 6.

(About 20 calories per serving)

Cucumbers with Lemon, Parsley & Chives

Cucumbers are wonderful served as a warm vegetable. They prepare in minutes and are an interesting accompaniment to roast chicken or baked fish.

3	medium cucumbers, peeled and halved (about 1 pound). With a spoon, scoop out the seeds.
4	tablespoons chicken broth
1	tablespoon lemon juice or more to taste
1	tablespoon chopped parsley leaves
3	tablespoons chopped chives

In a saucepan, cook together first 3 ingredients until cucumbers are limp, about 3 minutes. Stir in parsley and chives. Serves 4.

(About 20 calories per serving)

Sweet & Sour Red Cabbage with Apples & Currants

1   onion, chopped
2   cloves garlic, minced
1   teaspoon oil

1   cup beef broth
4   tablespoons lemon juice
1   small head red cabbage (about 1 pound), cored and shredded
2   apples, peeled, cored and grated
2   tablespoons dried black currants (optional)

In a Dutch oven casserole, saute onion and garlic in oil until onions are soft. Add the remaining ingredients, cover pan, and simmer mixture for about 30 minutes, or until cabbage is tender. Nice to serve with roast meat. Serves 8.

(About 49 calories per serving-with currants)
(About 43 calories per serving-without currants)

Cauliflower with Tomatoes & Onions

1   can (1 pound) stewed tomatoes, chopped. Do not drain.
1   onion, chopped
1   clove garlic, minced

2   packages (10 ounces, each) frozen cauliflower, cut into
        small florets
3   tablespoons lemon juice
1   teaspoon sugar
1   tablespoon minced parsley
    white pepper to taste

In a saucepan, cook together first 3 ingredients until onions are soft. Stir in the remaining ingredients and continue cooking until cauliflower is tender, about 7 minutes. Serve with chicken or fish. Serves 6.

(About 55 calories per serving)

Baked Eggplant with Tomatoes & Ricotta

This is a nice vegetarian quiche, with the eggplant acting as a crust. It is a nice healthy lunch and very adequate for dinner.

1   small eggplant (about 3/4 pound), cut into 1/4-inch slices. Do not peel.
1/4   cup chicken broth

1 1/2   cups ricotta cheese
1/4   cup crumbled Feta cheese (1 ounce)
1/4   cup grated Parmesan cheese
4   eggs, beaten
1/2   teaspoon dried dill weed

1   tomato, thinly sliced
1   tablespoon grated Parmesan cheese

In a 9x13-inch baking pan, place eggplant slices and drizzle with broth. Cover pan tightly with foil, and bake in a 350-degree oven for 25 minutes, or until eggplant is soft. Allow to cool a little and then place eggplant slices in a clean 9x13-inch baking pan, lining the bottom evenly.

Beat together the next 5 ingredients until blended. Spread cheese mixture evenly over the eggplant slices and place tomato slices evenly on top. Sprinkle top with grated Parmesan. Bake in a 350-degree oven for about 40 minutes, or until eggs are set and top is golden brown. Serve with Pink Orzo with Tomatoes & Onions as a delicious accompaniment. Serves 8 for lunch and 12 as a vegetable course for dinner.

(About 145 calories per serving-serving 8)
(About 97 calories per serving-serving 12)

Mushrooms & Tomatoes in Wine Sauce

1   pound mushrooms, sliced
2   medium tomatoes, peeled, seeded and chopped
3   shallots, minced
3   cloves garlic, minced
1/4 teaspoon thyme flakes
1   tablespoon minced parsley leaves
1/4 cup dry white wine
     pinch of cayenne pepper

In a saucepan, cook together all the ingredients until liquid rendered is evaporated and mushroom mixture is not soupy.   Serves 6.

(About 41 calories per serving)

Mushrooms with Dill & Yogurt Stuffing

1   pound mushrooms, cleaned and stems removed (about 24). Chop stems finely.

1   onion, minced
1/4 cup minced celery
1/2 teaspoon dried dill weed
1   teaspoon oil

1/2 cup garlic croutons, finely crushed
3/4 cup unflavored non-fat yogurt

2   tablespoons grated Parmesan cheese
     paprika

Prepare mushrooms and place them on a non-stick baking pan. In a skillet, saute together mushroom stems and next 4 ingredients until onion and celery are soft and liquid rendered is evaporated. In a bowl, mix together onion mixture, garlic croutons and yogurt until blended. Fill mushrooms with about 1 tablespoon filling and sprinkle tops with grated Parmesan and paprika. Bake at 350-degrees about 20 minutes. Broil for a few seconds to brown tops. Serve with beef or veal. Serves 8.

(About 49 calories per 3 mushroom serving)

Honey & Brandy Glazed Onions

1   pound baby white onions, stemmed
2   teaspoons butter
2   teaspoons Cognac or brandy
1   tablespoon honey
2   tablespoons minced parsley

In a large saucepan, cook onions in 1 quart boiling water until onions are firm tender and drain. Slip off the skins. In a skillet, heat together the remaining ingredients, add the onions and continue cooking and turning until onions are shiny and lightly browned, and most of the liquid rendered is evaporated. Place glazed onions around roast beef or veal or serve in a shallow vegetable dish. Serves 6.

(About 54 calories per serving)

Onions with Raisins

2   onions, thinly sliced
1   teaspoon sugar
1/4   cup beef broth

1/4   cup beef broth
1/4   cup raisins
1   tablespoon parsley

In a covered skillet, over very low heat, cook onions in sugar and broth until onions are soft and just beginning to take on color, about 30 minutes. Do not allow to brown. (This process is called "sweating", and the onions will darken but not "fry".) Add the remaining ingredients, and simmer mixture, uncovered, until broth is almost evaporated. Nice to serve with roast chicken or pork. Serves 4.

(About 51 calories per serving)

Onion & Mushroom Saute

1   pound baby pearl onions

1   pound mushrooms, sliced
1   teaspoon oil

1/4   cup chicken broth
2   tablespoons chopped parsley

Cook onions in boiling water for 10 minutes and drain. Allow to cool and slip off the skins. Saute the mushrooms in oil until tender. Combine onions and mushrooms in a Dutch oven casserole and add the broth. Cook for a few minutes, uncovered, until the broth is almost evaporated. Stir in the parsley and serve. Serves 8.

(About 44 calories per serving)

Potatoes Roasted with Garlic

8   baby potatoes, scrubbed (about 1 pound). Peel off 1-inch of skin
        from the center.
1   teaspoon olive oil
4   cloves garlic, thinly sliced
     pepper to taste

Line a 10-inch round baking pan with foil, extending the sides 6-inches. Toss together all the ingredients, place in pan, and fold the foil to seal the potatoes. Bake in a 350-degree oven for 25 minutes or until potatoes are tender. (You can pierce a potato with a skewer to test.) Open the foil package and broil the potatoes, turning once, until they are golden brown on all sides. Serves 4.

(About 104 calories per serving)

Country Baked Potatoes

6   medium potatoes (about 1 1/2 pounds), peeled
2   teaspoons melted margarine
     onion powder and paprika

Brush the peeled potatoes with melted margarine and sprinkle generously with onion powder and paprika. Bake uncovered at 350-degrees until potatoes are tender and golden brown, about 45 minutes. Can be held in a 300-degree oven for 20 minutes. However, do not prepare these in advance. Serves 6.

(About 104 calories per serving)

Sweet Potatoes Baked with Sugar & Spice

This is a nice dish to serve with turkey on Thanksgiving. It is slimmed down a lot using only 1 tablespoon of butter and brown sugar. Use the dark brown sugar for it imparts an attractive color.

2   large sweet potatoes, peeled and cut into 1/2-inch slices,
        (3/4 pound)
1   tablespoon butter or margarine, melted
1   tablespoon dark brown sugar
1/2 teaspoon cinnamon
     pinch of ground nutmeg

Place potatoes in one layer in a non-stick baking pan. Drizzle top with butter and sprinkle with brown sugar, cinnamon and nutmeg. Bake at 350-degrees until potatoes are tender, about 30 minutes. Serves 4.

(About 112 calories per serving)

Roasted Red Pepper, Potato & Onion Cake

This is a beautiful dish and delicious too. Potatoes prepared with sweet red peppers and green onions add excitement to a meal.

- 3   medium potatoes, peeled and grated
- 1   red pepper, cored, seeded and cut into thin strips
- 6   green onions, chopped
- 1   egg
- 1/4   cup cracker crumbs
-    black pepper to taste

- 1   teaspoon olive oil

In a large bowl, toss together first group of ingredients until nicely mixed. Place mixture into a 9x9-inch non-stick baking pan. Drizzle top with oil. Bake at 350-degrees about 40 to 45 minutes, or until top is golden brown and crisp. Serves 6.

(About 84 calories per serving)

Note: This can be baked in a 9-inch deep-dish pie plate, in which case, cut into wedges to serve.

Potato & Onion Cake

This is a variation of the old favorite, potato pancakes. The taste is great and you save at least 1/2 cup of oil. It is a nice accompaniment to roast chicken, veal, beef and other homey dishes. It is delectable served with 1 teaspoon half and half sour cream (7 calories) and 1 tablespoon unsweetened applesauce (7 calories), but that is optional.

- 6   medium potatoes, peeled and grated (1 1/2 pounds). Allow to stand in a bowl of cold water until ready to use and then drain. Dry with paper towelling.
- 2   medium onions, grated
- 2   eggs, beaten
- 1/2   cup cracker crumbs
-    salt and pepper to taste

In a large bowl, toss together all the ingredients until nicely blended. Spread mixture evenly in a lightly oiled non-stick 9x13-inch baking pan. Bake at 350-degrees for about 50 minutes, or until top is crusty and golden brown. Run a knife along the edge, cut into 12 servings, remove from pan and serve. Serves 12.

(About 79 calories per serving)

Garlic Potatoes with Onions & Rosemary

The success of this dish rests mainly with the tastiness of the broth. The richer the broth, the more succulent the taste. Prepare this in a porcelain baker (one with its own stand) and it will go from oven to table without the bother of transferring to a serving platter.

1	onion, chopped
6	cloves garlic, minced
1/2	cup chicken broth
1	teaspoon oil
1	teaspoon dried rosemary
6	medium baking potatoes, (about 1 1/2 pounds), scrubbed and cut into 1/4-inch thick slices. Do not peel.
	freshly ground black pepper
1/4	cup chicken broth

Stir together first 5 ingredients until nicely mixed. In a 9x13-inch non-stick baking pan, toss together the potatoes and onion mixture and spread evenly. Cover pan tightly with foil and bake at 375-degrees for 30 minutes.

Remove the foil and drizzle remaining chicken broth evenly over all. Return to oven, uncovered and bake for another 20 to 30 minutes, or until potatoes are tender, top is browned and broth is almost absorbed. Serves 6.

(About 109 calories per serving)

Steamed Baby Potatoes with Parsley & Dill

12	baby potatoes, (about 1 1/2 pounds) peeled
2	teaspoons melted butter
2	tablespoons chopped parsley
1/2	teaspoon dried dill weed

Line a 10-inch round baking pan with foil, extending the sides 6-inches. Toss together all the ingredients, place in pan, and fold the foil to seal the potatoes. Bake in a 350-degree oven for 25 minutes or until potatoes are tender. Serves 6.

(About 104 calories per serving)

Spinach Pate with Onions, Peppers, Carrots & Fresh Tomato Sauce

This is another of those lovely pates that are so good, and good for you, too. It is a wholesome combination of vegetables, proteins, dairy and starch. A good choice for lunch. Pate slices better when cold. It can be presliced and warmed at 350-degrees for 15 minutes.

    2   packages (10 ounces, each) frozen chopped spinach, defrosted and
          drained
    1   red pepper, seeds removed and finely chopped
    1   package (10 ounces) frozen sliced carrots
    1   small onion, grated
    1   cup non-fat cottage cheese
    1/3 cup grated Parmesan cheese
    1/2 cup fresh whole wheat bread crumbs (1 slice bread)
    2   eggs, beaten
        pepper to taste

Prepare vegetables. Drain spinach, parboil red pepper and carrots and coarsely chop in a food processor. In a large bowl, stir together all the ingredients until they are thoroughly mixed.

Place mixture into a lightly oiled 8x4-inch loaf pan, that has been lined with wax paper. Place pan in a larger pan with 2-inches boiling water. Bake in a 350-degree oven for about 55 minutes, or until pate is set and top is taking on color. Allow to cool in pan and then refrigerate until firm. To serve, remove from pan, remove wax paper and cut into slices to serve. Serve warm or at room temperature with a spoonful of Fresh Tomato Sauce. Serves 8 to 10.

(About 97 calories per serving-serving 8)
(About 77 calories per serving-serving 10)

Fresh Tomato Sauce:
    3   medium tomatoes, peeled, seeded, chopped and drained
    1/4 cup chopped chives
    2   tablespoons minced cilantro
    1   tablespoon minced parsley
    2   tablespoons lemon juice (or a little more to taste)

Stir together all the ingredients until blended. Serve at room temperature. Yields about 1 cup.

(About 6 calories per tablespoon)

Broiled Tomatoes with Garlic Cheese Crumbs

These are a lovely accompaniment to broiled meats, chicken or fish. They can be assembled earlier in the day and broiled before serving.

2   medium tomatoes, remove stems and cut in half crosswise

2   cloves garlic, mashed
2   tablespoons bread crumbs
2   tablespoons grated Parmesan cheese
2   tablespoons chopped chives
2   teaspoons chopped parsley
2   teaspoons lemon juice
1   teaspoon melted butter
    white pepper to taste

Place tomatoes, cut side up, in broiling pan. Mix together the remaining ingredients and spread evenly over the tomatoes. Broil until tops are browned, 2 to 3 minutes. Serves 4.

(About 46 calories per serving)

Baked Zucchini in Lemon Tomato Sauce

2   pounds small zucchini, cleaned and cut on the diagonal into
        1/2-inch slices

1   can (1 pound) stewed tomatoes, finely chopped. Do not drain.
1   small onion, grated or minced, about 1/4 cup
2   tablespoons chopped parsley
1   teaspoon sugar
3   tablespoons lemon juice
1/2 teaspoon dried dill weed
    freshly ground black pepper to taste

2   teaspoons grated Parmesan cheese

In a 9x13-inch pan, place zucchini. Stir together the next 7 ingredients and pour evenly over the zucchini. Sprinkle top with grated cheese. Bake in a 350-degree oven for about 30 minutes, or until zucchini is tender, but firm. Serves 6 to 8.

(About 53 calories per serving-serving 6)
(About 40 calories per serving-serving 8)

Zucchini Frittata with Tomatoes Vinaigrette

This is an attractive and colorful casserole to serve on a buffet. To prevent its getting soupy, it is important to squeeze the zucchini to remove excess liquid. Low-fat Ricotta cheese (320 calories per cup) is a little drier than the non-fat cottage cheese (140 calories per cup), but the savings in calories is marked and worth the looser texture.

2 pounds zucchini, grated. (Cut off ends, but do not peel.)

2 cups non-fat cottage cheese
1/4 cup cracker crumbs
1 egg
1/4 cup grated Parmesan cheese
1/2 teaspoon, each, oregano and sweet basil flakes
black pepper to taste

2 medium tomatoes, thinly sliced
2 tablespoons grated Parmesan cheese

Place zucchini in a dish towel and squeeze out some of the liquid. In a large mixing bowl, mix the zucchini with the next 6 ingredients until nicely blended. Spread mixture evenly into a lightly-oiled 9x13-inch baking pan and place tomatoes over the top. Sprinkle with the Parmesan cheese and bake in a 350-degree oven for 50 minutes to 1 hour or until top is golden brown. Serve hot, with a little Tomatoes Vinaigrette on the side. Serves 8.

(About 93 calories per serving)

Tomatoes Vinaigrette:
2 tomatoes, peeled, seeded and very finely chopped
3 tablespoons minced chives
1 tablespoon minced parsley
2 tablespoons red wine vinegar

Stir together all the ingredients until blended. Place sauce in a lovely boat and refrigerate. Remove from the refrigerator 20 minutes before serving. Yields a little more than 1/2 cup.

(About 7 calories per tablespoon)

Ramekins of Zucchini, Onions & Cheese

6 medium zucchini, (about 1 1/2 pounds), peeled and grated. Place
   zucchini in a towel and squeeze to remove excess liquid.
1 medium onion, grated
3 eggs, beaten
1/4 cup cracker crumbs
1/2 cup non-fat cottage cheese
1/4 cup grated Parmesan cheese

2 tablespoons grated Parmesan cheese

In a bowl, stir together first 6 ingredients. Divide mixture between 12 ramekins that have been lightly oiled. (1 drop oil in each cup is sufficient.) Sprinkle tops with 1/2-teaspoon grated cheese. Bake at 350-degrees for about 40 minutes, or until tops are golden brown. Run a knife along the edge, remove from pan and serve. Serves 12.

(About 55 calories per serving)

Baked Zucchini with Tomatoes & Cheese

2 pounds zucchini, unpeeled. Scrub, remove ends and cut into
   1/4-inch slices.
3 tomatoes, peeled, seeded and thinly sliced

1 clove garlic, minced
2 tablespoons, each, chopped parsley and chives
1/2 teaspoon sweet basil flakes
2 tablespoons cracker crumbs
2 tablespoons grated Parmesan cheese
   black pepper to taste
   pinch of cayenne

2 teaspoons olive oil (optional)

In a 9x13-inch pan, place zucchini. Top with sliced tomatoes. Toss together the remaining ingredients and sprinkle on top of the tomatoes. Drizzle with optional olive oil (a nice addition, but not necessary). Bake in a 350-degree oven for 30 minutes, or until zucchini are tender. Broil for a few minutes to brown the top. Serves 8.

(About 49 calories per serving-using olive oil)
(About 38 calories per serving-without olive oil)

Zucchini with Tomatoes & Onions

6   medium zucchini, (about 1 1/2 pounds), ends cut and sliced
      1/4-inch thick
1   medium onion, minced
1   clove garlic, minced
1   can (1 pound) stewed tomatoes, chopped and drained.
1   teaspoon parsley flakes
1/2 teaspoon Italian Herb Seasoning
1   tablespoon lemon juice
1   teaspoon olive oil
    pepper to taste

In a Dutch oven casserole, place all the ingredients. Bring mixture to a boil, cover pan, and lower heat. Simmer mixture for 30 minutes, or until onion is soft and zucchini is tender. Serves 6.

(About 48 calories per serving)

Baked Zucchini Crisps

Save hundreds of calories by baking, instead of frying, these zucchini crisps. These are nice to serve as an accompaniment to dinner or as small first course.

1   pound zucchini. Scrub, but do not peel. Slice on the diagonal
      into 1/2-inch thick slices.
1   tablespoon low-calorie, low-cholesterol mayonnaise
2   tablespoons chicken broth

1/3 cup savory cracker crumbs
1/3 cup grated Parmesan cheese

Stir together mayonnaise and chicken broth. Spread each slice of zucchini, on both sides with a thin coating of mayonnaise mixture.. Combine crumbs and cheese and sprinkle on both sides of zucchini. Place zucchini on a plastic-coated cookie sheet and bake at 400-degrees until golden brown, about 20 minutes. Carefully turn and brown other side. Serves 6 to 8.

(About 50 calories per serving-serving 6)
(About 38 calories per serving-serving 8)

Broiled Mixed Vegetable Platter

The beauty of this dish lies in the myriad of colors and shapes, and the large cuts of vegetables. Using chicken broth, instead of oil, makes this truly low calorie. Other vegetables can be used, broccoli, cauliflower, carrots, asparagus. Potatoes are also good, but should be cooked before using. Baby vegetables are especially attractive. Just recount the calories and have a feast.

- 2   leeks, white and tender green part only. Cut in half, lengthwise, and rinse off every trace of sand.
- 8   green onions. Trim the whiskers and any frayed tops and leave whole.
- 4   zucchini, about 1 pound. Scrub and do not peel. Cut into long 1/2-inch slices on the diagonal.
- 1   sweet red bell pepper, cut into 1-inch slices
- 2   cloves garlic, sliced
- 1/2   teaspoon dried dill weed
- 1   cup rich chicken broth

In a 9x13-inch broiling pan, place all the vegetables, sprinkle with dill and pour chicken broth over all. Place pan under the broiler and broil, 4-inches from the heat, turning the vegetables now and again, for 20 minutes or until they are tender. Serves 4.

(About 53 calories per serving)

Stir-Fried Mixed Vegetable Platter

The following can take on a totally different character with different seasonings. To take on an Oriental mood, add 1 tablespoon low-sodium soy and 1/4 teaspoon ground ginger. Herbs are nice. Sweet basil flakes, oregano or thyme add interest. Curry to taste is another good choice. Other vegetables can be used...cauliflower, broccoli, asparagus. Keep it varied and you will never feel bored.

- 8   green onions, cut into 1-inch strips, on the diagonal
- 4   carrots, peeled and sliced on the diagonal
- 1   sweet red bell pepper, cut into 1/2-inch slices
- 1   green bell pepper, cut into 1/2-inch slices
- 4   stalks celery, cut into thin slices
- 4   cloves garlic, sliced
       seasoning of your choice

- 2   teaspoons oil
- 2   tablespoons rich chicken broth

Prepare the vegetables. In a wok or large skillet, over high heat, heat the oil and broth until bubbling. Add the vegetables, and continue cooking, over high heat, tossing and turning, until vegetables are tender, but still firm. Serves 4.

(About 62 calories per serving)

Desserts

From my notebook:

Well, here we are; I hope you've made it to the end. Because in this chapter you will find some interesting low-calorie desserts, that will round out a meal rather nicely and not leave you craving a little "something sweet."

There are several recipes that I want to point out that are so delicious and so satisfying that you will never feel deprived or wanting. This is what I meant, in the introduction, by "natural and normal" eating.

Orange & Walnut Torte is one of the tastiest of tortes, fresh and refreshing with the tartness of orange and peel. The Walnut Cake with the Raspberry & Lemon Glaze is one of the best, for taste and texture. Skinny Chocolate Torte ala Sacher has the character of the famous cake, (chocolate cake, apricot glaze and chocolate frosting) and is truly rapturous. Lemon Cheesecake with Strawberry Sauce is another very memorable dessert. These are all grand for the finest dinner party. While relatively low in calories, they still have calories, so keep the portions as directed.

For a very low calorie dessert, Angel Cake with Fresh Strawberry Sauce (92 calories) is about the most satisfying. It is quite a generous portion too. The Chocolate Sponge (113 calories) is also exceedingly low and is very versatile. It can be rolled, cut into layers or cut into pastries. Lady Finger Spongecake Base (40 calories) is great when topped with fresh fruit and a generous serving of Low-Calorie Whipped Cream. Basic Orange & Lemon Spongecake (98 calories) is one of my favorites. It is tart and fruity, and served with a few crushed strawberries and Low-Calorie Whipped Cream...delicious!

There are certain fruit recipes that I want to make note of...Apples Baked in Orange Juice is one of the very best. It can be prepared as an accompaniment to roast chicken, as apple sauce (it is the best), as a topping to ice milk, or sponge cake. Spiced Peaches with Cinnamon & Cloves is also great. Apricots can be substituted. It is a great dessert and a beautiful accompaniment to Chicken and Veal. It is recommended in various recipes.

Baked Bananas is another very delicious recipe. Serve it as dessert or as an accompaniment to Caribbean Chicken. Spiced Compote of Dried & Winter Fruit (98 calories) served warm, is a good choice on a chilly night. Banana Ice Cream (58 calories) is amazing. It is no more than a frozen banana, pureed in a food processor and flavored slightly. Excellent snack, also.

Apple Tart (126 calories) or Strawberry Tart (120 calories) are excellent low-calorie choices for dessert. As are the Cobblers. Basic Fruit Souffle (39 calories) is very light and delicious. A cookie can be added and dessert will still be very low.

Ices are low in calories and are a refreshing finale to a meal. Add a cookie and the calories are still low. If possible, invest in an electric ice cream maker and you will be able to produce ices with excellent texture and in the minimum amount of time.

Many of the cookies are made with oats, oat bran and whole wheat flour. The Brownie is not like its high-caloried cousin. It has half the fat, so don't overbake it or it will be too dry. Also, it is intensely chocolate and you might want to reduce the cocoa by 1 tablespoon.

The Low-Calorie Vanilla Creme Fraiche is a variation of the Creme Fraiche I created way back in 1968...only then, I called it Creme Vanilla. It is still one of the most delectable sauces. Now, it is equally delicious made with low-fat sour cream and half and half. "One" tablespoon of Creme Fraiche (20 calories) will add a good deal of taste and pleasure to a dessert. The accent is on the word "one."

Low-Calorie Whipped Cream (2 calories per tablespoon) is made with cold skim milk and in minutes in a food processor. It is really very pleasant and, flavored with a little vanilla, it does add a little character to dessert. It is so low in calories and so innocent in content, that you can enjoy it as often as you like.

A few dessert beverages to add a little pleasure to dessert. Hot Spiced Apple Cider with Orange & Lemon (50 calories) is nice around the winter holidays. Cappuccino (35 calories) or Café Kahlua (25 calories) deliver a lot of satisfaction and will round out a lovely dinner.

Remember, keep it moderate...It is the overeaters of the world that have given good food a bad reputation.

Orange & Walnut Torte with Orange Glaze

This cake assembles in minutes, yet it tastes as if it took hours to prepare. It is one of the most delicious and flavorful with the rich taste of orange and apple. It is a low cake, so don't think anything went wrong.

2	eggs
3/4	cup sugar
1	cup chopped walnuts
1/4	cup flour
1	teaspoon baking powder

1/2	orange, grated (3 tablespoons fruit, juice and peel)
1	medium apple, peeled and grated

In a food processor, blend together first 5 ingredients for 40 seconds, or until nuts are ground. Add the orange and apple and blend for 15 seconds, or until fruit is finely chopped. Spread batter into a paper-lined 10-inch springform pan and bake at 350-degrees for about 20 to 25 minutes, or until top is browned. Allow to cool in pan. When cool, remove from pan and drizzle top with Orange Glaze. Serves 12.

Orange Glaze:
Stir together 1/4 cup sifted powdered sugar, 1 1/2 teaspoons orange juice and 2 teaspoons grated orange zest until blended.

(About 150 calories per serving)

Walnut Cake with Raspberry & Lemon Glaze

If you love nut cakes, this is a nice one to consider. It will be deliciously moist if you do not overbake it. Apricot spread can be substituted for the raspberry spread.

3/4	cup non-fat milk
2	tablespoons oil
1	egg
1	teaspoon vanilla

1 1/2	cups flour
1/2	cup sugar
3	teaspoons baking powder
1/2	cup chopped walnuts

Beat together first 4 ingredients until blended. Beat in remaining ingredients until blended. Pour batter into a paper-lined 10-inch springform pan and bake at 350-degrees for about 25 minutes, or until top is golden brown. Allow to cool in pan. When cool, remove from pan and spread top with Raspberry Spread and drizzle top with Lemon Glaze. Serves 12.

(Cake-146 calories per serving)

Raspberry Spread:
Heat 3 tablespoons Raspberry Spread (sweetened with fruit juice), until liquefied. (This can be done in 15 seconds in a microwave and facilitates spreading.) Quickly spread over cooled cake. This makes a very thin layer. (Add 7 calories per serving.)

Lemon Glaze:
Stir together 1/4 cup sifted powdered sugar and 1 1/2 teaspoons lemon juice until blended. (Add 10 calories per serving)

(About 163 calories per serving-using Raspberry Spread and Lemon Glaze)

Angel Cake with Fresh Strawberry Sauce

This is perhaps one of the most benign of cakes, very light, very low in calories and delightful with fresh fruit and frozen non-fat yogurt or ice milk. It is a generous portion, as well.

6	egg whites, at room temperature
1/4	cup sugar
3/4	teaspoon cream of tartar
3/4	teaspoon vanilla or lemon juice
1/2	cup flour
1/4	cup sugar

Beat egg whites until foamy. Continue beating, adding sugar, 1 tablespoon at a time until whites are stiff. Beat in cream of tartar and flavoring. Stir together flour and 1/4 cup sugar and gently fold into egg white mixture.

Spread batter evenly into an ungreased 10-inch tube pan and bake at 375-degrees for about 20 minutes, or until top is golden brown. Remove from oven and invert cake until cooled. Serve with a tablespoonful of Fresh Strawberry Sauce or 2 tablespoons softened frozen non-fat strawberry yogurt, or both. Serves 12.

Fresh Strawberry Sauce:

1	cup strawberries
1	teaspoon sugar
2	tablespoons orange juice
2	teaspoons lemon juice

In a blender or food processor, puree strawberries with sugar and juices. Refrigerate until serving time. Yields about 3/4 cup (12 tablespoons) sauce.

To prepare Chocolate Angel Cake:
Reduce flour to 3/8 cup and add 2 tablespoons sifted cocoa. All other instructions remain the same.5

Angel Cake, about 85 calories per serving
Strawberry Sauce, about 7 calories per tablespoon
Frozen Non-fat Yogurt, about 14 calories per 2 tablespoons
Chocolate Angel Cake, about 84 calories per serving

Skinny Chocolate Torte ala Sacher

I have literally exhausted myself, trying to bring you a magnificent chocolate torte that will only contain around 150 calories per serving...and here it is. It's a beauty. The frosting does contain 1/2 ounce of chocolate and 1 teaspoon butter, but drizzled over 12 servings, it only adds 13 calories per serving. This is a divine cake, beautiful for a dinner party, yet easy enough to make at any time.

2	eggs
1	cup walnuts
3/4	cup sugar
2	tablespoons cocoa
1/4	cup flour
1/4	cup unflavored non-fat yogurt
1	teaspoon baking powder
1/2	teaspoon vanilla

In a food processor, blend all the ingredients for about 1 minute, or until the nuts are very finely chopped. Pour batter into a paper-lined 10-inch springform pan and bake at 350-degrees for 30 minutes or until a cake tester, inserted in center, comes out clean. Allow to cool in pan. When cool, spread top with warm Apricot Spread and drizzle Chocolate Glaze on top. Serves 12.

Apricot Spread:
Melt 3 tablespoons Apricot Spread (sweetened with fruit juice) until liquefied.

Chocolate Glaze:
Stir together 1/2 ounce (1 rounded tablespoon) semi-sweet chocolate, melted, and 1 teaspoon melted butter until blended.

(About 156 calories per serving)

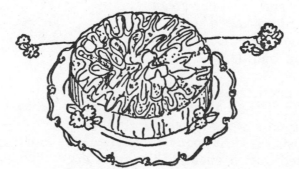

Chocolate Sponge For Buches or Pavés

You will hardly believe that this elegant Chocolate Sponge is so low in calories. It is truly delicious. If you are planning to make a Christmas log (buche), a jelly roll, or a 15-inch 3-layer loaf cake (pavé), this recipe is a good choice. Be certain to beat the eggs for the full amount of time so as to get full volume. The frosting is a slimmed down version of my Sour Cream Frosting, omitting the chocolate and using cocoa. This is not a lot of frosting, but it is very satisfying and the total calories is very low.

4	eggs, at room temperature
2/3	cup sugar
2/3	cup flour
3	tablespoons sifted cocoa
1	teaspoon baking powder

Lightly grease a 10x15-inch jelly roll pan, and line it with wax paper, extending 4-inches extra on the sides. Lightly grease wax paper. Preheat oven to 375-degrees. Wet a dish towel and wring it out until it is just damp.

In the large bowl of an electric mixer, beat eggs on high speed until foamy. Continue beating at high speed, gradually adding the sugar, until eggs have tripled in volume and have thickened, about 6 minutes. Meanwhile, sift together flour, cocoa and baking powder. Gently fold 1/3 flour mixture into stiffly beaten eggs, and repeat with remaining flour. Spread batter evenly into prepared pan and bake for 20 minutes, or until edges slightly pull away from the sides of the pan.

Remove cake from oven and cover with damp dish towel until cool. Invert cake on dish towel, remove wax paper and cut off any dry edges. Cut cake into 3x15-inch layers. Place 1 layer on serving plate and cover with 1/4 cup frosting. Repeat with second layer. Frost top and sides with remaining frosting. Yields 14 servings.

Chocolate Sour Cream Frosting:

1	cup half and half sour cream
1/4	cup sifted powdered sugar
1	tablespoon sifted cocoa
1	teaspoon vanilla

In a bowl, stir together all the ingredients until mixture is blended and sugar is dissolved. If the half and half sour cream has small lumps that you cannot stir out, then sieve it through a strainer.

(Unfrosted cake is about 81 calories per 1-inch serving)
(Frosted cake is about 113 calories per 1-inch serving)

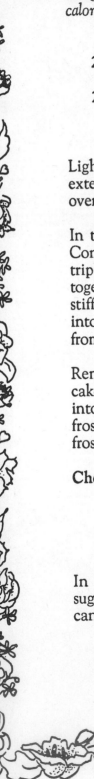

Cinnamon-Marbled Orange Walnut Cake

This lovely coffee cake is truly satisfying with the flavors of cinnamon and orange. The nutty texture adds a little crunch. Leftovers can be sliced thin and toasted.

1/4	cup oil
1/4	cup orange juice
1/2	cup water
3	tablespoons grated orange peel
1/2	cup sugar
2	eggs
1	teaspoon vanilla

1 3/4	cups flour
2 1/2	teaspoons baking powder

1/4	cup chopped walnuts

2	teaspoons cinnamon
1	tablespoon sugar

Beat together first group of ingredients until blended. Combine the next 2 ingredients and add, all at once, beating until blended. Stir in the walnuts. Pour 1/2 the batter into a lightly greased 10-inch tube pan. Combine cinnamon and sugar and sprinkle over the first layer. Spoon the remaining batter evenly over the cinnamon mixture, and spread to even.

Bake at 350-degrees for 35 to 40 minutes, or until a cake tester, inserted in center, comes out clean. Allow to cool in pan. Remove from pan and sprinkle with 1 teaspoon sifted powdered sugar. Serves 12.

(About 166 calories per serving)

Apple Cinnamon Coffee Cake

Another basic cake that can be prepared with any number of fruits...pears, peaches, apricots, cherries. This is a low cake, fruity and not very sweet.

1	egg
1/2	cup sugar
2	tablespoons oil
1 1/4	cups buttermilk
1	teaspoon vanilla

1	cup whole wheat flour
1	cup all-purpose flour
2	teaspoons baking powder

1	apple, peeled, cored and thinly sliced. (Use the slicing side of a 4-sided grater.)
2	tablespoons cinnamon sugar

More →

Apple Cinnamon Coffee Cake (Continued)

Beat together first 5 ingredients until blended. Beat in the next 3 ingredients until blended. Place batter in a lightly oiled 10-inch springform pan and place apples decoratively on top. Sprinkle top with cinnamon sugar.

Bake at 350-degrees for about 35 to 40 minutes, or until a cake tester, inserted in center, comes out clean. Allow to cool in pan. When cool, remove from pan and sprinkle with 1 teaspoon sifted powdered sugar. Serves 12.

(About 149 calories per serving)

Orange & Apple Oatmeal Cake

This benign cake, with oats and whole wheat flour, sparkled with orange and apple, and spicy with cinnamon is a true caloric bargain. It yields 24 generous servings and freezes beautifully. Because this contains a high quantity of oats, you cannot test with a cake tester, so look for the top to be nicely browned.

2	tablespoons oil
2/3	cup sugar
1	cup non-fat buttermilk
1	egg
1/2	orange grated (about 3 tablespoons fruit, juice and peel)
1	medium apple, peeled and grated
1 1/2	cups oats
1	cup whole wheat flour
1/2	cup all-purpose flour
1	teaspoon baking powder
1	teaspoon baking soda
2	teaspoons cinnamon

In the large bowl of an electric mixer, beat together first 4 ingredients until blended. Stir in orange and apple. Stir together the remaining ingredients and add, all at once, beating until blended. Do not overbeat.

Spread batter evenly into a 9x13-inch non-stick baking pan and bake at 350-degrees for 30 minutes, or until top is golden brown. Allow to cool in pan. When cool, drizzle top with Orange Glaze. Serves 24.

Orange Glaze:

1/2	cup sifted powdered sugar
1	tablespoon orange juice
2	teaspoons grated orange zest (orange part of the peel)

Stir together all the ingredients until blended.

(About 95 calories per serving)

Spicy Applesauce Cake

A delightful cake to serve around the winter holidays. This cake is very moist, so don't think anything went wrong. A tablespoon or two of Low-Calorie Whipped Cream is nice. Serve with a cup of spicy, hot cider and who would guess we're counting...

1	egg
1/2	cup sugar
3	tablespoons oil
1 1/4	cups unsweetened applesauce
2	teaspoons vanilla
1 3/4	cups flour
1	teaspoon baking powder
1/2	teaspoon baking soda
2	teaspoons pumpkin pie spice
1	teaspoon cinnamon
1/4	cup dried currants
1/4	cup chopped walnuts

In the large bowl of an electric mixer, beat together first 5 ingredients until blended. Combine the remaining ingredients and add, all at once, beating until nicely blended. Do not overmix. Pour batter into a lightly greased 10-inch tube pan and bake at 350-degrees for 35 to 40 minutes, or until a cake tester, inserted in center, comes out clean. Allow to cool in pan. When cool, remove from pan and sift 1 teaspoon powdered sugar on top. Serves 12.

(About 161 calories per serving.)

Ladyfinger Spongecake Base

This is a thin, delicate spongecake that is an excellent base for fruit, frozen non-fat yogurt or frozen non-fat ice milk. It is exceedingly low in calories (less than an average cookie) and very satisfying. Piled high with 1/2 cup frozen yogurt, which is about (64 calories) and drizzled with 1 tablespoon Low-Calorie Strawberry Sauce (10 calories), no one could feel deprived. And the total for the dessert is a mere 114 calories.

2	egg whites
1/3	cup sifted powdered sugar
1/2	teaspoon vanilla
2	egg yolks
1/4	cup flour

Beat whites until foamy. Slowly add powdered sugar while beating until whites are stiff. Beat in vanilla. Beat in yolks, one at a time, until nicely blended. Fold in the flour. Spread batter into a wax paper-lined 10-inch springform pan and bake at 350-degrees for 10 minutes. Invert onto a serving platter and remove wax paper. Yields 10 servings.

(About 40 calories per serving)

Basic Orange & Lemon Sponge Cake

This is an adaptation of my classic sponge cake. It is an excellent base for fruit or a small amount of lemon or chocolate sauce. With a dollup of non-fat frozen yogurt and a few crushed strawberries, it is pure pleasure. Using the whole wheat flour makes it a little more substantial but still very good. This recipe can be prepared as a 10-inch cake, 10 individual ramekins or 20 muffins. Instructions follow for the different sizes.

4	eggs
1/2	cup sugar
2/3	cup whole wheat flour
1/2	teaspoon baking powder
2	tablespoons grated orange (fruit, juice and peel)
1	tablespoon grated lemon (fruit, juice and peel)
1	teaspoon vanilla

In the large bowl of an electric mixer, beat eggs and sugar at high speed for at least 10 minutes, or until eggs have tripled in volume and are light and frothy. Stir together flour and baking powder and fold it into the egg mixture. Fold in the remaining ingredients.

Spread batter evenly into an ungreased 10-inch springform pan and bake at 350-degrees for about 30 to 35 minutes or until top is browned and a cake tester, inserted in center, comes out clean. Do not overbake. Remove from oven, and allow to cool.

Run a knife along the sides and bottom of the pan and place cake on a lovely serving platter. Serve with 1 pint crushed fresh strawberries and 3 cups non-fat frozen vanilla yogurt or Low-Calorie Whipped Cream. Serves 10.
(About 98 calories per cake serving)
(About 40 calories for strawberries and frozen non-fat yogurt)

To prepare as 10 individual ramekins:
Divide batter between 10 individual ramekins that have been sprayed with vegetable spray. Bake at 350-degrees for 15 minutes, or until tops are browned. While still warm, run a knife along the sides and ease cakes gently from the ramekins. Or serve in the ramekins with crushed fruit and a complimentary non-fat yogurt or Low-Calorie Whipped Cream.

To prepare as 20 muffins:
Divide batter between 20 non-stick muffin cups that have been sprayed with vegetable spray. Bake at 350-degrees for 15 minutes, or until tops are browned. While still warm, run a knife along the sides and ease muffins gently from the pan. Place 2 muffins on a dessert dish and serve as above.

Old-Fashioned Raisin Ginger Cake

Very spicy, aromatic and flavorful, this little gingerbread is just as delicious as its high-calorie cousin. With only 2 tablespoons of oil, it is still moist. This is a low cake, dense and chewy.

2	tablespoons oil
3/4	cup water
1/2	cup brown sugar
2	tablespoons molasses

2	cups flour
1 1/2	teaspoons baking soda
1	teaspoon ground ginger
1	teaspoon cinnamon
1/4	teaspoon ground nutmeg
1/4	cup chopped raisins

In the large bowl of an electric mixer, beat together first 4 ingredients until blended. Combine the remaining ingredients and add, all at once, beating until blended. Do not overmix. Spread batter evenly into a lightly greased 10-inch tube pan and bake at 350-degrees for 30 to 35 minutes, or until a cake tester, inserted in center comes out clean. Allow cake to cool in pan. When cool, drizzle top with Orange Glaze. Serves 12.

Orange Glaze:

1/4	cup sifted powdered sugar
2	teaspoons orange juice
1	teaspoon grated orange peel

Stir together all the ingredients until blended.

(143 calories per serving-with glaze)
(135 calories per serving-without glaze)

Cranberry, Orange & Walnut Cake

This is a nice low-calorie coffee cake to serve during the Winter holidays. It is on the tart side and fruity with orange flavor. The walnuts on top add a little texture. Stir in the cranberries quickly to avoid discoloring the batter.

2	tablespoons oil
1/3	cup orange juice
1/2	cup water
3	tablespoons grated orange peel
1/2	cup sugar
2	eggs
1	teaspoon vanilla

More →

Cranberry Orange & Walnut Cake (Continued)

      2   cups flour
   2 1/2   teaspoons baking powder

      1/2   cup fresh or frozen cranberries, sliced in half
      1/4   cup chopped walnuts

Beat together first group of ingredients until blended. Combine the next 2 ingredients and add, all at once, beating until blended. Quickly stir in the cranberries. Pour the batter into a lightly greased 10-inch tube pan and sprinkle top with walnuts.

Bake at 350-degrees for 40 to 45 minutes, or until a cake tester, inserted in center, comes out clean and top is golden. Allow to cool in pan. Remove from pan and sprinkle with 1 teaspoon sifted powdered sugar. Serves 12.
(About 150 calories per serving)

To make into an Apple Cake:
Substitute 1 large apple, peeled, cored and grated for the cranberries.

To make into a Carrot Cake:
Substitute 1 cup grated carrots for the cranberries.

Peach & Macaroon Crumb Cobbler

Apples can be substituted for the peaches in this recipe. If you enjoy the fruit simply baked, then omit the cookie crumbs. 2 tablespoons coarsely chopped walnuts can be added to the cookie crumbs. It is an addition I recommend, as the taste is heightened far above the calories consumed.

      6   medium-sized peaches, peeled, pitted and thinly-sliced or
               1-pound bag frozen sliced unsweetened peaches, thawed
      1/4   cup orange juice
      2   teaspoons cinnamon sugar

      1/2   cup macaroon cookie crumbs
      2   tablespoons coarsely chopped walnuts (optional)
      1/2   teaspoon ground cinnamon
               dash each of ground nutmeg and ground cloves

In a 10-inch round baking pan or pie pan, lay peaches in a circle. Pour orange juice over the peaches and sprinkle with cinnamon sugar. Bake in a 350-degree oven for 15 minutes.

Meanwhile toss together crumbs (optional walnuts) and spices and sprinkle over the peaches. Return to oven and bake for an additional 15 minutes, or until crumbs are lightly browned and peaches are tender. Serves 6.
(About 102 calories per serving)

Spicy Peach Cobbler with Oat Topping & Vanilla Cream Sauce

4 peaches, washed, pitted and thinly sliced. Do not peel. (1 pound)
4 tablespoons orange juice

1/2 cup quick-cooking oats
4 tablespoons dark brown sugar
1/2 teaspoon cinnamon
4 teaspoons melted butter

In 4 individual ramekins, divide the peaches and drizzle with 1 tablespoon orange juice. Stir together the remaining ingredients and divide mixture over the peaches. Place ramekins on a cookie sheet and bake at 350-degrees for about 20 to 25 minutes or until peaches are soft and top is browned. Serve warm, topped with 2 tablespoons of Vanilla Cream Sauce. Serves 4.
(About 160 calories per serving)

Vanilla Cream Sauce:
You can make a delicious dessert sauce by allowing frozen vanilla non-fat yogurt or vanilla ice milk to partially melt in the refrigerator. Using as little as 2 tablespoons will enrich a dessert. It tastes much like partially whipped cream but with little or no fat. Remove the frozen yogurt or ice milk from the freezer and place in the refrigerator about 10 minutes before serving.

(About 7 calories per tablespoon)

Blueberry & Lemon Cobbler

This is another basic recipe that can be prepared with any number of fruits. Peaches, apricots, apples, pears, plums all work well with the oatmeal topping.

1/3 cup whole wheat flour
1/2 cup quick-cooking oats (not instant oats)
1/4 cup sugar
2 tablespoons melted butter
1 teaspoon vanilla

2 pints blueberries (fresh or frozen)
1/4 cup sugar (optional)
1 tablespoon grated lemon zest
1 tablespoon lemon juice

Stir together first 5 ingredients until mixture is crumbly. Toss together blueberries with sugar (optional), lemon juice and zest and place in a 10-inch round baking pan. Sprinkle top with oat mixture. Bake at 350-degrees for 30 minutes. Serves 8.

(About 129 calories per serving)

Chocolate Cheesecake with Creme Vanilla

All ingredients should be at room temperature to assure a nice creamy texture without lumps. Ricotta cheese does not produce as smooth a cheesecake as cream cheese.

1/4   cup chocolate cookie crumbs

1   carton (15 ounces) low-fat ricotta cheese, at room temperature
1   cup low-fat sour cream
2   eggs
1/2   cup sugar
4   tablespoons sifted cocoa
2   teaspoons vanilla

Spread crumbs evenly into a 10-inch springform pan. Beat together the remaining ingredients until blended and pour evenly over the crumbs. Bake at 350-degrees for 45 minutes. (Center will still be a little soft.) Allow to come to room temperature and then refrigerate for several hours or overnight. Cut into wedges to serve and serve with 2 teaspoons of Creme Vanilla. Serves 12.

(About 150 calories per serving with sauce)
(About 15 calories per 2 teaspoons sauce)
(About 135 calories per serving for cheesecake)

Creme Vanilla:
In a jar with a tight-fitting lid, stir together 1/4 cup low-fat sour cream and 1/4 cup half and half. Allow to stand at room temperature for 1 hour. Stir in 2 teaspoons sugar and 1/2 teaspoon vanilla. Cover jar and refrigerate. Yields 1/2 cup sauce.

Note: To facilitate removing cheesecake from the pan, line the springform pan with parchment paper.

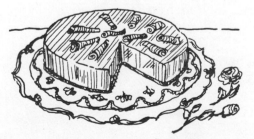

Lemon Cheesecake with Strawberry Sauce

This is a fairly delectable cheesecake, even though it is made with low-fat ingredients. Make certain that all the ingredients are at room temperature so that the cream cheese will beat smoothly. If it is cold, it will form small lumps.

1/4	cup vanilla wafer crumbs
1	pound low-fat cream cheese, at room temperature
2	cups low-fat sour cream
3/4	cup sugar
2	eggs
2	egg whites
4	tablespoons grated lemon (use fruit, juice and peel)
2	teaspoons vanilla

In a 10-inch springform pan, sprinkle crumbs evenly. Beat together the remaining ingredients until nicely blended. Do not overbeat. Pour mixture into prepared pan and bake at 350-degrees for 45 minutes. (Center will be soft.) Allow to come to room temperature and then refrigerate for several hours or overnight. Cut into wedges to serve and serve with 1 tablespoon of Strawberry Sauce on top. Serves 16.

(About 145 calories per serving including sauce)

Strawberry Sauce:
Stir together 1 cup mashed strawberries and 3 tablespoons undiluted frozen orange juice concentrate. Yields 1 1/4 cups sauce.

Note: To facilitate removing cheesecake from the pan, line the springform pan with parchment paper.

Chocolate Marbled Cheesecake

This is a variation of the Lemon Cheesecake yet is totally different in character. It is attractive with large chocolate swirls on top. The almond extract adds a little dimension to the cheesecake and should not be overlooked. As with all cheesecakes, ingredients should be at room temperature to avoid small lumps.

    1/4   cup vanilla or chocolate wafer crumbs

      1   pound low-fat cream cheese, at room temperature
      2   cups low-fat sour cream
    3/4   cup sugar
      2   eggs
      2   egg whites
      2   teaspoons vanilla
      1   teaspoon almond extract

      2   tablespoons sifted cocoa

In a 10-inch springform pan sprinkle cookie crumbs evenly. Beat together the next 7 ingredients until nicely blended. Pour 1/2 the cream cheese mixture over the crumbs. Stir the cocoa into the remaining cream cheese mixture until blended. Drop the chocolate filling by large dollups on top and with a knife swirl it around to marbleize. Bake at 350-degrees for 45 minutes. Allow to cool in pan and then refrigerate for several hours until firm, or overnight. Cut into wedges to serve. Serves 16.

(About 136 calories per serving)

Note: To facilitate removing cheesecake from the pan, line the springform pan with parchment paper.

Basic Brownies

The world would be a very sad place without a brownie once in a while. These are low-calorie with half the sugar and half the fat. Not the devilish brownie, but a compromise. Adding the chocolate chips, adds 6 calories per brownie (and is recommended)...adding the walnuts, adds 7 calories per brownie. Raspberries are fabulous and festive. These are not sweet, so if you are serving them plain, dust the top with a little sifted powdered sugar. Enjoy these once in a while and in moderation.

1/2	cup margarine (1 stick), at room temperature
1/2	cup sugar
2	eggs
2	teaspoons vanilla
1/2	cup all-purpose flour
4	tablespoons cocoa
1/2	teaspoon baking powder

Optional:
1/4	cup chopped walnuts
1/3	cup semi-sweet chocolate chips
1/2	cup fresh raspberries

Beat together margarine and sugar until blended. Beat in eggs and vanilla until blended. Beat in remaining ingredients until blended. Don't overbeat, or they will be too airy. Stir in walnuts or chocolate chips or raspberries (optional). Spread batter into a very lightly oiled 8x8-inch baking pan and bake at 350-degrees for 18 to 20 minutes or until top looks dry. Do not overbake. Divide each side into fifths and cut into 25 squares when cool. Sprinkle with a little sifted powdered sugar to serve.

(About 65 calories per basic brownie)
(Add 7 calories per brownie-using walnuts)
(Add 6 calories per brownie-using chocolate chips)
(Raspberries are a negligible 1 calorie addition)

Oatmeal & Raisin Bar Cookies

This chewy cookie, full of oats and raisins, can be prepared and baked in minutes. It is very good with milk and for snacking after school. It tastes very much like the classic oatmeal raisin cookie, but far less sweet. If you add 2 teaspoons of cinnamon to the batter, the cookie takes on a totally different character.

1/4	cup margarine, softened
1/2	cup sugar
1	egg
2/3	cup low-fat milk
1	teaspoon vanilla

1	cup whole wheat flour
1 1/2	cups oats
2	teaspoons baking powder
1/2	cup chopped raisins

Beat together first group of ingredients until blended. Beat in the remaining ingredients until blended. Spread batter evenly into a non-stick 9x13-inch baking pan and bake at 350-degrees for 15 minutes or until top looks dry and lightly browned. Allow to cool in pan. When cool, cut into 48 bars.

(About 35 calories per cookie)

Oat Bran & Apricot Cookies

These are nice to serve as an after school snack and can substitute for a breakfast bar, made as they are with oat bran, whole wheat flour and yogurt. These are soft and cake-like cookies. Normally, cookies made with 2 cups of flour would use 1 cup of butter or margarine. Using only 1/4 cup margarine saves 1200 calories.

1/4	cup margarine, softened
1/2	cup sugar
1	egg
2/3	cup unflavored non-fat yogurt
1	teaspoon vanilla

1	cup whole wheat flour
1	cup oat bran
2	teaspoons baking powder
1/2	cup chopped apricots (2 ounces)

Beat together first group of ingredients until blended. Beat in the remaining ingredients until blended. Spread batter into a non-stick 9x13-inch baking pan and bake at 350-degrees for 20 minutes. Allow to cool in pan. When cool, cut into 1 1/2-inch squares. Yields 48 cookies.

(About 37 calories per cookie)

Ginger-Spice Apple Cookies

Please don't expect a Toll House cookie for this one. It is definitely not sweet, but fruity and spicy. However, you are saving 1 1/2 cups of sugar, or 1230 calories. An extra 1/2 cup of brown sugar can be added, increasing each cookie by about 10 calories.

3/4	cup butter or margarine, softened
1/2	cup brown sugar
1	egg, beaten
1	teaspoon vanilla
1	apple, peeled, cored and grated
1/2	medium orange, grated, about 3 tablespoons. Use fruit, juice and peel
2	cups whole wheat pastry flour
1	teaspoon baking soda
1	teaspoon cinnamon
1/2	teaspoon ground ginger
1/2	teaspoon ground cloves
2	tablespoons cinnamon sugar

Beat together first 4 ingredients until blended. Stir in apple and orange. Mix together the next 5 ingredients, and beat into butter mixture until blended.

Spread batter evenly into a non-stick 9x13-inch baking pan and sprinkle top evenly with cinnamon sugar. Bake at 350-degrees for 20 minutes or until top is lightly browned. Do not overbake. Cut into 48 bars.

(About 56 calories per cookie)

Spiced Compote of Dried & Winter Fruit

1/2   cup dried apricot halves
1/2   cup soft pitted prunes
2   apples, peeled, cored and sliced
2   pears, peeled, cored and sliced
2   thin slices lemon

3/4   cup orange juice
1   tablespoon sugar
1   teaspoon cinnamon
1/8   teaspoon ground cloves
1/8   teaspoon ground nutmeg

In a 9x12-inch baking pan, lay the fruit. Stir together the remaining ingredients and pour over the fruit. Cover pan with foil and bake in a 350-degree oven for 35 minutes, or until apples are tender. Remove lemon slices and serve warm. Serves 8.

(About 98 calories per serving)

Spiced Peaches with Cinnamon & Cloves

8   peaches, peeled, halved and stoned, about 2 pounds

1/2   cup orange juice
1   teaspoon sugar
1/4   teaspoon cinnamon
1/8   teaspoon ground cloves

2   tablespoons chopped walnuts (optional, but nice)

In a 8x12-inch baking, place peaches cut-side down. Stir together the next 4 ingredients and pour over the peaches. Bake, uncovered in a 350-degree oven for 20 minutes. Sprinkle walnuts on top and bake another 10 minutes. Serve warm or at room temperature. Serves 8

(About 57 calories per serving)

Baked Apples with Orange, Macaroon & Walnut Sauce

In this recipe, the orange juice and honey is baked until it becomes very concentrated and intense in flavor. Crumbs and walnuts can be omitted, but they are a nice addition.

1	cup orange juice
1	tablespoon sugar
1/2	teaspoon cinnamon
1/4	teaspoon nutmeg
1/4	teaspoon ground cloves
6	apples, peeled, cored and sliced (about 4-ounces, each)
6	tablespoons macaroon cookie crumbs (3 cookies)
6	tablespoons finely chopped walnuts

Stir together first 5 ingredients until blended. Place apples in a 10x2-inch round baking pan and place orange juice mixture over all. Bake in a 350-degree oven until apples are tender and most of the juice has evaporated, about 40 minutes. Sprinkle top with cookie crumbs and walnuts and bake an additional 5 minutes. Serve warm (not hot), at room temperature or cold. Serves 8.

(About 120 calories per serving)

Substituting Fruits:
To Bake 6 Pears: Bake at 350-degrees for 20 minutes.
To Bake 10 Peaches: Bake at 350-degrees for 30 minutes.
To Bake 10 Apricots: Bake at 350-degrees for 30 minutes.

Substituting Juice: Instead of the orange juice, 1 cup apricot nectar or 1 cup apple juice can be substituted.

Baked Bananas with Orange & Walnuts

3	bananas, peeled and cut into 1/4-inch slices
1/4	cup orange juice
1	teaspoon finely grated orange zest
2	tablespoons brown sugar
4	sprinkles cinnamon, nutmeg and ground cloves
2	tablespoons finely chopped walnuts

In a 10-inch round porcelain baker, lay banana slices. Drizzle with orange juice and sprinkle with zest, brown sugar and spices. Bake at 400-degrees for 5 minutes, sprinkle with walnuts, and bake for another 5 minutes. Serve warm or at room temperature (not hot or cold). For a really glamorous touch, spoon 1 tablespoon of half and half around each serving. Serves 4.

(About 126 calories per serving-without half and half)
(About 146 calories per serving-with half and half)

Apples Baked in Orange Juice

Of all fruit desserts, this is one of the easiest and the best. It is very satisfying and wonderful served "natural" or as a topping for ice cream or sponge cake. It can be served warm or cold, but not hot. I recommend a porcelain baking dish for this recipe, as it can be baked and served without changing pans.

    6   medium apples, peeled, cored and sliced (4 ounces, each)
    1   cup unsweetened orange juice
    1   tablespoon grated orange peel
    2   teaspoons sugar
    1/2   teaspoon cinnamon
    1/8   teaspoon ground cloves or nutmeg (optional)

In a 10-inch round baking dish, place apples evenly. Stir together the remaining ingredients and pour over the apples. Bake in a 350-degree oven for about 40 minutes. Apples will be tender (not mushy) and orange juice will have thickened to a syrup. Serves 6.
(About 82 calories per serving)

Option 1. To prepare this as an **Apple Cobbler,** sprinkle top with 1/4 cup macaroon cookie crumb (about 2 cookies) after 30 minutes of baking. Continue baking for 10 minutes. **(Add 20 calories per serving.)**

Option 2. To prepare this as **Apple Sauce,** cover baking dish with foil and bake for an additional 20 minutes or until apples are very soft. **(No change in calories.)**

Option 3. To prepare this as a **Danish-Style Apple Cake,** chop the apples and bake them as above. Sprinkle the baked apples with 10 crushed vanilla wafers made into crumbs. Drizzle top with 2 tablespoons melted raspberry spread and 1 tablespoon chopped walnuts. Bake at 350-degrees for 20 minutes. **(Add 52 calories per serving.)**

Option 4. Serve with 1/4 cup of non-fat Vanilla Frozen Yogurt and a sprinkling of cinnamon. **(Add 32 calories per serving.)**

Mocha Parfaits with Kahlua

Purchase the frozen yogurt several hours before serving and store it in the freezer. Many of the yogurt companies now feature non-fat yogurt (which is truly delicious) and usually contains only 12 to 15 calories per ounce.

    3   cups (24 ounces) non-fat vanilla frozen yogurt
    1 1/2   teaspoons instant coffee granules
    4   teaspoons Kahlua liqueur
    4   teaspoons finely chopped toasted almonds (optional)

Just before serving, layer 3/4 cup yogurt and coffee granules in 4 parfait glasses and spoon each top with 1 teaspoon liqueur and 1 teaspoon chopped almonds. If preparing earlier, can be held in freezer for 30 minutes. Serves 6.
(About 77 calories per serving)

Iced Vanilla Glace
with Strawberries Grand Marnier

Strawberries Grand Marnier:
- 1 cup sliced strawberries, pureed and seived
- 1 teaspoon sugar
- 1 teaspoon Grand Marnier
- 1 teaspoon vanilla

Glace:
- 8 egg whites
- 2 tablespoons sugar

Stir together strawberries, sugar, Grand Marnier and vanilla and allow to stand until sugar is dissolved. Meanwhile, in the large bowl of an electric mixer, beat whites until foamy. Slowly add the sugar and continue beating until whites are stiff and glossy, but not dry.
Fold in strawberry mixture.

Divide between 8 paper-lined muffin cups and freeze until firm. Decorate top with a strawberry half and a faint sprinkle of macaroon cookie crumbs. Also delicious flavored with Peach & Triple Sec, or Rum & Raisins or Toasted Almonds. Simply substitute any of the following for the strawberry flavoring. Serves 8.

(About 40 calories per serving)

Substitutions for the Strawberries Grand Marnier:
Peach & Triple Sec: (No change in calories)
- 1 cup sliced peaches, peeled and pureed
- 1 teaspoon sugar
- 1 teaspoon Triple Sec Liqueur

Rum & Raisin: (Add 10 calories per serving)
- 1/4 cup raisins, finely chopped
- 1 teaspoon rum
- 1 teaspoon sugar
- 1 tablespoon orange juice

Toasted Almond: (Add 6 calories per serving)
- 1 ounce chopped toasted almonds (3 tablespoons)
- 1 tablespoon brown sugar
- 1/2 teaspoon almond extract

Basic Berry Granité

Strawberries, raspberries, blackberries all produce a lovely and light refreshing dessert. A granité (sometimes called "granita") is basically an ice made with a simple syrup and different flavorings. Berries are especially nice.

Simple Syrup:
>   2   cups water
>   1/2 cup sugar

Fruit:
>   1   pint strawberries, raspberries, blackberries, (fresh or frozen)
>   mashed and pressed through a sieve to remove seeds
>   1   tablespoon lemon juice

In a saucepan, simmer together water and sugar until sugar is dissolved. Allow to cool. Stir in fruit pulp and lemon juice until blended. Freeze in an ice cream maker according to manufacturer's instructions. Serves 8.

(About 60 calories per serving)

Basic Fruit Juice Ices

Practically any unsweetened juice can be made into an ice for a nutritious and low-calorie dessert. I would suggest you invest in an electric ice cream maker so that you can prepare these lovely, pure ices at any time. Using an ice cream maker produces a smoother ice. The addition of 1 or 2 tablespoons lemon juice or lime juice adds a little character to the ice.

>   2   cups fresh fruit juice (orange, tangerine, pineapple, apricot or any
>   combination)
>   1   tablespoon lemon juice (optional)
>   1   tablespoon sugar (optional)

Stir together fruit juice and optional lemon juice and sugar and allow to stand until sugar is dissolved. Freeze in an ice cream maker according to manufacturer's instructions. Serves 6.

(About 42 calories per serving-using 1 tablespoon sugar)

Espresso Granité with Kahlua

>   2   cups hot espresso coffee (freshly brewed or made from instant
>   granules)
>   2   tablespoons sugar (or a little more to taste)
>   2   tablespoons Kahlua coffee-flavored liqueur
>   1/2 cup low-fat milk

Stir sugar into hot coffee until sugar is dissolved. Stir in remaining ingredients. Place mixture in an ice cream maker and freeze according to the manufacturer's instructions. Serves 4.

(About 64 calories per serving)

Banana Iced Cream

What could be easier than freezing sliced bananas and whipping them up in a food processor to produce a delicious frozen dessert? There are many variations to this theme. You can add a few frozen strawberries to add color and flavor. A few drops of vanilla gives it a totally different air. A teaspoon or 2 of almonds or pecans, finely chopped, are an excellent addition. A little orange peel, cinnamon or nutmeg add interest and excitement.

     2   large bananas, peeled and sliced
    1/4 teaspoon vanilla

Freeze bananas in a plastic freezer bag. (If freezing for more than 2 or 3 days, then brush bananas with a little lemon juice, so that they do not darken.) In a food processor, whip bananas and vanilla until mixture is as smooth as silk. If necessary, add a few drops of non-fat milk to loosen. Serve with a few raspberries or sliced strawberries on top. Serves 4.

(About 58 calories per serving)

Frozen Strawberry Yogurt in Meringue Shells

This is one of the easiest desserts to prepare, as the shells and frozen yogurt can be purchased. It is, also, a beautiful choice for a formal or informal summer dinner. It looks spectacular with its white base, a mountain of frozen pink yogurt and red strawberries, sparkled with liqueur, on the top and sides. The meringue shells can be purchased in most bakeries and can be filled with the yogurt earlier in the afternoon and stored in the freezer. Remove from the freezer 10 minutes before serving, if yogurt is frozen solid. (I would recommend that the frozen yogurt be purchased in the late afternoon to avoid its freezing too firm.) Spoon the fresh strawberries on the top and sides just before serving. See Index for Meringue Shell recipe if you choose to make your own.

    6   meringue shells, about 4-inches in diameter
    3   cups frozen non-fat strawberry yogurt
    1   pint strawberries, sliced (reserve 4 large strawberries for
          decorating the tops)
    2   tablespoons Grand Marnier liqueur
    4   teaspoons chopped toasted almonds (optional)

Pile yogurt into meringue shells in a high swirl, (4 ounces in each), and freeze until serving time. Mix together sliced strawberries and Grand Marnier about 1 hour before serving and store in the refrigerator. To serve, spoon the strawberries over the yogurt and place one whole strawberry on top. A sprinkling of chopped toasted almonds is a nice addition. Serves 6.

(About 150 calories per serving-with almonds)

Note: Fresh peaches and peach yogurt can be substituted for the strawberries.

Basic Lemon Ice

This is a basic recipe for making ice with simple syrup. It is exceedingly low in calories and a refreshing end to a meal but not substantial enough for a satisfying dessert. I would suggest serving fresh fruit or cookies with ices, sherbets or granités. For an especially festive touch, serve a scoop of ice in a stemmed glass and pour 1 or 2 ounces of champagne on top. Serve with small spoons or colorful straws for sipping.

Ices are best made in an ice-cream maker according to the manufacturer's instructions. Ice cream makers produce a smoother more velvety ice. Ices can be prepared in a home freezer, but if left too long, they tend to freeze solid and are difficult to serve.

Simple Syrup:
- 2 cups water
- 1/2 cup sugar

Flavoring:
- 1/2 cup lemon juice
- 1 tablespoon grated lemon zest (the thin yellow outer layer of the peel)

Simmer together water and sugar until sugar is dissolved. Stir in lemon and zest. Refrigerate until ready to prepare. Freeze in an ice-cream maker, following the instructions of the manufacturer. Serves 6.

(About 68 calories per serving)

Orange Ice:
Substitute 1/2 cup undiluted frozen orange juice for the lemon juice and use orange zest.

Lime Ice:
Substitute 1/2 cup lime juice for the lemon juice and use lime zest.

Apple Ice:
Substitute 1/2 cup undiluted frozen apple juice for the lemon juice.

Pineapple Sherbet

- 2 cups unsweetened pineapple juice
- 2 egg whites
- 1 tablespoon sugar

In a plastic bowl, chill pineapple juice in freezer until mushy. Beat egg whites until foamy. Continue beating, adding the sugar slowly, until whites are a stiff meringue. Beat in pineapple juice. (Egg whites will deflate a bit. This is O.K.) Place in an ice cream maker and freeze according to manufacturer's instructions. Serves 6.

(About 58 calories per serving)

Basic Tea Sherbet

Did you know that herbal teas are a lovely flavor base for ices or sherberts. There are infinite varieties and combinations you can use. Orange, lemon, spice or almond flavored teas are especially delicious. The addition of the egg white gives it a creamier texture with very few added calories. The following is basic. Use your own favorite flavors.

- 2 orange cinnamon herbal tea bags
- 2 lemon or almond herbal tea bags
- 2 cups boiling water

- 1/2 cup orange juice
- 1/4 cup lemon juice
- 1 tablespoon sugar

- 1 egg white
- 1 teaspoon sugar

In a bowl, stir together tea bags and water and allow to steep for 5 minutes. Discard tea bags and stir in juices and sugar, stirring until sugar is dissolved. Place mixture in an ice-cream maker and start to freeze according to manufacturer's instructions.

Meanwhile beat the egg white with the 1 teaspoon of sugar until it is stiff, but not dry. Stir beaten egg white into the tea mixture after about 10 minutes of churning. Continue freezing according to manufacturer's instructions. Serves 6.

(About 24 calories per serving)

Low-Calorie Pumpkin Orange Spice Mousse

At about 70 calories, a small cookie may be added and total dessert calories will still remain low.

1/2	cup orange juice
1 1/3	envelopes unflavored gelatin (1 tablespoon plus 1 teaspoon)
1	teaspoon pumpkin pie spice
3	tablespoons sugar
1	cup canned pumpkin (pureed)
1	cup unflavored non-fat yogurt
4	tablespoons grated orange (use fruit, juice and peel)
2	teaspoons vanilla

In a metal measuring cup, soften gelatin in orange juice. Place metal cup in a larger pan with simmering water, and stir until gelatin is totally dissolved. (Little dots of gelatin will no longer appear on the spoon.) Stir in pumpkin pie spice and sugar, and stir until sugar is dissolved.

In a bowl, stir together the remaining ingredients until blended. Stir in the dissolved gelatin until blended. Divide mixture between 6 lovely stemmed glasses and refrigerate until firm. Serve with sprinkling (1 teaspoon) of macaroon cookie crumbs on top (optional). Serves 6.

(About 71 calories per serving)

Oatmeal & Raisin Cookies

While these are not markedly low in calories, they are made with oats, wheat germ and whole wheat flour, with very little fat or sugar.

1/4	cup softened margarine
1/3	cup dark brown sugar
1	egg
1	teaspoon vanilla
3/4	cup rolled oats
1/3	cup wheat germ
1/3	cup whole wheat flour
1/2	teaspoon baking powder
1/3	cup raisins

In the large bowl of an electric mixer, beat together first 4 ingredients until nicely blended. Add the remaining ingredients and beat until blended. Drop batter (it will be very thick and crumbly) by the heaping teaspoon onto a non-stick baking pan, and bake at 350-degrees for about 12 minutes or until tops are just beginning to take on color. Remove from pan and cool on brown paper. Yields 24 cookies.

(About 58 calories per cookie)

Peach & Strawberry Vanilla Rum Mousse

If you prepare this dessert from frozen unsweetened fruit, then it must be defrosted and drained. While I recommend the frozen peaches, be certain to get good quality frozen strawberries. (Frozen strawberries are sometimes too mushy for my taste.) Raspberries can be substituted for the strawberries.

1 1/3	envelopes unflavored gelatin (1 tablespoon plus 1 teaspoon)
1/2	cup water
3	tablespoons sugar
2	tablespoons rum
1	cup skim milk

3	egg whites
2	tablespoons sugar
1	teaspoon vanilla

3/4	cup sliced fresh strawberries
3/4	cup chopped fresh peaches, pitted and peeled
6	teaspoons macaroon cookie crumbs

In a saucepan, stir together first 4 ingredients until gelatin is softened. Cook mixture, over very low heat, until gelatin and sugar are dissolved. Stir in milk and refrigerate for 20 minutes. (Do not allow mousse to gel. It should look no firmer than unbeaten egg whites.)

Meanwhile, in the large bowl of an electric mixer, beat egg whites until foamy. Slowly add the sugar, while still beating, until whites are stiff, but not dry. Beat in the vanilla. Beat in the gelatin mixture, on very low speed, until blended. (This will deflate the egg whites a little. This is O.K. as you want the mousse to have a little character and not be light as air.)

Layer mousse and fruit into 6 lovely stemmed glasses and refrigerate until firm. Decorate tops with cookie crumbs and additional strawberry halves. Serves 6.

(About 101 calories per serving)

Low-Calorie Vanilla Creme Fraiche

1/2	cup sour half and half cream
1/2	cup half and half cream
1/2	teaspoon vanilla
2	teaspoons sugar

In a jar, stir together all the ingredients, and allow to stand at room temperature for 4 hours. Cover jar and refrigerate. Spoon as a topping on cakes, pies, puddings or ice cream. Yields 1 cup.

(About 22 calories per tablespoon)

Crisp Cookie Crust for Fruit Tarts

This is a virtuous crust, a bit on the crisp side, but with only 4 tablespoons of margarine it can be considered fabulous. The dough spreads easily with the fingertips. It is a thin and lovely base for fresh or cooked fruits.

- 1 cup flour
- 1 tablespoon sugar
- 4 tablespoons margarine
- 2 teaspoons grated lemon peel

- 1 egg
- 2 teaspoons water

In the bowl of a food processor, blend first 4 ingredients until the margarine is evenly distributed. Beat together egg and water until blended, add all at once, and process mixture for 4 or 5 pulses or until egg is distributed and mixture is crumbly. Do not overprocess or crust will toughen up.

Press dough on the bottom and a little up the sides of a greased 10-inch tart pan with a removable bottom. Bake at 350-degrees for 20 minutes, or until crust is lightly browned. Serves 10.

(About 92 calories per serving)

Flaky Crust

This little gem is as tasty and flaky as the high-caloried cousin. It assembles in a minute and is easy to handle. It can be used for sweet pies or savory quiches.

- 1/4 cup oil
- 1/4 cup water
- 1 cup flour
- pinch of salt (optional)

In a large bowl, place oil and water. Stir in flour (and optional salt) and lightly stir until flour is incorporated. Dough is soft but not sticky. Pat dough evenly on the bottom and 1/2-inch up the sides of an ungreased 10-inch springform pan. Bake at 350-degrees for 20 minutes or until very lightly browned. Crust will serve 10.

(About 90 calories per serving)

Suggested uses:
1. Brush crust with 4 tablespoons melted no-sugar apricot spread, top with 1/2-pound apricots or peaches, sliced. Brush fruit with 4 tablespoons melted apricot spread. **(Add 22 calories per serving.)**

2. Brush crust as above, but use melted no-sugar strawberry spread, top with 1 pint sliced strawberries. Brush fruit with melted strawberry spread. **(Add 22 calories per serving.)**

Strawberry Tart
(Method for Fresh Fruit Tart)

This very low-calorie tart will surprise you as it looks and tastes just as good as its roly poly cousin. It can be made with any number of fresh fruits...peaches, apricots, nectarines, raspberries. Use a complimentary fruit spread to glaze.

1   10-inch Crisp Cookie Crust, baked
4   tablespoons strawberry fruit spread, heated until liquefied, for glazing
2   pints fresh strawberries, stemmed and sliced

Baste bottom of crust with 1/2 the fruit spread and arrange sliced strawberries attractively on top. Brush strawberries with remaining fruit spread. Serves 10.

(About 120 calories per serving)

Apple Tart
(Method for Cooked Fruit Tart)

This method is for fruit that will be cooked in the crust. Pre-bake the crust for 15 minutes, or until it is just beginning to take on color and then fill with fruit. Bake for 20 to 30 minutes or until fruit is tender. Pears can be substituted for the apples.

1   10-inch Crisp Cookie Crust (baked for only 15 minutes)
4   medium apples, peeled, cored and thinly sliced
2   tablespoons cinnamon sugar
1   tablespoon grated orange peel
1   teaspoon flour

Bake crust for 15 minutes. Toss together apples, cinnamon sugar, orange peel and flour until blended and arrange apple mixture attractively over the crust. Bake at 350-degrees for 30 minutes.   Serves 10.
(About 126 calories per serving)

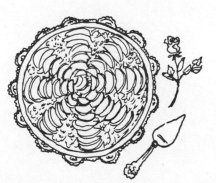

Basic Fruit Souffle

If you are looking for a dessert that is exceedingly low in calories and is attractive and festive, this is a good one to consider. It is glorious when taken from the oven all puffed and flecked with brown. At only 39 calories per serving, a cookie is a nice accompaniment and the total will still be under 100.

1	cup pureed stewed fruit, (peaches, apricots, apples or pears) about 1/2 pound, fresh or canned*
1	teaspoon grated lemon zest
2	teaspoons lemon juice
1	teaspoon cornstarch, sifted
4	egg whites
1/4	teaspoon cream of tartar
2	tablespoons sugar

In a bowl, stir together first 4 ingredients. Beat egg whites until foamy. Beat in cream of tartar. Gradually beat in the sugar and continue beating at high speed until whites hold stiff peaks. Place a dollup of beaten whites into fruit mixture to lighten it and then fold in the remaining whites.

Divide mixture between 6 individual ramekins and bake at 350-degrees for 20 minutes or until puffed and golden. Serve at once with 1 tablespoon or 2 of crushed strawberries or partially melted ice milk as a sauce. Serves 6.
(About 39 calories per serving)

*To stew fruit:
If you are using canned fruits, (apricots, peaches, apples, pears) you only need to drain and puree them in a food processor.

If you are using fresh fruit, peel, core and thinly slice it. Cook it in a covered saucepan with 1/4 cup orange juice and a sprinkling of cinnamon until it is tender, about 20 minutes. Drain and puree in a food processor.

Low-Calorie Whipped Cream

Don't think for a minute that this is the same as the roly-poly cream. However, it is tasty and satisfying and does give dessert a festive air. It has many uses...for mousses, molds and lightening sauces. Originally, it was made in an immersion blender, but I discovered that the food processor works exceedingly well. Hard to imagine that non-fat milk can look sinful, but it does. It requires no special, delicate handling. Use only non-fat milk, (low-fat milk will not whip), straight from the refrigerator (no need to partially freeze) and whip it up. Flavor it with a bit of sugar and a dash of vanilla...and Voila!...virtuous whipped cream. It does not hold for more than about 5 to 10 minutes, so it must be made just before serving. Uses for this versatile cream follows.

    1/2   cup cold non-fat milk

    1/2   teaspoon sugar
    1/4   teaspoon vanilla

In a food processor, with the steel blade, beat milk until it is light and foamy. Beat in sugar and vanilla. This will yield over 1 1/2 cups whipped topping.

(About 2 calories per tablespoon)

Uses:
1. Spoon over cakes, puddings, ice cream and other desserts as you would whipped cream.
2. Lighten sauces such as Bearnaise or Hollandaise.
3. Serve with stewed fruits.

No Sugar Hot Chocolate Sauce

In my numerous experiments to heighten taste and lower calories and cholesterol, this thick yummy sauce is one of the most pleasant discoveries. It is a great sauce to serve over non-fat frozen yogurt, spongecake, or iced milk. Please don't think it will replace a hot fudge sauce, but it is surprisingly delicious and very satisfying. At a very low 14 calories per teaspoon, with no fat, no cholesterol and NO sugar, it is a real treat. A dessert can become very extravagant with the addition of only 2 teaspoons of sauce. Any fruity spread, made with fruit juice, can be used. The ones I found best were seedless red raspberry and seedless black raspberry. Apricot was also quite good. The principle is simple. Fruit made with juice sweetens the cocoa which holds the dominant taste. The sauce has overtones of the fruity spread used, but its taste is predominantly chocolate.

    1/2   cup seedless red raspberry fruit spread (made with fruit juice)
    1   tablespoon sifted cocoa

Stir together both ingredients. Heat in the microwave for 1/2 minute or in a saucepan, over low heat, until fruit is very soft. Stir once again. Spoon warm sauce over desserts as noted above. Yields 24 teaspoons sauce.

(About 14 calories per teaspoon)

Low-Calorie Devonshire Cream

Spread this on scones, and serve with fresh sliced strawberries and a faint sprinkling of chopped pecans. Truly delicious.

4	ounces Neufchatel cheese (low-fat cream cheese) softened
1/2	cup half and half sour cream
1	teaspoon sugar
1/4	teaspoon vanilla

Beat cream cheese until fluffy. Beat in remaining ingredients until blended. Place mixture in a bowl, cover with plastic wrap, and allow to stand at room temperature for 4 hours. Store in the refrigerator. Yields 1 cup.
(About 21 calories per tablespoon)

Fresh Apple & Cinnamon Sauce

One could never guess that this sauce is so low in calories. It is flavored with fresh fruit and juice. However, the taste relies heavily on the spices. Serve over ice milk, pancakes, French toast or sponge cake.

1	apple, peeled, cored and grated
1	teaspoon butter or margarine
1	cup unsweetened apple juice
1	cup fresh orange juice
2	tablespoons cornstarch
1	tablespoon sugar or honey
1/2	teaspoon cinnamon
1/8	teaspoon powdered cloves
1/8	teaspoon ground nutmeg

In a saucepan, saute apple in butter until softened. Stir together juices and cornstarch until blended. Add to apple mixture with the remaining ingredients and simmer mixture, stirring, until sauce is slightly thickened, about 10 minutes. Place in a jar with a tight-fitting lid and store in the refrigerator. Yields about 2 1/2 cups sauce.
(About 10 calories per tablespoon)

Chocolate Sauce

When you are looking for an innocent sauce to spoon over pound cake, angel cake or frozen ice milk, this is a nice sauce to consider. Considering it is made with non-fat yogurt, sweetened with a little sugar and flavored with cocoa and vanilla, it is just about as innocent as you could find.

> **1** cup non-fat unflavored yogurt
> **2** tablespoons sugar
> **1** tablespoon sifted cocoa
> **1** teaspoon vanilla

Stir together all the ingredients until mixture is blended and sugar is dissolved. Yields about 18 tablespoons.

(About 12 calories per tablespoon)

Meringue Shells

While these are available at some bakeries, I am including the recipe in the event they are not sold in you're bakery or market. The shells are attractive, filled with frozen strawberry yogurt and drizzled with crushed or sliced strawberries. Chocolate frozen yogurt, a drizzle of chocolate sauce and a sprinkle of toasted sliced almonds is also beautiful. Meringue shells are basically not baked but dried in the oven. Don't allow them to brown. And, also, very important, as they are brittle, do not allow them to touch when baking or they will crack.

> **3** egg whites, at room temperature
> **3/4** cup sugar

In the large bowl of an electric mixer, at medium speed, beat whites until they are foamy. Start adding the sugar, a tablespoon at a time and increase speed to high. Keep beating while adding the sugar slowly, until meringue is stiff and shiny. Line a cookie sheet with parchment paper and drop meringue by the heaping tablespoon onto the paper. Do not allow shells to touch.

With the back of a spoon, indent the center and build up the sides to form shells. Bake at 225-degrees for 1 hour, turn oven off and allow meringues to dry for several hours in the oven. Shells should not brown. Yields 12 shells.

(About 50 calories per shell)

To Make Meringue Kisses:
Follow instructions as above, but drop meringue by the teaspoonful onto parchment-lined pan. Yields 48 kisses.

(About 12 calories per kiss)

Hot Spiced Apple Cider with Orange & Lemon

1	quart apple cider
1/2	cup orange juice, plus strip of peel from 1/4 orange
2	tablespoons lemon juice, plus strip of peel from 1/8 lemon
1	tablespoon sugar
2	sticks cinnamon, broken into 1-inch pieces
1	teaspoon whole cloves
1/4	teaspoon ground nutmeg

In a large enamel pot, (not metal), heat together all the ingredients for 15 minutes. Do not allow to boil. Strain and serve hot. Yields 10 servings.

(About 50 calories per 3 1/2 ounce serving)

Cappuccino

3 cups espresso, freshly brewed or made from instant coffee, and sweetened with 2 teaspoons sugar. (Decaffeinated espresso coffee can be found in most markets.)

4 teaspoons Creme de Cacao liqueur

1/2 cup cold non-fat milk, whipped in a processor until thick sprinkling of cinnamon and sifted cocoa

Divide hot coffee between 4 espresso glasses. Float 1 teaspoon of liqueur over each and top with whipped non-fat milk and a sprinkling of cinnamon and cocoa. True, cappuccino is made with foamy hot milk, but whipped non-fat milk will not chill it markedly and it is easily made without special equipment. Serves 4.

(About 35 calories per serving)

Note: To whip cold non-fat milk, place milk in blender or food processor and whip until thick. See Low-Calorie Whipped Cream for other uses.

Café Kahlua

2	teaspoons sugar
4	teaspoons Kahlua liqueur
3	cups strongly brewed hot coffee

Place 1/2 teaspoon sugar and 1 teaspoon Kahlua into 4 coffee cups. Pour 3/4 cup coffee into each cup and serve at once. Yields 4 servings.

(About 25 calories per serving)

Calorie Chart

Alcohol	1 1/2 oz	95
	1 T	32
	1 t	11
Almonds	1 cup	777
Apple	4 oz	60
Apple Juice	1 cup	117
	6 oz	87
Applesauce, unsweetened	1 cup	100
Apricots, dried	2 oz	135
Apricot, fresh	1 med	18
	3 med	55
Artichokes		
marinated	6 oz	175
drained		75
frozen	10 oz	120
Asparagus		
fresh	1 lb	66
frozen	10 oz	60
Baking Powder	1 t	4
Calumet	1 t	2
Banana	1 med	101
	1 small	81
BBQ Sauce	1 T	10
Beans		
Canellini	15 oz can	340
Garbanzo	1 cup	220
	3/4 cup	165
	1 lb can	385
Great Northern	15 oz can	340
Green, fresh	1 lb	128
Kidney, red	1 lb can	385
Lima, frozen	10 oz	390
Beef Broth, canned	1 cup	16
from Stock Base		
(makes 1 cup)	1 t	8
Beef		
Chuck	1 lb	993
Trimmed of Separable fat	1 lb	717
Round	2.5 oz	135
	1 lb.	864
Sirloin steak	2.5 oz	150
	1 lb	960
Spencer steak	2 oz	130
Beer & Ale	12 oz	148
	1/2 cup	50
Blueberries	1 cup	80
Bran		
All-Bran Cereal	1/2 cup	70
	1 cup	140
Millers Bran Flakes	1 T	17
	1 cup	272
Brandy, Cognac	1 1/2 oz	105
	1 T	35

Bread Crumbs, dry	1/2 cup	211
	1 cup	422
	1/3 cup	141
	2 T	53
Bread Crumbs (fresh)	1/2 cup	80
	1/3 cup	70
	1/4 cup	40
	1 T	10
	1 t	3
Bread, French	1 oz	80
Bread, Fresh	1 oz slice	80
Broccoli, spears or chopped		
raw	1 lb	69
frozen	1 pkg-10oz	91
Brussel Sprouts, trimmed		
raw	1 lb	204
frozen	10 oz	138
Bulgur	1 cup	600
Butter	1 T	100
	1 t	33
Buttermilk	1 cup	100
Skim Buttermilk	1 cup	88
Cabbage		
Red	1 lb jar	240
raw	1 lb	111
White, raw	1 lb	86
Carrots, raw	1 lb	156
	1 medium	10
frozen	10 oz	129
Cauliflower, raw	1 lb	49
frozen	10 oz	84
Celery	1 lb	58
	1 lrg. stalk	7
Chick Peas (Cici Peas)	1/2 cup	110
Chicken Broth		
canned	1 cup	30
homemade	1 cup	4
seasoned stock base		
(makes 1 cup)	1 t	8
bouillon (makes 1 cup)	1 cube	7
Chicken , Cooked	1/2 cup	120
	4 oz	154
Chicken, Raw		
Breast	4 oz	193
Fryer	2 1/2 lb	805
Chiles	1 oz	6
	4 oz	24
	7 oz	42
Chili Powder	1 t	10
Chive	1 T	1
Chocolate	1 oz	145
Choc. Chips	1 cup(6oz)	870
	1 heap.T	73

Calorie Chart

Cinnamon	1 t	5
Clam Broth	1/2 cup	15
Clams, Chopped	4 oz	60
	7 oz	105
Cocoa	1 T	14
Cognac	1 T	35
Cornstarch	1 t	10
Cottage Cheese, Non-Fat	1 cup	140
	1/2 cup	70
	1/4 cup	35
	1 T	9
Cous Cous	1 oz	100
Cracker Crumbs		
Ritz Cracker	1	17
Ritz Crackers	4	68
Cracker Crumbs	1 cup	366
	1/4 cup	92
Soda Cracker	1 cup	307
Cracker Meal	1 cup	400
	1/4 cup	100
	1 T	25
Cranberries	1/2 cup	22
Cream 1/2 & 1/2	1 oz	40
	1 T	20
	1 t	3+
Cream, Sour, Lo-fat (also known as Sour Half & Half)	1 oz	40
	1 t	3+
Cream Cheese (Lo-Fat)	1 oz	74
Creme Fraiche (Low Cal)	1 T	20
Crouton	1/2 cup	65
Cucumbers	8 oz	30
Currants	1/4 cup	100
	1/2 cup	200
	2 T	50
Dates, Chopped	1/2 cup	235
Egg, Whole, Large	1	80
White, large	1	17
Yolk, large	1	60
Eggplant	1 lb	86
	3/4 lb	69
	1/4 lb	23
Feta Cheese	1 oz	76
Fish & Shellfish		
Halibut	1 lb	336
Lobster	1 lb	430
Scallop	1 lb	368
Sea Bass	1 lb	428
Shrimp	1 lb	400
Snapper	1 lb	420
Sole	1 lb	360
Tuna	1 lb	576

Flour, Spooned (not packed)		
White	1 cup	400
	1/2 cup	200
	1/4 cup	100
	1 T	28
Whole Wheat	1 cup	392
	1/4 cup	98
Fruit Spread	1 t	14
	1 T	42
Garlic	1 clove	4
Gelatin, Knox	1 pk.	25
Grand Marnier Liqueur	1 T	50
	1 t	17
	1 oz	100
Green Onions	1 cup	44
	1/2 cup	22
	1/4 cup	11
Honey	1 T	62
	1/4 cup	247
	1/2 cup	494
Horseradish	1 t	3
Ketchup	1 T	17
Lamb Leg, lean	1 lb	1007
Trimmed of Separable Fat	1 lb	830
Leeks	4 oz	30
Lemon juice	1 T	4
Lentils	1 cup	649
	1/2 cup	325
	1/2 lb	771
Lettuce, chopped	1 cup	8
Lime juice	1 T	4
Liqueur	2 T	95
Mayonnaise Lo-Calorie	1 T	40
Merinque Shell	1 (4 in.)	63
homemade	1 (4 in.)	53
Milk, Dry	1 cup	436
	1/4 cup	109
Milk, NonFat	1 cup	85
Low Fat	1 cup	120
Regular	1 cup	150
Molasses	1 T	40
	1/4 cup	160
	1/2 cup	320
Mozzarella Cheese	1 oz	90
Mushrooms	1/2 lb	62
Mustard, Dijon	1 t	6
Mustard	1 T	15

Calorie Chart

Noodles		
Dry, any shape	1 oz	110
Linguini	1 lb	1660
Vermicelli	8 oz	880
Oatmeal	1 cup	280
Oil	1T	124
	1 t	41
Oil, Olive	1T	119
Olives, black, sliced	1/2 cup	26
Onions		
raw, yellow	1 lb	132
pearl	1 lb	176
Orange	1	64
Orange juice		
California	1 cup	120
Florida	1 cup	100
Papaya 1/2	1/2 lb	60
Parmesan cheese,grated	1 cup	340
	1/2 cup	170
	1/4 cup	85
	1/3 cup	113
	2T	41
	1T	20
	1 t	7
Parsley	1T	1
Peas (frozen)	10 oz	207
Peaches (4 to a lb)	1 lb	150
Peanuts	1/4 cup	210
	2T	105
	1T	53
	1 t	18
Peanuts,chopped	1/4 cup	202
Pears	1 lb	250
Pecans, chopped	1T	48
Pepper, Bell		
Green	1 med. 4oz	20
Red	1 med. 4oz	20
Pimientos, Jar	2 oz	20
	8 oz	80
Pineapple Juice,unswt.	6 oz	100
Pine nuts	1 oz	156
Plum Jam	1T	53
Pork Loin,		
Boneless, trimmed of separable fat & skin	1 lb	1250
Raw with bone, trimmed of separable fat	1 lb	495
Potatoes, raw	1 lb	360
canned	1 lb	180
Prunes	2 oz	140
Pumpkin, puree	1/2 cup	35
	1 cup	70

Raisins, packed	1/2 cup	237
	1T	30
	1/4 cup	119
Raspberries, Red	1 cup	70
Relish	1T	23
Rice		
brown long grain	1 cup	666
white long grain	1 cup	666
	1/2 cup	333
	1/4 cup	166
Ricotta cheese	1 oz	40
	1/4 cup	80
	1 cup	320
Rock Cornish Hen	l lb	768
(1 lb. yields 8 oz.)		
	1/2 lb	354
Rum	1T	32
Sauce,		
BBQ	1T	10
Soy, Low Sodium	1T	9
Teriyaki	1T	17
Sesame seeds	1T	47
	1 t	16
Shallots	1 med.	5
Snow Peas	1 lb	228
Spinach	1 lb	85
Spinach, Frozen	10 oz	68
	10 oz drain.	51
Strawberries	1 cup	55
Stuffing Mix	1/2 cup	110
Sugar		
brown	1T	48
packed	1 cup	791
unpacked	1 cup	541
granulated, white	1 t	15
	1T	46
	1 cup	750
	1/3 cup	250
	1/2 cup	375
Powdered, sifted	1T	31
	1 cup	366
	1/3 cup	122
	1/4 cup	91
Sweet Potato	4 oz	155
Tea, Herbal	1 bag	2
Tofu	4 oz	82
Tomato	1 medium	25
	1 lb	100
Tomato Juice	1 cup	40
Tomato Paste	1 cup	215
	6 oz	139
	1/2 cup	110
	1/4 cup	55
	1/3 cup	67
	1T	15

Calorie Chart

Tomato puree	1 cup	100		Wheat germ	1 T	28
Tomato Sauce	1 cup	75			1/2 cup	224
	1/4 cup	18			1 cup	448
	4 T	18			1/3 cup	150
	2 T	9				
Tomato, Sun-dried	1	25		Wine		
Tomato, Stewed	1 cup	50		red	1 cup	192
	2 cups	100			1 oz	25
	2 1/2 cups	125			1 T	12
Tortilla, corn	1 oz	76			3 1/2 oz	80
				white	1 cup	176
Turkey, white meat, raw	1 lb	800			1/2 cup	88
					1/3 cup	59
Vanilla	1 t	10			1/4 cup	44
Veal					1 T	11
leg, boneless	1 lb	821			3 1/2 oz	75
extra lean, ground	1 lb	785				
shank, with bone	1 lb	368		Yams	1 lb	394
Vegetables, mixed				Yeast	1 T	20
Broccoli, Carrots,					1 pkg-1/4 oz	20
Cauliflower	1 lb	88		Yogurt		
				nonfat	1 cup	110
Walnuts (1 cup=4 ounces)					1/2 cup	55
	1/2 cup	350			1/4 cup	28
	1/4 cup	175		non-fat, frozen	1 oz	14
	1 T	44				
Waterchestnuts	4 oz	90		Zucchini	1 lb	73

Calorie Values

Calorie values are not strictly uniform in the different publications nor in data submitted by the manufacturer. When small differences occurred, either an average or higher value was used. When serving-size varied, every attempt was made to give calorie value for the different numbers served, rather than the lower number alone. Where sauces or ingredients were optional, calories were noted with and without the option. Manufacturer's computations for similar products varied. Every care was taken to present the values as accurately as possible.

The preceding values were computed from the following sources:

1. Adams, Catherine F., "Nutritive Value of American Foods in Common Units", Agriculture Handbook No. 456, United States Department of Agriculture, Agricultural Research Service, Washington D.C., November 1975.
2. Gebhart, Susan E. & Matthews, Ruth H., "Nutritive Value of Foods", Home and Garden Bulletin Number 72, Human Nutrition Information Service, United States Department of Agriculture, Washington, D. C., Revised 1981.
3. Kraus, Barbara, "Calories and Carbohydrates", Sixth Revised Edition, New American Library, New York, 1985.
4. Nutrition Information submitted by the Manufacturer on the Label of the Product.

BASICS 35-42
- Basic Chicken Broth, 37
- Extra-Rich Chicken Broth, 37
- Fresh Strawberry Sauce, 42
- Hollandaise with Basil, 39
- Hollandaise with Chives, 39
- Hollandaise with Dill, 39
- Horseradish Sauce for Roast Beef, 40
- Light Mayonnaise, 41
- Low-Cal Fresh Strawberry Jam, 42
- Low-Calorie Béarnaise Sauce, 40
- Low-Calorie Cheese & Chive Spread, 38
- Low-Calorie Hollandaise Sauce, 39
- Low-Calorie Mayonnaise-Like Spread, 38
- Low-Calorie Sauce with Dill & Chives, 41
- Low-Calorie Sour Cream, 38
- Mayonnaise-Hollandaise & Chive Sauce, 41
- Seasoned Flour for Chicken & Fish, 36
- Sun-Dried Tomatoes, 36

BREADS & MUFFINS 43-56
Biscuits
- Hardy Whole Wheat with Chives, 56
- Whole Wheat Buttermilk with Poppy Seeds, 56
Breads
- Basic Non-Fat Whole Wheat Yeast, 54
- Basic Whole Wheat Quick, 55
- Crispettes of Cheese, 85
- Flatbread with Caraway, 53 with Garlic & Rosemary, 53
- Focaccio-Italian Flatbread with Red Peppers, 51
- Greek Sesame Flatbread with Lemon, Onions, 52
- Italian Croustades with Tomatoes, Chives & Cheese, 83
- Italian Flatbread with Onions & Cheese, 53
- Spicy Apricot & Carrot, 50
French Toast, Oven-Baked, 55
Muffins
- Apple & Orange Whole Wheat, 49

- Bran & Oatmeal Date Nut, 46
- Butter-Less Egg-Less Whole Wheat with Raisins, 45
- Buttermilk Oat Bran with Orange & Bananas, 47
- Buttermilk Orange Bran with Raisins & Walnuts, 48
- Cinnamon Cranberry & Orange, 47
- Low-Cal Cinnamon Orange Bran, 49
- Oat Bran & Carrot, 44
- Spicy Orange Bran & Oatmeal, 46
- Zucchini Oatmeal, 44

CASSEROLES 57-72
- Big Chile Chicken Relleno, 63
- Cabbage Rolls in Sweet Sour Tomato Sauce, 65
- Cauliflower with Potatoes & Tomatoes, 67
- Cheese Blintzes, 72
- Chili Beef with Red Beans, 59
- Crustless Quiche with Eggplant, & Cheese, 66
- Crustless Tart with Tomatoes & Goat Cheese, 62
- Eggplant Frittata with Onions & Cheese, 60
- Eggplant Lasagna with Tomatoes & Ricotta, 58
- Eggplant Stuffed with Ricotta, 70
- Fresh Vegetable Pizza, 69
- Frittata with Artichoke & Red Peppers, 62
- Greek Omelet with Tomatoes, Feta, 71
- High Protein Cottage Cheese Pancakes, 71
- Jambalaya Creole, 68
- Light Crepes for Cheese Blintzes, 72
- Old-Fashioned Stuffed Peppers, 64
- Omelet with Spinach & Cheese, 72
- Onion-Flavored Baby Baked Potatoes, 71
- Paella Valencia, 67
- Royal Artichoke & Spinach, 60
- Spinach Frittata with Cheese & Onions, 66

- Tomatoes Stuffed with Turkey, 61
- Vegetable Paella with Artichokes & Yellow Rice, 69

CREPES
- Cheese Blintzes, 72
- Light Crepes for Cheese Blintzes, 72

DESSERTS 209-244
Beverages
- Café Kahlua, 244
- Cappuccino, 244
- Hot Spiced Apple Cider, 244
Cakes & Tortes,
- Angel with Strawberry, 212
- Apple, Cinnamon, Coffee, 215
- Basic Orange & Lemon Sponge, 218
- Cinnamon-Marbled Orange Walnut, 215
- Chocolate Sponge for Jelly-Rolls, 214
- Cranberry, Orange, Walnut, 219
- Lady Finger Sponge Base, 217
- Old-Fashioned Raisin Ginger, 219
- Orange & Apple Oatmeal, 216
- Orange, Walnut Torte, 210
- Skinny Chocolate Torte ala Sacher, 213
- Spicy Applesauce, 217
- Walnut with Raspberry & Lemon Glaze, 210
Cheesecakes
- Chocolate with Creme Vanilla, 222
- Chocolate Marble, 224
- Lemon with Strawberry, 223
Cobblers
- Blueberry & Lemon, 221
- Peach & Macaroon, 220
- Spicy Peach with Oats, 221
Cookies
- Basic Brownies, 225
- Ginger-Spice Apple, 227
- Oat Bran & Apricot, 226
- Oatmeal & Raisin Bar, 226
- Oatmeal & Raisin, 236
Fruits
- Apples Baked in Orange Juice, 230
- Baked Apples with Orange Macaroon Walnut, 229

-Baked Bananas with Orange & Walnuts, 229
-Spice Compote of Dried & Winter, 228
-Spiced Peaches with Cinnamon & Cloves, 228
Glazes
-Lemon, 210
-Orange, 211
Ice Cream & Ices
-Banana Iced Cream, 233
-Basic Berry Granité, 232
-Basic Fruit Juice Ices, 232
-Basic Lemon Ice, 234
-Basic Tea Sherbet, 235
-Espresso Granité with Kahlua, 232
-Frozen Yogurt in Meringue Shells, 233
-Iced Vanilla Glacé, 231
-Mocha Parfaits with Kahlua, 230
-Pineapple Sherbet, 234
Meringues
-Kisses, 243
-Shells, 243
Mousses
-Low-Calorie Pumpkin Orange, 236
-Peach & Strawberry, Vanilla Rum, 237
Sauces
-Chocolate, 243
-Creme Fraiche, 237
-Creme Vanilla, 222
-Fresh Apple & Cinnamon, 242
-Fresh Strawberry, 42, 212
-Low-Calorie Devonshire Cream, 242
-Low-Calorie Vanilla Creme Fraiche, 237
-Low-Calorie Whipped Cream, 241
-No-Sugar Hot Chocolate, 241
Souffle
-Basic Fruit, 240
Tarts
-Apple on Cookie Crust, 239
-Crisp Cookie Crust, 238
-Flaky Crust, 238
-Strawberry on Cookie Crust, 239

EGGS
-Greek, with Tomatoes,Feta, 71
-with Spinach & Cheese, 72

FISH & SHELLFISH 107-128
FISH
-Chinese Whole Fish Steamed in Oven, 121
Bass
-in Salsa Español, 118
-Persillade with Yogurt & Tomatoes, 120
-with Low-Calorie Basil, 120
-with Mushrooms, Tomatoes & Leeks, 119
-with Tomatoes, Currants & Pine Nuts, 119
Red Snapper
-Fillets with Crumb Topping, 122
-Sesame with Ginger & Scallions, 122
-Teriyaki with Ginger & Scallions, 121
Sole
-in Artichoke & Tomato Sauce 115
-in Lemon Dill Cream Sauce, 117
-Italienne with Red Pepper, 114
-Mousse of Spinach, Yogurt & Chives, 113
-Provencal, Tomatoes & Onions, 116
-Stuffed with Spinach & Cheese, 111
-with Leeks & Tomatoes, 113
-with Garlic, Lemon, Chives, 112
-with Sun-Dried Tomatoes, 112
Tuna
-Steaks with Tomato Vinaigrette, 117

SHELLFISH
-Jambalaya Creole with Shellfish, 68
-Paella with Shellfish, 67
Lobster
-with Chile Salsa & Crumbs, 125
Sauces
-Honey Mustard Dill, 128
-Mexican Tomato Salsa, 128
-Tartar, 128
Scallops
-and Mushroom in Herb Sauce, 127
-in Wine Sauce, 127

Shrimp
-Best Herbed Scampi with Leeks & Shallots, 126
-Cajun in Red Hot Garlic Clam Sauce, 123
-in Honey Barbecue Sauce, 124
-in Honey Yogurt Lemon, 102
-Greco with Lemon & Feta, 125
-Red Hot Baby, Creole, 124

MEATS 161-174
Beef
-and Red Peppers Romano, 166
-Chili with Red Beans, 59
-German-Style Sweet & Sour Potted, 164
-Irish Stew with Mashed Potatoes, 165
-Old-Fashioned Hungarian Goulash, 164
-Oven-Baked Stew with Carrots & Potatoes, 162
-Paupiettes de Boeuf, 163
-Sweet & Sour with Cabbage, 162
-with Peppers & Onions, 165
Lamb
-Indienne with Garlic & Yogurt, 168
-Leg with Lemon, Garlic & Rosemary, 168
-Moroccan Dumplings with Apple, Raisin, 167
Pork
-Honey Glazed with Baked Apples, 169
-with Red Cabbage & Apples, 169
Veal
-and Vegetable Pate, 172
-Dumplings in Light Tomato Sauce, 171
-Italienne with Onions, Carrots & Tomatoes, 171
-Paupiettes with Apple Stuffing, 174
-Roast Persillade with Garlic, Tomatoes & Wine, 173
-Shanks in Tomato Wine Sauce, 170
-with Roasted Leeks & Carrots, 170

NOODLES, RICE & GRAINS, 175-186
  Grains
    -Bulgur with Lemon, Currants & Pine Nuts, 180
    -Chicken, Cous Cous & Currants, 97
    -Cous Cous, 167
    -Cous Cous with Chick Peas, 137
    -Cracked Wheat with Mushrooms & Onions, 177
    -Lentils with Carrots & Onions, 179
  Noodles
    -Pastina with Fresh Tomato & Basil Sauce, 185
    -Pink Orzo with Tomatoes & Onions, 186
    -Toasted Egg Barley with Onions & Mushrooms, 179
    -Toasted Fideos, 180
    -Toasted Orzo with Mushrooms & Onions, 185
  Rice
    -Brown and Lentils, Onions, 176
    -Brown with Leeks & Onions, Oven-Method, 178
    -Brown with Leeks & Onions, Stove-Top Method, 178
    -Brown with Mushrooms, Onions & Carrots, 116
    -Brown with Onions & Cinnamon, 135
    -Brown with Pimiento, 176
    -Confetti Brown with Scallions & Peppers, 176
    -Confetti with Onions, Peppers & Peas, 181
    -Dirty Rice, 143
    -Emerald with Parsley & Chives, 184
    -Fried with Green Onions, 183
    -Herbed, 183
    -Lemon with Leeks & Herbs, 183
    -Lemon with Onions & Pine Nuts, 181
    -Pink, 59
    -Pink Chili, 63
    -Pink Mushroom, 182
    -Pink with Chives & Parsley, 182
    -with Cheese & Chives, 184
    -with Lemon & Chives, 182
    -with Mushrooms, 184
    -Yellow Rice, 69

PASTAS & PIZZAS 73-80
  Pastas
    -Angel Hair, 139
    -Primavera with Tomato Basil Sauce, 79
    -Salad with Chicken & Vegetables, 95
    -with Artichoke, Red Pepper & Sun-Dried Tomatoes, 78
    -with Eggplant, Peppers & Sun-Dried Tomatoes, 80
  Pizzas
    -Basic Crust, 75
    -Fresh Vegetables, 69
    -Lowest-Calorie No-Oil Crust, 74
    -Mediterranean with Sun-Dried Tomatoes, 76
    -with Eggplant, Mushrooms, Leeks & Feta, 77
    -with Tomatoes & Chevre, 78

POULTRY 129-160
  Chicken
    -and mixed Vegetable, 140
    -and Pasta Salad, 95
    -Baked Breasts in Tomato, Artichoke Sauce, 150
    -Baroness with Artichoke & Mushrooms, 160
    -Big Chile Relleno, 63
    -Breasts Stuffed with Spinach & Cheese, 144
    -Breasts with Herbed Stuffing, 148
    -Breasts with Mushrooms, Red Peppers, 145
    -Caribbean with Apricots, 135
    -Creole in Hot Pepper Tomato Sauce, 158
    -Country with Potatoes & Carrots, 138
    -Dijonnaise with Mushroom, Pepper, Tomato, 151
    -Enchiladas with Chiles & Cheese, 142
    -Hot & Spicy Cajun Wings, 143
    -Indienne with Yogurt & Lemon, 146
    -in Dill & Wine, 132
    -in Honey, Lemon, Yogurt Sauce, 130
    -in Mushroom Wine Sauce, 154
    -in Tomato Vinaigrette, 149
    -Italienne in Red Pepper Sauce, 139
    -Kung Pao with Peanuts, 136
    -Mexican with Tomatoes & Chiles, 155
    -Moroccan with Raisins, 137
    -New Orleans with Apricots & Pecans, 153
    -Normandy with Apples & Wine, 157
    -Old-Fashioned Stew, 138
    -Paella with Tomatoes & Chiles, 133
    -Parmesan in Light Tomato Sauce, 131
    -Plum-Glazed Teriyaki, 130
    -Romano with Red Pepper & Garlic, 151
    -Salad with Cous Cous & Currants, 97
    -Smothered in Honey Onions, 155
    -with Apples & Honey Ginger Sauce, 157
    -with Carrots, Apples & Prunes, 153
    -with Honey Mustard Dill Sauce, 149
    -with Mushrooms & Onions in Burgundy Wine, 159
    -with Mushrooms in a Delicate Champagne Sauce, 147
    -with Red Cabbage, Apples & Cranberries, 134
    -with Tomatoes, Cabbage & Onions, 141
    -with Yogurt, Lemon & Garlic, 152
  Rock Cornish Hens
    -with Mushroom & Carrots, 156
  Turkey
    -Tomatoes Stuffed with, 61

SALADS & DRESSINGS 93-106
  Dressings
    -Basil Garlic Vinaigrette, 106
    -Basil Pimiento, 104
    -Cucumber Dill for Poached Salmon, 104
    -French Mustard Vinaigrette, 106
    -Imperial Verte, 105
    -Lemon-Dill Yogurt, 104
    -Tomato & Chile Salsa, 105
    -Yogurt Lemon, 106

Salads
-Artichoke, Red Pepper & Potato, 96
-Asparagus Vinaigrette with Cheese & Chives, 102
-Carrot & Snow Pea, 97
-Chicken with Cous Cous & Currants, 97
-Confetti Cole Slaw with Horseradish, 98
-Cucumber with Parsley & Chives, 94
-Eggplant with Tomato with Lemon & Dill, 100
-Eggplant with Tomatoes & Cheese, 98
-Leeks & Tomatoes, 100
-Low-Calorie Pineapple Cole Slaw, 101
-Marinated Red Pepper, 99
-Middle Eastern Cracked Wheat with Tomatoes, 103
-Pasta with Chicken &Vegetables, 95
-Raw Vegetable, 95
-Shrimp in Lemon Honey Yogurt , 102
-Spinach, Mushroom & Red Onion, 96
-Tomato, Mushroom & Mozzarella, 94
-Tomato & Onion with Basil, 99
-Tomatoes, Onion & Feta, 94
-Tomatoes with Garlic & Parmesan, 101
-White Bean with Tomatoes & Scallions, 103

SAUCES
-Cucumber Dill for Poached Salmon, 104
-Dilled Mushroom Cream, 148
-Hollandaise with Basil, 39
-Hollandaise with Chives, 39
-Hollandaise with Dill, 39
-Honey Mustard Dill, 128
-Horseradish for Roast Beef, 40
-Lemon Dill Yogurt, 104
-Light Mayonnaise, 41
-Low-Calorie Béarnaise, 40
-Low-Calorie with Dill & Chives, 41
-Mayonnaise-Hollandaise with Dill & Chives, 41

-Mexican Tomato Salsa, 128
-Tartar, 128

SOUPS 81-92
-Best Country Cabbage & Tomato, 84
-Best Old-Fashioned Stew, 86
-Bouillabaisse, 110
-Carrot with Apples & Cinnamon, 89
-Chicken CiCi Pea Stew, 91
-Cioppino, 83
-Cold & Creamy Dilled Zucchini, 92
-Costa del Sol Chowder, 108
-Cucumber & Chive with Lemon & Dill, 84
-Dill Potato & Cucumber, 92
-Easiest & Best Clam Chowder, 85
-Healthy & Homey Lentil, 82
-Italian Vegetable & Bean, 87
-Leek & Potato & Chives, 90
-Leek & Tomato with CiCi Peas, 88
-Low-Calorie Farm House Vegetable, 91
-Mexican Chicken & Chile Bean Stew, 90
-New Orleans Hot & Spicy Fish Stew, 109
-Spinach with Lemon & Vermicelli, 88
-Thanksgiving Honey Apple Pumpkin, 89

VEGETABLES 187-208
-Broiled Mixed Vegetable Platter, 208
-Stir-Fried Mixed Vegetable Platter, 208
Artichokes
-and Mushrooms with Cheese, 188
-and Potatoes with Green Onions, 188
-and Vegetable Paella, 69
-Frittata & Red Peppers, 62
-Red Pepper & Potato Salad, 96
-Royal & Spinach Casserole, 60
-with Pasta & Sun-Dried Tomatoes, 78

Asparagus
-in Lemon Chive Sauce, 189
-Vinaigrette with Cheese & Chives, 102
-with Lemon, Garlic & Cheese, 189
Beans
-Green with Parsley Sauce, 190
-Green with Tomatoes, 190
-Lima with Onions, 190
Broccoli
-Broth-Fried with Ginger, 191
-Frittata with Mushrooms, 192
-with Garlic & Shallots, 191
Brussel Sprouts
-with Lemon Chive Sauce, 192
-with Mushrooms & Shallots, 193
Carrots
-and Potato Cake, 194
-and Snow Peas, 97
-Honey & Brandy Glazed, 199
-Honey & Butter Glazed, 194
-Pureed with Cinnamon, 193
Celery
-in Lemon Dill Sauce, 195
Cucumbers
-with Lemon ,Parsley &Chives 195
Cabbage
-Rolls in Tomato Sauce, 65
-Sweet & Sour Red, with Apples & Currants, 196
Cauliflower
-with Tomatoes & Onions, 196
-with Tomatoes & Potatoes, 67
Eggplant
-and Tomato Salad, 100
-Baked with Tomatoes & Ricotta, 197
-Crustless Quiche with Onions & Cheese, 66
-Frittata with Onions & Cheese, 60
-Lasagna with Tomatoes & Ricotta, 58
-Pizza with Mushrooms, Leeks & Feta, 77
-Salad with Tomatoes & Cheese, 98
-Stuffed with Ricotta, 70
-with Pasta & Red Peppers, 80
Mushrooms
-and Tomatoes in Wine, 198
-Spinach & Red Onion Salad, 96

The Index

-Tomato & Mozzarella, 94
-with Dill & Yogurt Stuffing, 198

Onions
-and Mushroom Saute, 199
-with Raisins, 199

Peppers
-Artichoke & Potato Salad, 96
-Frittata with Artichokes, 62
-Marinated Salad, 99
-Old-Fashioned Stuffed, 64

Potatoes
-and Artichoke, Red Pepper Salad, 96
-and Onion Cake, 134, 201
-Cauliflower & Tomatoes, 67
-Country Baked, 200
-Garlic with Onion & Rosemary, 202
-Mashed, 166

-Onion Flavored Baby, 71
-Roasted Red Pepper & Onion Cake, 201
-Roasted with Garlic, 200
-Steamed Baby with Dill, 202
-Sweet Baked with Sugar & Spice, 200

Snow Peas
-and Carrot Salad, 97

Spinach
-Frittata with Cheese & Onions, 66
-Mushroom & Red Onions, 96
-Omelet with Cheese, 72
-Pate with Onions & Carrots, 203
-Royal Artichoke & Spinach, 60

Tomatoes
-and Onion Salad, 99
-Broiled with Garlic Cheese Crumbs, 204
-Cauliflower & Potatoes, 67
-Crustless Tart & Goat Cheese, 62
-Leeks & Lemon Dressing, 100
-Mushroom & Mozzarella, 94
-Onions & Feta, 94
-Stuffed with Turkey, 61

Zucchini
-Baked Crisps, 207
-Baked in Lemon, 204
-Baked with Tomatoes & Cheese, 206
-Frittata with Tomato Vinaigrette, 205
-Ramekins of Onions & Cheese, 206
-with Tomatoes & Onions, 207

Additional Copies of the Simply Delicious
RENNY DARLING COOKBOOKS
can be purchased at your local bookstore or ordered directly from:

ROYAL HOUSE PUBLISHING CO., INC.
P.O. Box 5027   Beverly Hills, CA 90210